# The Twilight of Jewish Philosophy

# The Twilight of Jewish Philosophy

EMMANUEL LEVINAS' ETHICAL HERMENEUTICS

## Tamra Wright

*Jews' College*
*London, UK*

**harwood academic publishers**
Australia • Canada • China • France • Germany
India • Japan • Luxembourg • Malaysia
The Netherlands • Russia • Singapore • Switzerland

Amsteldijk 166
1st Floor
1079 LH Amsterdam
The Netherlands

**British Library Cataloguing in Publication Data**

Wright, Tamra
  The Twilight of Jewish Philosophy : Emmanuel Levinas'
  ethical hermeneutics
  1. Levinas, Emmanuel – Philosophy   2. Judaism – Sacred books –
  Hermeneutics   3. Judaism – Theology   4. Philosophy, Jewish
  5. Ethics, Jewish
  I. Title
  296.3'092

  ISBN: 90-5702-350-4

FOR ADINA AND JOE

# CONTENTS

# ACKNOWLEDGEMENTS

I owe a great debt of gratitude to Andrew Benjamin and David Wood who not only introduced me to Levinas' philosophy, but helped to arrange for Alison Ainley, Peter Hughes and myself to interview Levinas at his home in 1986. (David Wood and Robert Bernasconi subsequently published the interview in *The Provocation of Levinas: Rethinking the Other*.)

The bulk of the research for this book was carried out at the University of Essex, in the course of my doctoral studies. I am grateful to Robert Bernasconi and David Pollard, who supervised the early stages of the work and to Simon Critchley, who, with admirable patience, guided me through to completion.

Many thanks are due to the following bodies, without whose financial support my doctoral studies would not have been possible: the Association of Commonwealth Universities, the Social Sciences and Humanities Research Council of Canada, and the Imperial Order of the Daughters of the Empire.

The Social Sciences and Humanities Research Council of Canada also funded two years of post-doctoral research (1992–94), which enabled me to examine the relationship between Levinas' thought and that of Emil Fackenheim and to expand my work on Levinas for publication in the current form. I am grateful to Jay Bernstein and Simon Critchley for their help during the first year of this period, which was spent at Essex. The second year was spent at the School of Oriental and African Studies, University of London. Many thanks to John Hinnels and the Department for the Study of Religions for their warm welcome and for extending 'academic hospitality' to me.

Thanks also to Tudor Parfitt for arranging a further period of academic hospitality at SOAS through the Centre for Jewish Studies, and to Jews' College, London, for accommodating me as a Research Fellow for the academic year 1994–95.

I am grateful to Emmanuel Levinas, z"l, and Basil Blackwell for permission to quote lengthy extracts from 'Revelation in the Jewish Tradition' and 'Assimilation and New Culture'; to Duquesne University Press for permission to reprint material from *Totality and Infinity*; and to Kluwer Academic Publishers for permission to quote extensively from *Otherwise than Being or Beyond Essence* (originally published by Martinus Nijhoff).

Finally, a gesture of thanks to the person whose direct and indirect contributions to this work are too numerous to list in full: my husband, Ian Gamse.

# GLOSSARY

**Aggada**  Non-legal sections of the Talmud and *Midrash*, comprising ethical and moral teachings, legends, and so forth.

**Akiva, Rabbi**  (c 50–135 c.e.) One of the outstanding *tannaim* (teachers of the Oral Law) who, following the Bar Kokhba revolt against Roman rule in 132 c.e., was imprisoned and executed for teaching the Torah in defiance of a Roman edict. Akiva was tortured to death by having his flesh ripped from his body with iron combs. The Talmud relates that he welcomed this chance to fulfil the commandment 'Thou shalt love the Lord thy God with all thy heart and with all thy soul [...] even if you must pay for it with your life' (*Berakhot* 61b).

**Amalek**  The first enemy encountered by the Israelites after the crossing of the Sea of Reeds.

**Amoraim**  Plural of *Amora*, speaker or interpreter. Name given to the Rabbinic teachers of the 3rd to 5th centuries.

**Gemara**  The traditions, discussions and rulings of the *Amoraim*, commenting on or supplementing the *Mishna*.

**Halakha**  The Law. The term can be used to designate either a particular law or the entire legal side of Judaism.

**Kiddush Hashem**  Literally, sanctification of the (divine) name. Martyrdom or act of strict integrity in support of Judaic principles.

**Midrash**  From the root '*darash*', to inquire. The term designates a body of Rabbinic literature which uncovers meanings other than the literal in the Bible.

**Mishnah**  Earliest codification of the Oral Law, edited at the end of the 2nd century c.e.

**Mitzvot**  Plural of *mitzvah*, 'commandment'.

**Rashi**  Acronym of Rabbi Shlomo Itzhaki (1040–1105 c.e.). Author of the most famous commentaries on the Bible and Talmud.

**Sanhedrin**  The supreme Jewish religious and judicial body in Palestine during the Second Temple and Roman periods.

**Shema**  (or *Keri'at Shema*) Recitation of biblical passages (Dt 6: 4–9; Dt 11: 13–21; Nu 15: 37–41) containing the declaration of God's unity and of acceptance of the 'yoke of the commandments'.

**Shoah**  The destruction of European Jewry by the Nazis and their accomplices between 1933 and 1945; the term is used by many Jewish thinkers in preference to 'Holocaust' because of the latter's theological implication.

**Talmud**  Compendium of discussions of the Mishnah by several generations of scholars in the academies of Babylon over (primarily) the 4th and 5th centuries. The Jerusalem Talmud is the equivalent product of the scholarship of the Palestinian academies of the 4th century.

**Talmud torah**  Study of Torah, in its widest sense; considered by rabbinic Judaism as one of the major constituents of religious life and elevated in some circles (particularly, in the context of this study, by R. Hayyim of Volozhyn) into a quasi-mystical activity.

**Torah**  The entire body of Jewish law and lore; also used specifically for the Pentateuch.

# INTRODUCTION

The Talmud relates that Ben Dima, the nephew of Rabbi Yishmael, once asked the rabbi whether, having already learnt the whole of the Torah, he ought to study Greek wisdom. In reply, Rabbi Yishmael cited the verse 'This book of the Torah shall not depart out of thy mouth; but thou shalt meditate therein day and night' (Joshua 1: 8) and said 'Find an hour which is neither day nor night and study Greek wisdom then'.[1] Although the obvious meaning of Rabbi Yishmael's response might seem to be a blanket prohibition of the study of Greek wisdom,[2] the task of finding an hour which is neither day nor night is not as difficult as it sounds. Someone who, like Ben Dima, had learnt the whole of the Torah, would surely be familiar with the halakhic concept of *bein ha-shemashot*,[3] the period between sunset and night which belongs neither fully to the day nor to the night. Perhaps, then, Rabbi Yishmael was allowing his nephew to study Greek wisdom, but only for this limited period each day?[4]

Emmanuel Levinas has suggested a different interpretation: 'an hour that is neither day nor night' might be a metaphorical allusion to 'the twilight hours [...] hours of uncertainty when the recourse to Greek wisdom would be possible, perhaps even necessary.'[5] For Levinas, this twilight period is one in which Israel is neither master of Judaism's 'difficult wisdom', nor blindly submitted to Jewish tradition.[6] According to this interpretation of Rabbi Yishmael's reply, Greek wisdom—which Levinas here equates with philosophy—'would be necessary during times of wavering, being capable, as it is, of reducing multidimensional questions to the disjunction 'yes or no?'[7] Thus, we might say that Rabbi Yishmael's equivocal answer to the question 'Should I study Greek wisdom?' was paradoxically a refusal of this 'rationalism of yes and no' which at the same time left room for recourse to such rationalism.

Is Jewish philosophy—or the recourse of Judaism to philosophy—a legitimate enterprise? This question is often asked from the perspective of philosophy,[8] but it should also be posed from that of Judaism itself.[9] Levinas' commentary on the exchange between Ben Dima and Rabbi Yishmael does exactly this: it seeks a Jewish justification of Jewish philosophy (or perhaps a Jewish justification of philosophy *tout court*).

Elsewhere, Levinas has defined the task of Jewish philosophy as that of translating the Bible into Greek,[10] by which he means expressing the ethical teaching of Judaism in the abstract and universal language of western philosophy. However, as his comments on the exchange between Ben Dima and Rabbi Yishmael make clear, Levinas does not believe that such a translation can ever be an unqualified success: it is not possible to summarise Judaism,[11] nor can its reasoning be reduced without remainder to the philosophical 'rationalism of yes and no'.

Nevertheless, although the translation can never be entirely adequate, the task must be undertaken. It should be noted, however, that Levinas does not seek legitimation of philosophy in terms of the eternal quest for truth. Instead, it is justified in terms of a historically determinate period of need—a translation of the Torah, for all its failings, would be better than no Torah at all.[12] Indeed, although Levinas interprets Rabbi Yishmael's twilight as a period between mastery of Jewish tradition and 'blind submission' to it, the darkness that threatens us in the twentieth century is in fact not unquestioning obedience to, but total ignorance of, Judaism.

In Levinas' view, the forgetting of Judaism would be a tragedy not just for the Jewish people, but for humanity itself. A world without Judaism would be a world of night, not only because it would mean a total 'posthumous victory' for Hitler,[13] but because the ethical message of the Bible, which Judaism bears,[14] is a perennially necessary corrective to the totalising (but equally necessary) forces of western thought.

The relationship between 'Hebrew' and 'Greek' thought is one of the recurring themes not only within Levinas' own corpus, but in the secondary literature on his work. This is a question to which we shall be returning throughout the course of this study. However, one issue which has troubled commentators needs to be dealt with at the outset: Levinas both stresses the 'incomparability of Judaism and philosophy' and yet makes Judaism 'available to philosophy'.[15] How does this paradox affect the credibility of his discourse?

The argument of this book is that Levinas' rapprochement (despite their differences) of Judaism and philosophy works because each can be understood as a response to the 'pre-philosophical experience' of the self's inescapable responsibility for the other(s). Admittedly, the ethical concern for the other is much easier to discern in the texts of Judaism than in those of western philosophy. However, despite his scathing criticisms of the 'Greek' disciplines of philosophy and politics, Levinas insists not only that they are necessary, but that they too emerge from the pre-original encounter with the other. Levinas does not set out to destroy philosophy, but to remind it of its proper role, that of serving ethics.

Levinas' account of the 'ethical relation', or 'face-to-face', as it is presented in *Totality and Infinity*, is the focus of the first chapter. Subsequent chapters are concerned with showing how this quasi-phenomenological account of the ethical relation provides the orientation for Levinas' approach to interpreting the texts of both Judaism and western thought, his 'ethical hermeneutics'.

Although the term 'hermeneutics' has been used in various senses in the modern era,[16] we will be concerned primarily with two senses of the word: the older meaning of biblical interpretation, and the modern use of the word to refer to the general field of theory of interpretation.

The theory of interpretation *per se* is not a major concern in Levinas' philosophical writings. However, we will see that his philosophy makes an important contribution to contemporary hermeneutics. Emil Fackenheim has defined the central problem of biblical hermeneutics as that of overcoming the historical chasm separating the 'here and now' of contemporary readers from the 'then and there' of the Bible.[17] Levinas' approach to the Bible, via the rabbinic commentaries, shows that Scripture retains its meaning in any era when read as ethical teaching. We will see in Chapter 5 that the ethical approach to interpretation is not limited to the Bible, and thus that Levinas' work is of importance not only for biblical exegesis, but for the general theory of interpretation as well.

However, Levinas' ethical philosophy must be considered on its own before we can discuss its significance for hermeneutics. Chapters 2 through 4 focus on three key terms in Levinas' discourse: 'humanism', 'God' and 'Judaism' respectively. All three of these terms cry out for interpretation in an age which claims to have witnessed the death of the subject, the author and God—an age in which the proclaimed goal of Jewish studies was to provide Judaism 'with a magnificent funeral'.[18]

Each of these chapters is mainly taken up with close readings of central texts by Levinas. Chapter 2 examines Levinas' rehabilitation of the term 'humanism', both in his early essays on Judaism,[19] in which he writes of 'Hebraic humanism', and in his philosophical essays collected under the title of 'Humanisme de l'autre homme'. Chapter 3 analyses Levinas' use of the word 'God' (that 'overwhelming semantic event')[20] in the hope of alleviating the fears of readers who suspect that he writes theology in the guise of philosophy.

With Chapter 4 we turn to the specifically Jewish (but nonetheless universally significant) question of the meaning of Judaism in a post-Holocaust world. Since Fackenheim is the thinker who has devoted himself to this question in the most rigorous and determined way, we begin with a discussion of the relationship between Fackenheim and Levinas, exploring both the affinities between the two thinkers and some of the crucial differences in their approach to the Jewish tradition. In particular, Fackenheim's insistence on reading the 'naked text' of the Bible is contrasted with Levinas' argument for the necessity of approaching Scripture via the rabbinic commentaries. It is then argued that Levinas' analysis of the significance of the commandments and the meaning of revelation in Judaism facilitate an understanding of Judaism that does not begin with (or necessarily culminate in) belief in 'God', one that is neither destroyed by the Holocaust, nor called into question by higher Bible criticism.

Chapter 5 examines the writings that constitute Levinas' most distinctive contribution to Jewish thought: his talmudic commentaries. We begin by looking at the content of three commentaries, in order to clarify the relationship between Levinas' 'confessional' and philosophical writings. On the basis of this analysis, we discuss the sense in which Levinas can be appropriately described as a 'Jewish philosopher', and his work understood as a translation of 'Hebrew' wisdom into 'Greek'. Finally, we look to the 'form' of the talmudic readings, to see how Levinas' ethical hermeneutics works in practice.

1 *Menachot*, 99b.

2 Rashi, for example, understands the statement in this way.

3 See Glossary for an explanation of these and other Hebrew terms.

4 Since Levinas insists (as we will see in Chapter 5) on approaching the Talmud via the traditional commentaries, it is worth noting that the commentators do not generally understand Rabbi Yishmael's reply in this way. However, the comments of *Netsiv* (Naphtali Zvi Yehuda Berlin) on this passage and parallels in Mekhilta (*Beshallah*) and Midrash Tehillim, 1.1 lend some support to Levinas' decision to understand Rabbi Yishmael's reply as an allusion to twilight. *Netsiv* understands 'day and night' in Joshua 1: 8 as 'the time when day and night are joined' (*Meromey Sadeh*, published by *Netsiv*'s grandsons, Jerusalem 1958, *ad loc*).

5 *L'Au-delà du verset: Lectures et discours talmudiques*, Paris, Editions de Minuit, 1982, p. 42. Hereafter cited as *L'Au-delà du verset*.

6 Idem.

7 Idem. It should be noted, however, that this is only one stage in his commentary on the talmudic text. Later on, Levinas points out that in the Talmud 'Greek wisdom' sometimes signifies the scientific and artistic splendours of Greece, and the clarity of its reasoning; at other times, it signifies rhetoric, diplomacy, a certain duplicity (Ibid., p. 43).

8 One way of phrasing the question is to focus on the universality of philosophy: If philosophy is a 'universal, rational inquiry into the truth', is the notion of Jewish philosophy any more meaningful than that of Jewish physics or mathematics? (José R. Maia Neto, 'The String that Leads the Kite: Steven S. Schwarzschild's (1924–1989) View of Jewish Philosophy', *Judaism*, Issue 158, vol. 40, no. 2, Spring 1991, p. 225).

9 As Gillian Rose has pointed out, even by formulating the question 'Is there a Jewish philosophy?', we permit 'philosophy to identify Judaism, and, in so doing, [philosophy] reduces it to an epithet of philosophy.' *Judaism and Modernity: Philosophical Essays*, Oxford, Blackwell, 1993, pp. 12–13. Hereafter cited as *Judaism and Modernity*.

10 'We are faced with the great task of articulating in Greek those principles of which Greece had no knowledge. Jewish singularity awaits its philosophy.' 'Assimilation and New Culture', translated by Roland Lack in *The Levinas Reader*, edited by Seán Hand, Oxford, Blackwell, 1989, p. 287. (Translation slightly altered.)

11 *Hors Sujet*, Paris, Fata Morgana, 1987, p. 30.

12 See Levinas' comments on the translation of the Septuagint, in *A l'heure des nations*, Paris, Editions de Minuit, 1988, p. 59.

13 For a discussion of the relationship between Levinas' thought and that of Fackenheim, see Chapter 4.

14 See 'Useless Suffering', translated by Richard Cohen in *The Provocation of Levinas: Rethinking the Other*, edited by Robert Bernasconi and David Wood, London, Routledge, 1988, p. 163.

15 Gillian Rose, *Judaism and Modernity*, p. 14. A similar paradox is pointed out by Robert Gibbs in his discussion of the meanings of 'Greek' in Levinas' talmudic discourses. Levinas argues that 'Hebrew' provides nourishment for the philosopher. Gibbs points out that this digestive metaphor is paradoxical because 'Levinas claims that the inadequacy of "Greek" is precisely that it knows not by doing responsibility for the other, but by assimilating the other into the same.' *Correlations in Rosenzweig and Levinas*, Princeton University Press, 1993, p. 164. (Hereafter cited as *Correlations*.)

16 See Robert C. Holub, *Reception Theory: A Critical Introduction*, London, Methuen, 1984, p. 36. Holub lists Schleirmacher's psychology of understanding, Dilthey's methodology of the human sciences, and Gadamer's linking of hermeneutics with Heideggerian ontology. Another well-known writer in the field of hermeneutics, whose relationship to Levinas deserves a study in its own right, is of course Paul Ricoeur.

17 *The Jewish Bible after the Holocaust: A re-reading*, Manchester, Manchester University Press, 1990, p. 4 ff.

18 Levinas cites the famous saying to this effect of Leopold Zunz, the founder of both liberal Judaism and the 'science' of Judaism, in *Hors Sujet*, p. 17.

19 Collected in *Difficile liberté: Essais sur le judaïsme*, Paris, Albin Michel, 1976. Hereafter cited as *Difficile liberté*.

20 *Otherwise than Being Or Beyond Essence*, translated by Alphonso Lingis, The Hague, Martinus Nijhoff, 1981, p. 151. Hereafter cited as *Otherwise than Being*.

# Chapter 1

## ETHICAL PHILOSOPHY

INTRODUCTION

'Everyone will readily agree that it is of the highest importance to know whether we are not duped by morality.'[1] The opening line of *Totality and Infinity* indicates the orientation not only of the work itself, but of Levinas' mature philosophical œuvre in its entirety. He is concerned with the fate of the notions of morality and ethics in a world which has witnessed 'two world wars, the totalitarianisms of right and left, Hitlerism and Stalinism, Hiroshima, the Gulag, and the genocides of Auschwitz and Cambodia.'[2] For Levinas, the essential problem for twentieth century consciousness (and not just for philosophers) is 'Can we speak of morality after the failure of morality?'[3]

How is a philosopher to address this question? Traditionally, ethics has been seen as a branch of philosophy, one of several areas of enquiry to which the philosopher could turn his attention and to which he could apply his rigorous conceptual thought. Within this framework the philosopher would respond to the question 'are we duped by morality?' by, for example, trying to establish whether moral propositions are true, or at least meaningful, according to the criteria laid down by philosophy. Philosophy, in other words, would adjudicate the claims of morality.

Levinas does not write 'philosophy' in this sense of the word. Instead of placing philosophy in the position of judge, he casts it in the role of the accused: western philosophy, with its relentless insistence on totalisation, on reducing all otherness to sameness, is condemned as 'violent'. It is a philosophy of power which results in tyranny.[4]

For Levinas, 'ethics' is not just one branch of philosophy; instead, the ethical provides the standpoint from which philosophy itself can be judged, and from which it must receive its orientation. He insists that philosophy must abandon its self-definition as 'the love of wisdom' and regard itself instead as 'the wisdom of love at the service of love'.[5] Dedication to the Good must guide the search for the True. Ethics must become 'first philosophy'.[6]

The word 'ethics' in Levinas' discourse has a very particular meaning. Levinasian ethics is neither a set of laws or moral rules, nor a theory of such rules.[7] Instead, Levinas uses the word 'ethics' to refer to the 'face-to-face', or ethical, relation to the human Other.[8] He defines ethics as 'the putting into question of my spontaneity by the presence of the Other.'[9] As Simon Critchley explains, 'Ethics, for Levinas, is critique; it is the critical *mise en question* of the liberty, spontaneity, and cognitive emprise of the ego that seeks to reduce all otherness to itself.'[10]

This chapter examines Levinas' account of the face-to-face relation as the basis for an affirmation that ethics and morality are meaningful even (or perhaps especially) in a post-Holocaust world.[11] Yet we will see that Levinas' answer to the philosophical question of morality becomes a questioning, a calling into question, of philosophy itself.

## LEVINAS' CRITIQUE OF WESTERN PHILOSOPHY

Levinas' critique of western philosophy is directed to the entire tradition, from Parmenides to Heidegger.[12] He claims that western philosophy is unable to offer an adequate account of human existence because it consistently fails to recognise transcendence.[13] This criticism does not amount to the simple claim that philosophy denies the existence of a 'transcendent' Being named 'God'.[14] Rather, Levinas is concerned with philosophy's failure to recognise the transcendence of the other person, the fact that he[15] is radically different from me, wholly other. Since, in Levinas' view, it is recognition of the other's alterity that makes ethics and justice possible, philosophy's insistence on reducing all alterity to sameness has profound implications for morality.

Levinas' claim that recognition of the radical alterity of the other is the *sine qua non* of ethics appears to be a reversal of our ordinary way of thinking about ethical behaviour. Christianity's 'golden rule', for example, is indicative of a tendency to think of ethics as having to do with sameness, not difference.[16] Yet Levinas is claiming that my concern for ethics originally arises not from recognition that others are the same as me, but out of respect for their alterity.

The alterity that he has in mind is not merely that of the specific qualities that make another person different from me. He insists that the other's alterity is not relative, but absolute.

> The Other is not other with a relative alterity as are, in a comparison, even ultimate species, which mutually exclude one another but still have their place within the community of a genus—excluding one another by their definition, but calling for one another by this exclusion, across the community of their genus. The alterity of the Other does not depend on any quality that would distinguish him from me, for a distinction of that nature would precisely imply between us that community of genus which already nullifies alterity.[17]

Levinas is not denying that we can have a concept of 'man' or 'human being'. However, he insists that our experience[18] of encountering the other is not adequately described as a meeting with another member of the genus 'human'. Levinas is not interested in the logic of the I-Other relation, but in its phenomenological significance. He frequently argues that the relation is inconceivable in terms of 'formal logic'.[19]

Levinas, however, does not simply replace a logical analysis of the I-other relation with a phenomenological one. Although, as we shall we, he is deeply indebted to both Husserl and Heidegger, his own philosophical method constitutes a significant departure from, and critique of, both Husserlian phenomenology and Heidegger's 'fundamental ontology'. The description of the face of the Other, which lies at the heart of *Totality and Infinity*, is not, strictly speaking, phenomenological. Phenomenology is the study of phenomena.[20] Levinas insists that the face is not a phenomenon: it is neither an object of consciousness, the relation to which could be adequately described through intentional analysis,[21] nor an entity that can 'show itself in itself and from itself'.[22] A phenomenon is something that appears. Levinas argues that the face does not appear; it is ultimately refractory to phenomenology.

Robert Bernasconi has suggested that, in describing the face-to-face relation, Levinas 'follows the transcendental method to the point where it is halted and in order to sustain itself must draw on that which is radically exterior to it'.[23] Taking our cue from this insight, we will present the salient features of Levinas' account of the I-Other relation before considering in more detail Levinas' method and its relation to phenomenology.

ETHICAL PHILOSOPHY

Levinas' account of the I-Other relationship is written from the perspective of the 'I'. He describes the self's mode of being in the world as 'sojourning', maintaining that although the world is in many ways foreign and hostile, the self can overcome this hostility by using objects and creating a home.[24] He argues that the 'I' is at home in the world, and at home with itself. It is the being who has 'identity as [its] content',[25] self-identical not in the sense that it never changes, but that it represents changes to itself and thinks them.[26]

Prior to the encounter with the human other, the 'I' lives in a 'totality', a world in which all otherness can be overcome, reduced to sameness by possession or the exercise of another of the ego's powers.

> The 'at home' is not a container but a site where *I can*, where, dependent on a reality that is other, I am, despite this dependence or thanks to it, free. It is enough to walk, to *do [faire]*, in order to grasp anything, to take. In a sense, everything is in the site, in the last analysis everything is at my disposal, even the stars, if I but reckon them, calculate the intermediaries or the means. Everything is here, everything belongs to me; everything is caught up in advance with the primordial occupying of a site, everything is comprehended.[27]

The site where the 'I can' holds sway is also termed the world of 'enjoyment'. Levinas elaborates his description of the 'I of enjoyment' in the second section of *Totality and Infinity*. He criticises the privileging of representation in Husserl's work,[28] insisting that 'enjoyment' has a completely different structure from that of representation.[29] Whereas the intentionality of representation consists in suspending the exteriority of the object, the intentionality of enjoyment consists in 'holding on' to this exteriority. 'Representation', Levinas writes, 'consists in the possibility of accounting for the object as though it were constituted by a thought, as though it were a noema.'[30] The intentional relation of representation, he explains, differs from every other sort of relation in that 'in it the same is in relation with the other but in such a way that the other does not determine the same; it is always the same which determines the other.'[31] Levinas illustrates this idea that the same determines the other in representation with reference to both Husserl and Descartes. Husserl's theory of the primacy of the objectifying act leads, Levinas points out, to the affirmation that 'the object of consciousness, while distinct from consciousness, is as it were a product of consciousness'.[32] The idea that the object of representation is interior to thought also governs the Cartesian notion of the 'clear and distinct idea'.

> Descartes' clear and distinct idea manifests itself as true and as entirely immanent to thought: entirely present, without anything clandestine; its very novelty is without mystery.[...] *Intelligibility, the very occurrence of representation, is the possibility for the other to be determined by the same without determining the same, without introducing alterity into it; it is a free exercise of the same.*[33]

By contrast, in the intentionality of enjoyment, the same is determined by the other. The 'I' of enjoyment is the 'I' of the body positioned in the world. Although it is identified as the centre of the world it perceives, it is also, Levinas insists, conditioned by its own representation of the world. In the body, representation reverts into life, the subject that represents reverts into 'life which is sustained by these representations and lives of them'.[34] Because the body is essentially needy, it intends exteriority as exterior. Levinas explains that even negative actions, such as doubting, the destruction of obstacles and the killing of enemies, all assume objective exteriority rather than constituting it.[35]

The corporeal I, in assuming exteriority, is conditioned by it. Levinas terms the way in which the same is determined by exteriority 'living from', explaining that we 'live from' the contents of life: '"good soup", air, light, spectacles, work, ideas, sleep etc. [...] These are not objects or representations. We live from them.'[36] Rather than being tools or 'implements' in the

Heideggerian sense, the things from which we live are always, to a certain extent, objects of enjoyment. Things, Levinas explains, 'are always more than the strictly necessary; they make up the grace of life.' Labour, for example, ensures our subsistence; but we also live from our labour in that 'it fills (delights or saddens) life'.[37] Levinas defines life as 'love of life'. It is, he writes,

> [...] a relation with contents that are not my being but more dear than my being: thinking, eating, sleeping, reading, working, warming oneself in the sun. Distinct from my substance but constituting it, these contents make up the worth [*prix*] of my life.[38]

Life as love of life is enjoyment. Levinas insists that enjoyment is not simply one psychological state among others; rather it is 'the very pulsation of the I.'[39] Although it is below the level of reflection, enjoyment depends on memory. Even meeting the most basic needs of life is experienced as accomplishment; 'enjoyment is made of the memory of its thirst; it is a quenching'.[40] Levinas therefore rejects the Platonic interpretation of need as a simple lack. He insists that 'the human being thrives on his needs; he is happy for his needs'.[41] An essential characteristic of need is the fact that it is capable of satisfaction. As such, 'living from' is dependency, but one that, through satisfaction, 'turns into sovereignty, into happiness'.[42]

Although man's needs make him dependent on the world, it is through these very needs that the possibility of independence arises. In meeting our needs we overcome the alterity of the world and our dependence on it. Levinas sees nourishment, the meeting of needs, as the essence of enjoyment. Nourishment, he writes,

> is the transmutation of the other into the same, which is in the essence of enjoyment: an energy that is other, recognised as other, recognised, we will see, as sustaining the very act that is directed upon it, becomes, in enjoyment, my own energy, my strength, me. All enjoyment is in this sense alimentation.[43]

Not only is the alterity of the specific content overcome in meeting my needs (for example, the bread I eat becomes part of me) but my dependence on the world can be overcome by planning to meet these needs. Levinas insists that the factor of time is crucial to the relationship between the I of enjoyment and the world. My need for food, for example, makes me dependent on the world, but because I have time to plan for and meet these needs, I am not totally determined by the world.[44]

Levinas insists that enjoyment is not simply an affective state, but an 'exaltation' in which the self 'dawns'.[45] In other words, there is no 'self' prior to and separate from enjoyment. Rather, the 'substantiality of the I' is always implicated in happiness, in the egoism of existence for itself. Although, as we will see below, this self-sufficient existence is called into question by the presence of the Other, happiness remains constitutive of the self.

Moreover, Levinas insists that the I of egoism is a unicity, insofar as it remains 'outside the distinction between the individual and the general'. He realises that this is a 'logically absurd' structure, but insists that 'the refusal of the concept is not only one of the aspects of its [the I's] being, but its whole content; it is interiority'. In refusing the concept, the I is 'driven' into the 'dimension of interiority'. It is 'at home with itself'.[46]

It must be emphasised that the I at home with itself, the I of enjoyment, is not consciousness; it is the I of sensibility, not reflection or representation. We have seen that this I is characterised by its paradoxical relationship to the world; both dependent on the world to meets its needs and, through the possibility of labour, independent. In its independence, or 'separation', the I of enjoyment breaks with the totality of being by refusing to be subsumed in the generality of a concept. At the same time, the I is itself totalising, in that it reduces the alterity of the objects it needs. Although in enjoyment the I intends the world as exterior, when it acts upon an object it transmutes that other into the same.

We have also seen that this tendency towards totalisation is even more extreme in consciousness, which does not even intend exteriority as exterior. Levinas claims that in representation, which is the essence of consciousness, 'the distinction between me and the object, between interior and exterior, is effaced'.[47] For Levinas then, the self's mode of relating to the exteriority of the world, both on the level of consciousness and on the pre-reflective level of 'enjoyment', consists in reducing alterity to sameness.

However, with the appearance of the human other, the self's comfortable sojourn in the world is disturbed. Unlike the alterity of objects, the alterity of the other person cannot be suspended. I cannot grasp him through concepts or possess him the way I possess a thing. He is the 'Stranger' over whom 'I have no power'.[48] Levinas insists that the Other 'escapes my grasp by an essential dimension, even if I have him at my disposal. He is not wholly in my site.'[49]

In addition to being refractory to possession, the Other calls into question my being at home in the world, my possession of all that I had appropriated before his appearance. However, Levinas insists that my realisation that the Other contests my possession of the world does not depend upon a recognition of the Other's similarity to me, that is, upon a line of reasoning which establishes that we each believe ourselves to be the centre of a world which we own and that we are, therefore, competitors. If this were the case, the Other's alterity would not be absolute. Nor does the Other contest my possession by entering into a struggle with me. The contest is not physical, but ethical. In the face of the Other I find not a threat, but the expression of need. Adopting biblical idiom, Levinas describes the Other as 'the stranger, the widow, the orphan'.[50] From my position in the world of enjoyment, I seem to have everything while the Other is destitute. At the same time, I feel obligated towards him because he appears from a 'dimension of height, a dimension of transcendence',[51] which confers the authority to command me. He commands me to 'welcome' him, to assume my responsibility for him, without trying to deny or neutralise his alterity.

The relationship between the self and the absolutely other is characterised not by need, but by a desire which Levinas describes as 'metaphysical'.

> The other metaphysically desired is not 'other' like the bread I eat, the land in which I dwell, the landscape I contemplate [...] I can 'feed' on these realities and to a very great extent satisfy myself, as though I had simply been lacking them. Their *alterity* is thereby reabsorbed into my own identity as a thinker or a possessor. The metaphysical desire tends toward *something else entirely*, toward the *absolutely* other.[52]

Unlike needs, which are characterised by the possibility of satisfaction, desire cannot be satisfied. Levinas calls it 'Desire for the invisible', explaining that 'invisibility does not denote an absence of relation; it implies relations with what is not given, of which there is no idea'.[53]

According to Levinas, vision amounts to an 'adequation of the idea with the thing'.[54] But the Other desired metaphysically is so radically other that it is impossible to have an adequate idea of it. Desire for the invisible is a desire which does not try to reduce the alterity of the other, but 'precisely understands [*entend*] the remoteness, the alterity and the exteriority of the other'.[55] Although there can be no adequate idea of this alterity, Levinas insists that it nevertheless has a meaning: it opens up the 'dimension of height' and makes goodness possible.[56]

The self's preoccupation with the Other leads it to discover itself as guilty before the Other. Levinas insists that the essence of conversation is apology. To be in conversation with the Other is simultaneously to recognise the Other's right over the egoism, and to assert oneself.[57] However, Levinas insists that even whilst feeling guilty for its appropriation of objects, the self can never completely overcome its egoism. Conversation, or the face-to-face relationship, requires two partners.

> A relation whose terms do not form a totality can [...] be produced within the general economy of being only as proceeding from the I to the other, as a *face-to-face*, as delineating a distance in depth—that of conversation, of goodness, or Desire—irreducible to the distance the synthetic activity of the understanding establishes

between the diverse terms, other with respect to one another, that lend themselves to its synoptic operation. [...] Alterity is possible only starting from me.[58]

Levinas terms the bond between the self and the absolutely other 'religion',[59] and draws upon the Cartesian notion of the 'idea of the Infinite' to describe it. According to Descartes, the 'idea of the Infinite' provided a proof of the existence of God. Descartes reasoned that, since the idea of perfection could not have originated in an imperfect being, the fact that he had the idea of 'Infinity' or 'perfection' proved that a perfect being (i.e. God) must exist, being the only possible source of the idea of perfection. Levinas, however, is not interested in this proof of God's existence, but in the differences between the 'idea of the Infinite' and all other ideas. 'We could', Levinas writes, 'conceivably have accounted for all the other ideas, other than that of infinity, by ourselves'.[60] He emphasises that it is impossible to have an adequate idea of the infinite. 'The idea of infinity is exceptional in that its *ideatum* surpasses its idea, whereas for the things the total coincidence of their "objective" and "formal" realities is not precluded.'[61]

Because the infinite cannot be known, it maintains its alterity; the I and God remain separate. Levinas stresses that the 'distance' between the *cogito* and the infinite is

> [...] not equivalent to that which separates the mental act from its object in all our representations, since the distance at which the object stands does not exclude, and in reality implies, the possession of the object, that is, the suspension of its being.[62]

Transcendence, the relationship with the infinite, is unique, in that 'the distance that separates *ideatum* and idea' is itself the content of the *ideatum*.

> Infinity is characteristic of a transcendent being as transcendent; the infinite is the absolutely other. The transcendent is the sole *ideatum* of which there can be only an idea in us; it is infinitely removed from its idea, that is, exterior, because it is infinite.[63]

For Levinas, then, the Cartesian idea of the infinite provides a model of a non-totalising relationship, in which the two terms remain absolutely separated. Such a relationship obtains when the I of enjoyment encounters the human other. Just as the infinite surpasses the *cogito*'s idea of it, so, Levinas claims, the Other always surpasses my idea of him.

Levinas uses the term 'face' to describe the other's way of presenting himself. Although the word 'face' evokes a visual image, the term in Levinas' usage does not refer to what we see when we look at the other. Instead, it evokes that which we can never see, perceive or comprehend. Levinas defines the face as 'the way in which the other presents himself, *exceeding the idea of the other in me*'.[64] The impossibility of comprehending the other is not simply a philosophical thesis. Rather, awareness of the inadequacy of my idea of the other belongs to the experience of the encounter. 'The face of the Other at each moment destroys and overflows the plastic image it leaves me, the idea existing to my own measure and to the measure of its *ideatum*—the adequate idea.'[65]

The positive significance of the face is described in the third section of *Totality and Infinity*. Insisting on the absolute alterity of the Other, the impossibility of comprehending him, Levinas remarks that 'the face is present in its refusal to be contained'.[66] However, he continues, the face is not a pure negation of the I, for even total negation itself refers to a prior relation.[67] Rather than focusing on the negative fact of the impossibility of comprehending the Other, Levinas turns his attention to discourse[68] which, he says, makes possible a relation with what remains transcendent.

[...] Absolute difference, inconceivable in terms of formal logic, is established only by language. Language accomplishes a relation between terms that breaks up the unity of a genus. The terms, the interlocutors, absolve themselves from the relation, or remain absolute within relationship. Language is perhaps to be defined as the very power to break the continuity of being or of history.[69]

Levinas begins his analysis of language by attempting to uncover the meaning of its 'formal structure'. He considers the situation in which I address the other. As we saw above, he maintains that I can never have an adequate idea of the Other; like the Cartesian idea of the infinite, my idea of the Other is, in itself, recognition of the inadequacy of this idea. I may use a word to thematise the Other, and this word may, momentarily, appear to contain him. But in his presence this word is addressed to him, and I immediately become aware that 'his presence is not reabsorbed in his status as a theme'.[70]

In discourse the divergence that inevitably opens between the Other as my theme and the Other as my interlocutor, emancipated from the theme that seemed a moment to hold him, forthwith contests the meaning I ascribe to my interlocutor.[71]

The fact that the Other contests any and every meaning I ascribe to him reveals, Levinas maintains, the meaning of the formal structure of language: it 'announces the ethical inviolability of the Other, and, without any order of the "numinous", his holiness'.[72]

The encounter with the absolutely Other, Levinas explains, opens up a new dimension in the I's existence, a relationship with something that remains absolute within the relation, remains exterior. As we saw above, the Other exceeds the self's idea of him, overflows it. Levinas clarifies this metaphor by insisting that it must be distinguished from the 'image of a liquid overflowing a vessel'.[73] The overflowing presence of the Other is, he emphasises, 'effectuated as a position *in face of* the same'.[74] He insists that the facing position has an ethical meaning. 'The facing position, opposition par excellence, can be only as a moral summons. This movement proceeds from the other.'[75]

Using an argument structurally similar to Descartes' ontological argument, Levinas insists that the exteriority of the Other is inscribed in its essence.

> The idea of infinity, the infinitely more contained in the less is concretely produced in the form of a relation with the face. And the idea of infinity alone maintains the exteriority of the other with respect to the same, despite this relation. Thus a structure analogous to the ontological argument is here produced: the exteriority of a being is inscribed in its essence. But what is produced here is not a reasoning, but the epiphany that occurs as a face.[76]

The emphasis on the concreteness of the face-to-face relation should be noted. Levinas does not simply define the Other, negatively, as a being of whom I can never have an adequate idea, a being whose 'exteriority [...] is inscribed in its essence'. Rather, he maintains that the other reveals himself to me, opposes me, challenges my idea of him. To respond to this opposition and this challenge is to 'welcome the face'.[77]

To welcome the Other, Levinas continues, is to respond to his revelation. The first word of this revelation, the 'primordial expression' is the commandment 'you shall not commit murder'.[78] Levinas' account of this commandment begins with a discussion of the essential difference between murder and other acts of destruction. Only murder 'aims at the face, which is not of the world'.[79] The face expresses itself in this world, while remaining exterior to it. Levinas explains that

> Murder exercises a power over what escapes power. It is still a power, for the face expresses itself in the sensible, but already impotency, because the face rends the sensible. The alterity that is expressed in the face provides the unique 'matter' possible for total negation. I can wish to kill only an existent absolutely independent, which exceeds my powers infinitely, and therefore does not oppose them but paralyses the very power of power. The Other is the sole being I can wish to kill.[80]

Levinas concedes that, empirically, the other is easily destroyed. However, the other can oppose me, that is, 'oppose to the force that strikes him not a force of resistance, but the very *unforeseeableness* of his reaction'. In doing so, Levinas writes, the Other opposes to me 'not a greater force [...] but the very transcendence of his being'. This constitutes 'a relation not with a very great resistance, but with something absolutely *other*: the resistance of what has no resistance—the ethical resistance'.[81]

The significance of the ethical impossibility of murder is not simply negative or formal, since it is conditioned by the relation with infinity.

Infinity presents itself as a face in the ethical resistance that paralyses my powers and from the depth of defenceless eyes rises firm and absolute in its nudity and destitution. The comprehension of this destitution and this hunger establishes the very proximity of the other. But thus the epiphany of infinity is expression and discourse.[82]

The essence of discourse and expression is not the communication of information about the other's interior world. Rather, the essence of expression is that one presents oneself, exposing oneself to the interlocutor's response and his questions.[83]

Levinas insists that, whereas I can choose not to engage with the world of objects, I cannot hide from the Other or be deaf to his appeal. He emphasises that the expression of the Other is not equivalent to a true representation. A true representation always refers to its opposite, the non-true, and thus can be doubted by the sceptic; the true 'ineluctably meets with the smile and the silence of the sceptic'.[84] However, there is no logical opposite of the expression of the face. Thus, Levinas argues, the discourse which the epiphany of the face opens cannot be evaded by scepticism and silence. My responsibility for the Other is irrecusable.

In the relationship between the self and the Other, where the expression of the Other establishes the inescapable responsibility of the self, Levinas finds the foundation of the universality of reason.

> The face opens the primordial discourse whose first word is obligation, which no 'interiority' permits avoiding. It is that discourse that obliges the entering into discourse, the commencement of discourse rationalism prays for, a 'force' that convinces even 'the people who do not wish to listen' and thus founds the true universality of reason.[85]

The claim that the encounter with the other 'founds the true universality of reason' is supported through an analysis of the relationship between language and objectivity. Objectivity, Levinas argues, results from language. With the appearance of the other, I cease to regard things simply in terms of the use I can make of them and begin, instead, to view them as offerable to the Other. Levinas emphasises that, prior to the encounter with the Other, I have no need to endow objects with a rational signification, or to designate them. Language does not simply arise from a process of symbolisation or abstraction which would occur within an isolated subject. Instead, it is the means by which the world is shared with the Other.

> In designating a thing I designate it to the Other. The act of designating modifies my relation of enjoyment and possession with things, places the things in the perspective of the Other. [...] Objectivity results from language, which permits the

putting into question of possession. This disengagement has a positive meaning: the entry of the thing into the sphere of the other. The thing becomes a theme. To thematize is to offer the world to the Other in speech.[86]

Levinas, of course, is not the first philosopher to claim that thought is indissolubly linked to language. He cites Husserl, Heidegger and Merleau-Ponty as thinkers who have debunked the notion that the function of words is simply to reflect thought. Levinas praises Merleau-Ponty for showing that 'thought consists in foraging in the system of signs, in the particular tongue of a people or civilization, and receiving signification from this very operation'.[87] However, he argues that Merleau-Ponty has overlooked the fact that 'the essence of language is the relation with the other'.[88] It would not be possible merely to add to Merleau-Ponty's analysis the notion of the Other as the addressee of language, for the relation with the Other orients even inward discourse.[89]

Levinas insists that the original signification is infinity or 'the Other'. The face 'establishes signification itself in being'.[90] He compares the relationship between this signification and perception to that between the symbol and the object symbolised. 'The symbol', he writes, 'marks the inadequateness of what is given in consciousness with regard to the being it symbolizes.'[91] Similarly, signification is 'an overflowing of the intention that envisages by the being envisaged'.[92] However, signification differs from symbolisation in that the epiphany of the face overflows consciousness and calls it into question. Signification is 'the ethical exigency of the face which puts into question the consciousness that welcomes it'.[93]

If it is the face-to-face that founds language, and the face that establishes signification in being, we must conclude that language is not simply the servant of reason, but reason itself. Levinas therefore rejects the notion of reason as an 'impersonal legality', arguing that this notion fails to recognize the plurality of interlocutors in discourse.[94] He also rejects the Hegelian understanding of reason, according to which language dissolves 'the ipseity of individual consciousness', either by transforming it into an "I think" which no longer speaks', or making it 'disappear into its own discourse, whereupon, having entered into the State, it could only undergo the judgment of history, rather than remain me, that is, judge that history'.[95] Levinas insists that if, as he has been arguing, 'reason lives in language' and 'the first intelligibility gleams forth in the face-to-face',[96] the pluralism of society would, contra Hegel, be the very condition of reason.

As Robert Gibbs points out, the identification of being 'me' with judging history is one of the key themes that Levinas develops from his reading of Rosenzweig.[97] Throughout *Totality and Infinity*, Levinas insists that both I and the Other, in different ways, escape from history. Since the Other is 'absolutely other' or transcendent, he cannot be encompassed by the historical totality.

> The absolutely other, whose alterity is overcome in the philosophy of immanence on the allegedly common plane of history, maintains his transcendence in the midst of history. The same is essentially identification within the diverse, or history, or system. It is not I who resist the system, as Kierkegaard thought; it is the other.[98]

In spite of this claim that 'It is not I who resist the system', Levinas also argues that subjectivity is itself refractory to totalisation. As we saw above, subjectivity is described as 'separated' existence. The I of enjoyment is characterised by its paradoxical relationship to the world: both dependent upon it and, at the same time, independent. The I breaks with the totality of being by refusing to be subsumed in the generality of a concept; this refusal drives it into the 'dimension of interiority'. Interiority, in turn, is described as instituting 'an order different from historical time'.[99]

Interiority's resistance to the totalisation of history is explained by returning to the Cartesian *cogito*. Levinas emphasises the chronological order of the movements in the *Meditations*, stressing that the *cogito* is discovered prior to the idea of the Infinite. This chronological order is different from the logical and causal order of the Cartesian system, in which God, as the Creator and First Cause, is prior to any other being, including the *cogito*. Yet the *cogito* discovers God only after discovering itself. For Levinas, this interval is crucial.

> That there could be a chronological order distinct from the 'logical' order, that there could be several moments in the progression—here is separation. For by virtue of time this being is not *yet*—which does not make it the same as nothingness, but maintains it at a distance from itself. It is not all at once. Even its cause, older than itself, is still to come. The cause of being is thought or known by its effect *as though* it were posterior to its effect.[100]

Levinas insists that this reversal is not an illusion, but a 'positive event'. The 'anteriority of the posterior' is not limited to the Cartesian discovery of the *cogito* and its creator, but is produced by memory and thought. In memory and thought, 'the After or the Effect conditions the Before or the Cause: the Before appears and is only welcomed.'[101] Levinas sees this inversion as a 'revolution in being', in that it shows that all thought, and the psychism itself, articulate separation. The Same is an independent being.

> The present of the *cogito*, despite the support it discovers for itself *after the fact* in the absolute that transcends it, maintains itself all by itself—be it only for an instant, the space of a *cogito*. That there could be this instant of sheer youth, heedless of its

slipping into the past and of its recovered self possession in the future [...] that there be the very order or distance of time—all this articulates the ontological separation between the metaphysician and the metaphysical.[102]

The existence of a separated being entails that time must be conceived in two distinct ways. There is chronological order, which is the time of history. Levinas insists that it is only in history that totalisation can be accomplished. Historiographers can totalise because they assume that the chronological order of history

> [...] outlines the plot of being in itself, analogous to nature. The time of universal history remains as the ontological ground in which particular existences are lost, are computed, and in which at least their essences are recapitulated.[103]

For the historiographer, interiority is a nothingness, and thus does not need to be taken into account. However, Levinas argues that, for a true pluralism to be possible in society, it is necessary to take interiority seriously, and to reject the notion that only historical time represents the real. Instead, interior intentions, 'the secrecy that interrupts the continuity of historical time',[104] must also be considered.

Levinas maintains that interior time differs from the time of historiographers both in its relation to the past and in its relation to the future. The essence of interior time is memory. Memory allows me to 'ground myself after the event, retroactively: I assume today what in the absolute past of the origin had no subject to receive it and had therefore the weight of a fatality'.[105] In addition to differing from chronological time with respect to the past, interiority also has a different view of the future from that of the historiographer. The historiographer thinks the death of the other in the person, as an end, as 'the point at which the separated being is cast into the totality, and [consequently...] the point from which the separated being will continue by virtue of the heritage his existence has amassed.[106] However, interiority resists this fate, refuses to see itself becoming 'nothing but past'. It is the conflict between historical time, which will continue after one's death and incorporate one's story, and interior time, which is about to cease, which constitutes the death agony.[107]

Levinas, however, insists that it is possible to triumph over death, through 'fecundity', a concern for the other who will continue to exist after my death. He emphasises that interiority's 'non-reference to the common time of history' entails that mortal existence 'unfolds in a dimension that does not run parallel to the time of history and is not situated with respect to this time as to an absolute'.[108] It is only because interiority interrupts historical time that human life is not meaningless.

[... The] life between birth and death is neither folly nor absurdity nor flight nor cowardice. It flows on in a dimension of its own where it has meaning, and where a triumph over death can have meaning. This triumph is not a new possibility offered after the end of every possibility—but a resurrection in the son in whom the rupture of death is embodied.[109]

Levinas argues that it is through interiority's refusal to submit itself to the cruel judgment of history that morality arises. He acknowledges the need for rational institutions to protect the freedom of the will. 'Freedom', he writes, 'is not realized outside of social and political institutions[...].'[110] However, these institutions pronounce judgment on the will, treating it as if it 'were dead and signified only in its own heritage.'[111] The individual, therefore, rejects the judgment of history, longing for a judgment which will not deny his singularity.[112] Such recognition of singularity takes place in what Levinas terms the 'judgment of God'. Unlike the judgment of history, the judgment of God takes the singularity of the individual into account. This judgment takes place through the ethical relation.

The invisible offence that results from the judgment of history, a judgment on the visible, will attest subjectivity to be prior to judgment or to be a refusal of judgment, if it is only produced as cry and protestation, if it is felt within me. But it is produced as judgment itself when it looks at me and accuses me in the face of the Other [...] The will is under the judgment of God when its fear of death is inverted into fear of commiting murder.[113]

This judgment does not consist of the impersonal pronouncement of a verdict arising out of universal principles. Instead, 'judgment is pronounced upon me in the measure that it summons me to respond.'[114] The 'judgment of God' does not simply take the singularity of the individual into account, but 'exalts' it.

The exaltation of the singularity in judgment is produced precisely in the infinite responsibility of the will to which the judgment gives rise. [...] The summons exalts the singularity precisely because it is addressed to an infinite responsibility.[115]

The notion of infinite responsibility is not quantitative. Rather, it is the notion of a responsibility that increases in the measure that it is assumed. 'The better I accomplish my duty the fewer rights I have; the more I am just the more guilty I am.'[116]

Levinas terms the taking up of infinite responsibility 'goodness'[117] and explains that its demands exceed those of universal justice. Justice, he writes, 'does not include me in the equilibrium of its universality'; rather, it 'summons me to go beyond the straight line of justice, [...] necessitating all the resources of a singular presence.'[118]

In Levinas' later work, the notion of a 'justice beyond justice' is clarified by introducing a distinction between 'ethics' and 'justice'. Whilst in *Totality and Infinity*, the terms 'ethics' and 'justice' are used interchangeably, in his later work Levinas uses the word 'ethics' to refer to the face-to-face relation and 'justice' to refer to the institutions that arise from this relation. He discusses the relationship between ethics and justice in 'The Paradox of Morality'.

> The other is unique, unique to such an extent that in speaking of the responsibility for the unique [...] I use the word 'love'. [...] What is a loved one? He is unique in the world.[...]

Now, when there are two unique beings, the genre reappears. From this moment on, I think of the other in the genre.[...] The thought of comparison, of judgment, the attributes of the subject, in short, the entire terminology of Greek logic and Greek politics appear. [...] But what I say, quite simply, is that it [justice] is ultimately based on the relationship to the other, on the ethics without which I would not have sought justice. Justice is the way in which I respond to the fact that I am not alone in the world.[119]

Having defined justice not as an impersonal system, but as 'the way in which I respond to the fact that I am not alone in the world', Levinas emphasises that the institutionalisation of justice never divests me of my responsibility for the other. He explains that

> [...] there is a violence in justice. When the verdict of justice is pronounced, there remains for the unique I that I am the possibility of finding something more to soften the verdict. There is a place for charity after justice.[120]

For Levinas, then, 'ethics' and 'justice' are not totally distinct from one another, but are inexorably linked together through the excessive responsibility of the self. However, given that the key to Levinas' thought is this notion of a surplus of responsibility, and that he recognises that there are always more than two of us in the world, one might wonder what need Levinas has of the notion of a 'face-to-face relation'. This question leads us back to the general question of Levinas' method.

Levinas deals briefly with the question of the role of the face-to-face relation in the interview cited above. After describing the ethical relation he remarks that a discussion of the I-Other relationship is 'only the beginning of the analysis, because the way in which we behave concretely is different.'[121] Concrete relationships are different because 'there are not only two of us in the world.'[122] Presenting what would appear to be a transcendental analysis, Levinas continues

[...] I think that everything begins as if we were only two. It is important to recognize that the idea of justice always supposes that there is a third. But, initially, in principle, I am concerned about justice because the other has a face.[123]

The face-to-face here seems to be the condition of the possibility of justice, rather than a concrete experience. Similarly, later in the interview Levinas presents the relationship between ethics and justice as a foundational one. He asks, 'if everything terminates in justice, why tell this long story about the face, which is the opposite of justice?' His first answer is that it is ethics which is the foundation of justice'.[124]

However, in the rest of the paragraph, Levinas seems to assign to ethics more than a transcendental role. He notes that 'justice is not the last word; within justice, we seek a better justice'.[125] He then, as we saw above, points out the violence inherent in the verdicts of justice, and the possibility for 'the unique I' to find a way to 'soften the verdict' and improve the universality of justice.[126] This appeal to the unique I does not appear to come from the system of justice itself, but from the ethical relation. Levinas therefore appears to be arguing that the face-to-face is somehow both the condition for the possibility of justice and a concrete experience.

Most interpreters of Levinas, however, have opted either for a 'transcendental' or an 'empirical' reading of *Totality and Infinity*. Moreover, as Bernasconi points out, 'Levinas himself seems unable to decide between these rival interpretations'.[127] Bernasconi suggests that *Totality and Infinity* is a work of neither transcendental nor empirical philosophy, nor again is it a 'transcendental empiricism'. Rather, it seems to him that

[...] Levinas is using the language of transcendental philosophy and the language of empiricism [...] in an effort to find a way between these twin options given to us by the philosophical—and non-philosophical—language we have inherited.[128]

Although an evaluation of this argument and a thorough discussion of the status of the face-to-face relation lie beyond the scope of the present work, a brief analysis of Bernasconi's essay will help to illuminate both the paradoxical structure of the ethical relation and the ambivalence of Levinas' relationship to empirical and transcendental philosophy.

Bernasconi highlights Levinas' hesitation before the terms 'transcendental' and 'experience' in *Totality and Infinity*. In the preface, for example, Levinas notes that 'the relation with infinity cannot [...] be stated in terms of experience, for infinity overflows the thought that thinks it.'[129] However, Levinas then goes on to suggest that 'experience' should be understood to mean 'a relation with the absolutely other', in which case 'the relation with infinity accomplishes experience in the fullest sense of the word.'[130] Bernasconi notes that, on the same page of the preface, Levinas both indicates 'his uneasiness before the word "transcendental"' and states that his approach resembles the transcendental method.[131] 'The word *resembles*,' Bernasconi argues, 'is the key here because by it Levinas attempts to distance himself from the common conception of the transcendental method.'[132]

Although Levinas criticizes transcendental philosophy at various points in *Totality and Infinity*, a clearer explanation of his reservations can be found in *De Dieu qui vient a l'idée*. In an interview published under the title 'Questions et réponses', Levinas states that while he considers his method to be phenomenological, he rejects the association of transcendental philosophy with a search for foundations.

> The transcendental method consists in always searching for the foundation. 'Foundation' is moreover an architectural term, a term which is made for a world one inhabits, for a world which is *prior* to everything it supports, an astronomical world of perception, an immobile world, rest *par excellence,* the Same *par excellence.* An idea is justified when it has found its foundation, when one has shown the conditions of its possibility.—On the contrary, in my way of proceeding which starts with the human and the approach of the human [...] there is another manner of justifying one idea by another: moving from an idea to its superlative, all the way to its emphasis.[133]

Levinas' 'emphatic' procedure will be discussed in Chapter Two, when we examine the notions of passivity and substitution. For the moment, however, let us focus on his criticism of transcendental philosophy. An intentional analysis which seeks 'foundations' would not be capable of describing the relation with infinity, because the very notion of 'foundation' belongs to the world of the Same.

Bernasconi points out that, according to Levinas, 'the face of the Other ruptures what is ordinarily called experience.'[134] He then asks whether transcendental philosophy, as a search for foundations, can survive this rupture.

> Does not the very process of tracking the transcendental conditions of experience require that a continuous path be drawn between experience and its condition? In other words, can a transcendental thinking maintain the thought of transcendence? Levinas answers this question and shows the way in which his thought only resembles the transcendental method in the following passage: 'We can proceed from the experience of totality back to a situation where totality breaks up, a situation that conditions the totality itself.'[135]

Bernasconi understands Levinas to mean that 'the conditions for the possibility of the experience of totality are at the same time the conditions for the impossibility of the experience of totality, in the sense that the rupture with totality shows that there never was a totality'.[136] Bernasconi's thesis is that

Levinas follows the transcendental method to the point where it is halted and in order to sustain itself must draw on that which is radically exterior to it. This exteriority is itself therefore the condition for that which had been revealed in transcendental thought and for transcendental thought itself.[137]

This understanding of Levinas' method is supported by a careful analysis of the second part of *Totality and Infinity*. In this section, Levinas argues that labour and objectifying thought are 'relations analogous to transcendence' which 'already imply the relation with the transcendent'.[138] His task is, therefore, twofold; he must first show 'the difference between transcendent relations and relations analogous to transcendence' and, secondly, show 'the former to be reflected in the latter'.[139]

As we saw above, in our discussion of enjoyment and representation, Levinas argues that these relations differ from the transcendent relation (the relation with the Other) in that they remain within the domain of the Same. In representation, 'the exteriority of the object represented appears to reflection to be a meaning ascribed by the representing subject to an object that is itself reducible to a work of thought'.[140] Similarly, although in enjoyment the object is intended as exterior, through nourishment, the meeting of needs, it is assimilated to the same.

However, in spite of this important difference between the transcendent relation and the relations of enjoyment and representation, Levinas characterises the latter as analogous to the I-Other relationship. Bernasconi explains that the similarity between the two types of relationship is their 'double origin', the paradoxical structure of the '*anterior posteriori*'.[141] We saw above that Levinas finds two origins in the Cartesian Meditations, namely the *cogito* and the Infinite. In the chronological order of the Meditations, the *cogito* is discovered first and posited as an origin. Yet it later discovers the Infinite as its creator, and therefore as chronologically prior to it. Bernasconi emphasises Levinas' insistence that 'the *cogito* and the infinite are both absolute starting points for Descartes'.[142] Indeed, as we have seen, Levinas presents the Cartesian double origin as the model of separation[143] and argues that the same structure is exhibited by memory and thought.[144]

Bernasconi argues that the *anterior posteriori* is also exhibited by enjoyment and representation, each of which is presupposed by the other.[145] In enjoyment, as we saw above, the I is both dependent on the world from which it lives, and independent. Although representation seems to be constitutive of objects, it continually reverts into enjoyment, thus restoring 'the antecedence of what I constitute to this very constitution'.[146] Most significantly for our purposes, Bernasconi argues that the relationship with the human Other also exhibits the *anterior posteriori* structure.[147]

In order to understand this argument, we must turn to Levinas' analyses of habitation and economic existence, which we omitted from our preliminary description of the I-Other relation. Levinas highlights the importance of man's ability to overcome his dependence on the world, through planning and working to meet the very needs that constitute this dependence. He argues that the labour and possession involved in this struggle for independence are only possible if man has first established a 'home' or 'dwelling' from which to approach the world, and to which he can retreat.[148] Having a home makes possible a break with the immediacy of enjoyment, of life in the 'element'. 'The hand,' Levinas explains, 'both brings the elemental qualities to enjoyment, and takes and keeps them for future enjoyment.'[149] In order to do the latter, one must have a home in which to store possessions.

> The hand *comprehends* the thing not because it touches it on all sides at the same time (it does not touch it throughout), but because it is no longer a sense-organ, pure enjoyment, pure sensibility, but is mastery, domination, disposition—which do not belong to the order of sensibility. An organ for taking, for acquisition, it gathers the fruit but holds it far away from the lips, keeps it, puts it in reserve, possesses it in a home. The dwelling conditions labor. The hand that acquires is burdened by what it takes; it does not found possession by itself.[150]

Levinas' terminology in the final two sentences quoted suggest that he is presenting a transcendental argument: the dwelling conditions labour and founds possession. Yet, when Levinas introduces the Other to this analysis, the analogy of foundations breaks down. On the one hand, Levinas insists that the home presupposes the Other. 'The possibility for the home to open to the Other,' he writes, 'is as essential to the essence of the home as closed doors and windows',[151] that is, as essential as the possibility of shutting oneself up in one's home. Thus the home, which 'founds' labour and economic existence, already refers to the Other. On the other hand, Levinas is equally insistent that to welcome the Other is to be ready to offer 'my' possessions to him. The face-to-face relationship, he writes, 'is not enacted outside of the world';[152] 'no face can be approached with empty hands'.[153] As Bernasconi explains, this is 'Levinas' way of saying that the relation with the absolutely Other who paralyses possession presupposes economic existence'.[154]

Although Levinas uses the language of transcendental philosophy, the instances cited here of the *anterior posteriori* structure belie attempts to understand the face-to-face relation as an ultimate ground or foundation.[155] At the same time, the method followed in *Totality and Infinity* is not simply a form of empiricism. Levinas writes that

The method practiced here does indeed consist in seeking the condition of empirical situations, but it leaves to the developments called empirical in which the conditioning possibility is accomplished—it leaves to the concretization—an ontological role that specifies the meaning [*sens*] of the fundamental possibility, a meaning invisible in that condition.[156]

As Bernasconi explains, this passage is not to be understood as an indication that 'the meaning given to the formal structures by concretization equip them with an irreducible cultural specificity'.[157] Instead, Levinas is acknowledging that 'although his method is transcendental (at least by resemblance)', it is not a pure formalism such as that of Descartes. Rather, Levinas' transcendental analyses uncover a *sens*, a meaningful direction, in the possibilities they reveal.[158] The ethical direction is revealed in the 'concretization' of the formal structures.

When asked in interviews whether the face-to-face relation is ever realised concretely, Levinas often relates the story of a group of South American students who asked him the same question.

I remember meeting once with a group of Latin American students, well versed in the terminology of Marxist liberation and terribly concerned by the suffering and unhappiness of their people in Argentina. They asked me rather impatiently if I had ever actually witnessed the utopian rapport with the other that my ethical philosophy speaks of. I replied, 'Yes, indeed—here in this room.'[159]

This example obviously does not contstitute a proof of the face-to-face relation, which is invisible from the outside.[160] Nor, for the reasons discussed above, can the face-to-face be seen as the transcendental foundation of the concrete experience of concern for the other. Instead, in Levinas' view, examples such as these reveal the true sense of human existence: the very humanity of the human is the ability to break with the *conatus essendi* and put the other's needs before my own.

Levinas' task as a thinker is to express the significance and implications of this possibility in the language of western philosophy. As Bernasconi has shown, neither transcendental philosophy nor empirical philosophy are adequate to this task. Thus, in *Totality and Infinity*, rather than creating a 'transcendental empiricism', Levinas attempts to

[...] find a way between these twin options given to us by the philosophical—and nonphilosophical—language that we have inherited. Only by employing both languages and drawing them into contradiction as he does in the notion of the *anterior posteriori* can he hope to introduce us to a way of thinking which rests on neither.[161]

As we will see in subsequent chapters, Levinas' struggle with the language of western philosophy continues throughout his work. Although in his later work Levinas abandons the ontological language of *Totality and Infinity* and uses different linguistic stratagems to express the ethical, the notion that to be a self is to be responsible for the Other is the hallmark of later works as well.

Levinas' 'transcendental' analyses of dwelling, labour, representation and language have revealed, in Bernasconi's terminology, an 'ethical direction', an orientation towards the Other. This orientation allows the self to escape from the totalising forces of history by judging that history and becoming responsible for it. This responsibility is not irrational, but is rationality itself. Levinas has argued that reason is language, and that language arises through the ethical relation. He has reversed the philosophical hierarchy which makes ethics one subject among many to which the philosopher may turn his attention and consider its truth claims. Instead, truth itself is seen to arise out of the ethical relation.

### THE HOLOCAUST AND WESTERN PHILOSOPHY

As discussed above, Levinas criticises the western philosophical tradition for failing to recognise and respect the alterity of the human other. This critique of philosophy does not amount to identifying an error that philosophy has made and could correct without undergoing fundamental changes in itself. It is not simply that philosophy, until Levinas, has been mistaken about the nature of the ethical relation; rather, Levinas insists that when philosophy fails to recognise the alterity of the other, it issues in violence.

Many thinkers have been troubled by the fact that the Holocaust was the product of twentieth century Germany, a country which until then seemed to exemplify the virtues of post-Enlightenment western culture. Emil Fackenheim and Irving Greenberg, amongst others, have suggested a degree of complicity between the universal culture of the Enlightenment and the *Shoah*.[162] Although *Totality and Infinity* does not deal specifically with the question of philosophy's responsibility for the Holocaust, Levinas' analysis of the 'violence' inherent in western philosophy provides a way of understanding this complicity.

In *Totality and Infinity* Levinas introduces a distinction between two different types of theoretical knowledge: 'ontology', which is violent, and 'critique', which is ethical. Ontology reduces all alterity to sameness through a third, neutral term. For example, the third term is often a concept; when I think conceptually about something, 'the individual that exists abdicates into the general that is thought'.[163] By reducing otherness to sameness, ontology 'promotes freedom—the freedom that is the identification of the same, not allowing itself to be alienated by the other'.[164] The second form of theory, 'critique', exhibits more respect for alterity. Critical thought calls into question 'the freedom of the exercise of ontology'.[165] This calling into question of spontaneity is brought about by the self's encounter with the other.

> We name this calling into question of my spontaneity by the presence of the other ethics. The strangeness of the Other, his irreducibility to the I, to my thoughts and my possessions, is precisely accomplished as a calling into question of my spontaneity, as ethics.[166]

Levinas argues that most western philosophy has amounted to ontology rather than critique. In the first chapter of *Totality and Infinity* he cites four examples of ontological philosophy: the Platonic doctrine of *maieutics*, Berkeley's idealism, Husserl's notion of horizon and Heidegger's affirmation of the priority of Being over existents.

For Levinas, Socratic epistemology constitutes an excellent example of ontological thought. To claim that teaching does not consist in transmitting new knowledge to the student, but in awakening knowledge already within him, is to reduce what appears to be other (knowledge) to sameness (something already in the knower). This epistemology thus amounts to an assertion of the sovereignty of the same, which Levinas sees as the ultimate meaning of freedom in the western philosophical tradition.

> Freedom does not resemble the capricious spontaneity of free will; its ultimate meaning lies in this permanence in the same, which is reason. [...] That reason in the last analysis would be the manifestation of a freedom, neutralizing the other and encompassing him, can come as no surprise once it was laid down that sovereign reason knows only itself, that nothing other limits it.[167]

Berkeley's idealism, Levinas claims, also neutralises alterity. By reducing the qualities of objects to the subject's lived experience of those qualities, idealism reveals the exterior object to be ultimately a part of the self. Similarly phenomenology, whether Heideggerian or Husserlian, is, he insists, no less ontological than idealism. The idea of 'horizon' in phenomenology plays a role similar to that of the concept in classical idealism. Just as, in idealism, an individual 'arises from a concept', so in phenomenology an existent arises upon a horizon, 'a ground that extends beyond it'. The horizon renders the existent comprehensible. 'An existent is comprehended in the measure that thought transcends it, measuring it against the horizon whereupon it is profiled.'[168]

Heidegger's affirmation of the priority of Being over existents is also criticised by Levinas, in many contexts, as being fundamentally unethical.[169]

> To affirm the priority of Being over existents is to already decide the essence of philosophy; it is to subordinate the relation with someone, who is an existent (the ethical relation) to a relation with the Being of existents which, impersonal, permits the

apprehension, the domination of existents (a relationship of knowing), subordinates justice to freedom [...] In subordinating every relation with existents to the relation with Being the Heideggerian ontology affirms the primacy of freedom over ethics.[170]

Levinas acknowledges that for Heidegger, 'it is not man who possesses freedom; it is freedom that possesses man'. However, he insists that 'the dialectic which thus reconciles freedom and obedience in the concept of truth presupposes the primacy of the same, which marks the direction of and defines the whole of western philosophy.'[171] According to Levinas, then, Heideggerian philosophy, in spite of its attempt to escape metaphysics by returning to the 'question of Being', continues the western tradition of reducing the other to the same.

It is often in the context of discussions of Heidegger that Levinas considers the political implications of totalising philosophies. In the first chapter of *Totality and Infinity*, Levinas argues that ontology, as first philosophy, amounts to a 'philosophy of power'.[172] Because it does not call into question the same, it is a philosophy of injustice, which issues in the tyranny of the state.

> The relation with Being that is enacted as ontology consists in neutralizing the existent in order to comprehend or grasp it. It is hence not a relation with the other as such but the reduction of the other to the same [...]. Thematization and conceptualization, which moreover are inseparable, are not peace with the other but suppression or possession of the other. For possession affirms the other, but within a negation of its independence. 'I think' comes down to 'I can'—to an appropriation of what is, to an exploitation of reality. Ontology as first philosophy is a philosophy of power. It issues in the State and in the non-violence of the totality, without securing itself against the violence from which this non-violence lives, and which appears in the tyranny of the State. Truth, which should reconcile persons, here exists anonymously. Universality presents itself as impersonal; and this is another inhumanity.[173]

Levinas argues that, while 'denouncing the sovereignty of the technological powers of man', Heidegger remains an ontological thinker because he 'exalts the pre-technological powers of possession'.[174] For Heidegger, 'obedience to the truth of Being' is accomplished through an existence as 'builder and cultivator, effecting the unity of the site which sustains space'.[175] Building and cultivating entail possession and a sedentary existence which, according to Levinas, amount to a reduction of alterity to sameness.[176] Levinas insists that because Heideggerian ontology 'subordinates the relationship with the Other to the relation with Being in general', it 'leads inevitably to another power, to imperialist domination, to tyranny'.[177] Contra Heidegger, he insists that tyranny does not result simply from extending technology to reifed men. Rather, its origin lies

[...] in the pagan 'moods', in the enrootedness in the earth, in the adoration that enslaved men can devote to their masters. Being before the existent, ontology before metaphysics, is freedom (be it the freedom of theory) before justice. It is a movement within the same before obligation to the other.[178]

In his essay 'Philosophy and the Idea of Infinity', Levinas suggests that the tyranny of National Socialism rested on possession and enrootedness.

When Heidegger calls attention to the forgetting of Being [...] when he deplores the orientation of the intellect toward technology, he maintains a regime of power more inhuman than mechanism (and which perhaps does not have the same source as it; it is not sure that National Socialism arises from the mechanist reification of men, and that it does not rest on peasant enrootedness and a feudal adoration of subjugated men for the masters and lords who command them).[179]

As we have seen, Levinas reverses the terms of ontology by showing that the obligation towards the other is prior to freedom and truth; objectivity itself is the product of language, which arises in the ethical relation. Levinas is not denying the need for truth; he insists that the ethical relation, whilst opposed to 'first philosophy which identifies freedom and power' is nevertheless 'not contrary to truth'.[180] Ontological thought is necessary. Without being able to form the concept 'human', the institutions which belong to the realm of 'justice' would not be possible. To borrow Buber's terminology (keeping in mind the differences between the I-Thou and the face-to-face), we cannot remain indefinitely in the I-Thou, but must always return to the I-It. Otherwise the world could not function. It is not ontological thought *per se* that Levinas is opposed to, but ontology as first philosophy.

If western philosophy is indeed ontological, and ontology issues, as Levinas argues, in tyranny, we must conclude that this philosophy is in some measure responsible for the Holocaust. It would be beyond the scope of the present study to provide an adequate evaluation of Levinas' charge that the history of western philosophy amounts to the history of ontology. However, if Levinas' claim that the theoretical 'tyranny' of ontology issues in political oppression could be justified, the charge that western philosophy is implicated in the Holocaust could then be upheld or dismissed on the basis of such an evaluation.

On one level, the charge that ontology is responsible for the Holocaust is a truism. It would be impossible for a State or any other institution to think 'ethically'; all institutions must be run according to ontological, conceptual thought. The Holocaust, a bureaucratic attempt at genocide, would represent an extreme case of the 'violence' that Levinas identifies as a necessary product of ontological thought and thus of all institutions.

However if, like Levinas, we consider historical developments to take place through the actions of individuals, a more profound case against ontology can be made. Levinas has argued that to be 'I' is to experience oneself as infinitely obligated, as responsible for the entire world. Although it is impossible to realise the ethical relation to the other, since there are always more than two of us in the world, the ethical relation does not become irrelevant once the system of justice it has inspired comes into play. Instead, it provides the unrealisable standard by which any system of justice can itself be judged. It is up to the individual, experiencing himself as uniquely responsible, to make this judgment and to seek a 'better justice'.[181]

Ontology as first philosophy, however, denies either the self's responsibility for the world or its capacity for influencing events, or both. The Socratic doctrine of *maieutics*, for example, denies the truth of this responsibility by precluding the possibility of a teaching that comes from the Other. Deterministic philosophies of any description also mitigate against the possibility of an individual behaving as if he were responsible for the entire world. It is, of course, possible for a determinist to act in a manner that would be described as 'ethical' or 'responsible'; it is not necessary to believe in free will in order to perform a 'right' action. For example, one might donate a large sum of money to charity whilst believing that one had no choice in the matter, that the action was the direct result of one's psychological make-up, the configuration of the celestial bodies, or 'fate'. However, the human tendency to act out of self-interest is readily observable, and a deterministic philosophy would seem more likely to encourage this tendency than to curb it. The same would certainly be true of any philosophy which, for whatever reason, denies the self's responsibility for the world.

It is, therefore, not necessary to argue that Hitler was a student of Hegel, or that Nazism is an adaptation of any particular ontological philosophy, in order to support the claim that western thought is to some degree responsible for the Holocaust. Instead, we may focus on the failure of western culture to provide the majority of Germans with a philosophy that would help them to resist the atrocities of Nazism.

One might object that, if Levinas is correct and the 'I' experiences itself as responsible for the world, the Holocaust, and any human evil, would have been impossible. However, it must be noted that Levinas' philosophy is not a naive altruism. As we saw above, he does not claim that murder is actually impossible, but that it is ethically impossible.[182] Indeed, for Levinas it is not human evil that stands in need of explanation, but goodness. The description of the face-to-face relation is a quasi-phenomenological account of the possibility for a human being to break with the *conatus essendi* of living beings and place the needs of the other above his own. Western philosophy has failed humanity by mitigating against this possibility in providing the individual with alibis for following his natural inclination towards self-preservation, rather than responding to the call of the Other.

To return to the question we raised above, if all states are necessarily violent, how were the Nazis any different from other institutionalized powers? In other words, does Levinas' philosophy provide any criteria for the evaluation of the different forms states and other institutions may take? Levinas has addressed this question in the interview cited above. Asked 'How would you respond to the suggestion that your ethics is too idealistic, because it does not offer any practical advice for solving political problems?' Levinas responded by asserting the superiority of the liberal state over other forms of government.

> The liberal state is a state which holds justice as the absolutely desirable end and hence as a perfection. Concretely, the liberal state has always admitted—alongside the written law—human rights as a parallel institution. It continues to preach that within its justice there are always improvements to be made in human rights. Human rights are the reminder that there is no justice yet. And, consequently, I believe that it is absolutely obvious that the liberal state is more moral than the fascist state, and closer to the morally ideal state.[183]

Levinas concedes that his thought is utopian.

> There is a utopian moment in what I say; it is the recognition of something which cannot be realized but which, ultimately, guides all moral action. This utopianism does not prohibit you from condemning certain factual states, nor from recognizing the relative progress that can be made. There is no moral life without utopianism— utopianism in this exact sense that saintliness is goodness.[184]

Levinas' commendation of the liberal state would appear to raise another difficulty: if western thought is fundamentally ontological and violent, how can the liberal state, which is a product of western thought, be moral? We will see in the next chapter that Levinas sees concern for the other as the underlying intention of western humanism. This, however, is not a contradiction of his indictment of ontology. The argument of *Totality and Infinity* is that ontology arises out of the ethical relation. It is only when ontology, forgetful of its roots, presents itself as first philosophy and denies the self's responsibility for the Other, that it must be overcome. Moreover, Levinas does not use the term 'moral' in an absolute way. Societies (or philosophies) can never be perfectly moral; in the measure that they encourage concern for the Other they are 'ethical' and insofar as they discourage it they are 'violent'.

CONCLUSION

This chapter opened with a philosophical question—is morality still meaningful in a post-holocaust era? Levinas' quasi-phenomenological account of the face-to-face relation both provides the basis for an affirmative answer to this question, and at the same time transforms the philosophical question of ethics into an ethical questioning of philosophy.

Questioning is, in the words of Ricoeur, 'the primitive hermeneutical phenomenon'.[185] The remainder of this book will be primarily concerned with exploring how the question of ethics, or more precisely, ethics as a calling into question, provides the basis for Levinas' hermeneutics, his approach to interpreting and understanding the texts and traditions of western thought.[186] In the process of showing how Levinas teaches us to read the texts of our culture, we will also be concerned with questions of a more immediate hermeneutical nature about how to read Levinas' own writings, particularly the problematic terms 'God', 'humanism', 'subjectivity' and 'Judaism'.

1  *Totality and Infinity: An Essay on Exteriority*, translated by Alphonso Lingis, Pittsburgh, Duquesne University Press, 1969, p. 21. Hereafter cited as *Totality and Infinity*.

2  'Useless Suffering', p. 162.

3  'The Paradox of Morality: An Interview with Emmanuel Levinas' in *The Provocation of Levinas*, p. 176. Hereafter cited as 'The Paradox of Morality'.

4  Levinas' critique of western philosophy will be analysed in more detail below.

5  *Otherwise than Being*, p. 162.

6  In *Totality and Infinity*, Levinas writes 'Morality is not a branch of philosophy, but first philosophy' (p. 304).

7  In his seminal essay on Levinas entitled 'Violence and Metaphysics: An essay on the Thought of Emmanuel Levinas', Derrida describes it instead as 'an Ethics of Ethics'. (In *Writing and Difference*, translated by Alan Bass, London, Routledge and Kegan Paul, 1981, p. 111; hereafter cited as 'Violence and Metaphysics'.)

8  As Simon Critchley explains, 'ethics is simply and entirely the event of this relation'. *The Ethics of Deconstruction*, Oxford, Blackwell, 1992, p. 5.

9  *Totality and Infinity*, p. 43.

10  *The Ethics of Deconstruction*, p. 5.

11  We are here following Levinas in using the Holocaust as a paradigm of the inhuman events of the twentieth century. In a footnote to the essay 'Useless Suffering', Levinas writes 'I think that all the dead of the Gulag and all the other places of torture in our political century are present when one speaks of Auschwitz.' *The Provocation of Levinas*, note 6, p. 167.

12  For Levinas, Heidegger represents the culmination of western philosophy. The relationship between the two thinkers is a highly complex one, which is analysed at length by Robert John Sheffler Manning in his book *Interpreting Otherwise than Heidegger: Emmanuel Levinas' Ethics as First Philosophy*, Pittsburgh, Pennsylvania, Duquesne University Press, 1993 (hereafter cited as *Interpreting Otherwise*). Manning argues that Levinas' philosophy bears a dialectical relation to Heidegger's; it is 'a constant arguing against and an interpreting otherwise than Heidegger's phenomenological ontology, but always within the context of and after the manner of Heidegger's phenomenological project in *Being and Time*' (p. 7). We will look at Levinas' critique of Heidegger at several points in this study, but will not enter into the debate about the accuracy or otherwise of Levinas' reading of Heidegger.

13  We will see below that Levinas identifies a few exceptional moments in this history; but even the thinkers, such as Plato and Descartes, who recognize transcendence, soon return to the ontologising mode of thought that dominates western philosophy.

14  It will be argued in Chapter Three that Levinas is not a 'theological' thinker.

15 Levinas uses masculine pronouns to refer to the other, except when he is explicitly concerned with the 'feminine'. In order to avoid confusion, we will follow suit throughout this study.

16 The Jewish tradition includes similar formulations, such as Hillel's 'What is hateful to you, do not to your fellow' (*Shabbat* 31a). Arguably, this negative rule is a less 'violent' formulation, respecting the alterity of the other and demanding only that one refrain from activity that may be hurtful.

17 *Totality and Infinity,* p. 194.

18 As we will see below, Levinas argues that the word 'experience' only applies to our encounter with the other if the word is understood to mean 'a relation with the absolutely other', in which case 'the relation with infinity accomplishes experience in the fullest sense of the word'. Ibid., p. 25.

19 *Totality and Infinity* p. 195.

20 We will not give a more detailed account of phenomenology at this point, since the question of Levinas' relationship to the phenomenological method will be explored below. For an introductory analysis of Levinas' relationship to Husserlian and Heideggerian phenomenology, see Manning, *Interpreting Otherwise,* pp. 15–57.

21 As Adriaan Peperzak points out, the key concept in Husserl's renewal of philosophy through a return to 'things in themselves' is 'intentionality'. Husserl, Peperzak writes, 'saw not only that all consciousness is a *cogito* of something (*cogitatum*), but also that the intentional structure of consciousness cannot be characterized as the relation between a representing subject and objects met by that subject'. Instead, there are many different types of nonrepresentational intentions and clusters of intentions, which it would be the task of phenomenology to analyse. A complete phenomenological analysis, Peperzak continues, 'would reveal the specificity of all real, necessary, and possible intentions constituting human consciousness' and would 'encompass a complete description of an all—embracing consciousness and of the totality of all beings capable of manifesting themselves'. *To the Other: An Introduction to the Philosophy of Emmanuel Levinas,* West Lafayette, Indiana, Purdue University Press, 1993, pp. 14–15. (Hereafter cited as *To the Other.*) Levinas, however, is concerned to show that the Other necessarily escapes this all-embracing consciousness.

22 In *Being and Time,* Heidegger writes that 'The signification of "phenomenon", as conceived both formally and in the ordinary manner, is such that any exhibiting of an entity as it shows itself in itself, may be called "phenomenology" with formal justification' (pp. 48–50). Levinas' criticisms of Heideggerian phenomenology will be discussed below.

23 'Robert Bernasconi, 'Rereading *Totality and Infinity*' in *The Question of the Other: Essays in Contemporary Continental Philosophy,* Edited by Arleen B. Dallery and Charles E. Scott. Albany, State University of New York Press, 1989, p. 24. Hereafter cited as 'Rereading'.

24 *Totality and Infinity,* p. 36.

25 Idem.

26 Idem.

27 Ibid., p. 37.

28 Ibid., p. 122.

29 Ibid., p. 126.

30 Ibid., p. 128.

31 Idem.

32 Ibid., p. 123.

33 Ibid., p. 124; emphasis added.

34 Ibid., p. 127.

35 Ibid., pp. 127–28.

36 Ibid., p. 110.

37 Ibid., pp. 111–12.

38 Ibid., p. 112.

39 Idem.

40 Ibid., p. 113.

41 Idem.

42 Ibid., p. 114.

43 Ibid., p. 111.

44 Ibid., p. 116.

45   Ibid., p. 118.
46   Idem.
47   Ibid., p. 124.
48   Ibid., p. 139.
49   Idem.
50   Ibid., p. 215.
51   Idem.
52   Ibid., p. 33.
53   Ibid. p. 34.
54   Idem.
55   Idem.
56   Ibid., p. 63.
57   Ibid., p. 40.
58   Ibid., pp. 39–40.
59   Ibid., p. 40.
60   Ibid., p. 49.
61   Idem.
62   Idem.
63   Idem.
64   Ibid., p. 50.
65   Ibid., pp. 50–51.
66   Ibid., p. 194.
67   See our analysis of Levinas' discussion of the intentionality of murder, below.
68   It should be noted that Levinas is not claiming that all speech acts or discourses constitute a rela-
     tionship with transcendence. Under the sub-title 'Rhetoric and Injustice', Levinas explicitly states
     that 'Not every discourse is a relation with exteriority.[…] Our pedagogical or psychagogical dis-
     course', he continues, 'is rhetoric, taking the position of him who approaches his neighbour with
     ruse.[…] It approaches the other not to face him, but obliquely […]' *Totality and Infinity,* p. 70.
69   Ibid., p. 195.
70   Idem.
71   Idem.
72   Idem.
73   Ibid., p. 196.
74   Idem.
75   Idem.
76   Idem.
77   Ibid., p. 197.
78   Ibid., p. 199.
79   Ibid., p. 198.
80   Idem.
81   Ibid., p. 199.
82   Ibid., p. 200.
83   Idem.
84   Idem.
85   Ibid., p. 201. Levinas is here alluding to Plato (*Republic*, 32b).
86   Ibid., p. 209.
87   Ibid., pp. 205–206.
88   Ibid., p. 207.
89   Idem.
90   Idem.
91   Idem.
92   Idem.
93   Idem.
94   Ibid., p. 208.

95   Idem.
96   Idem.
97   *Correlations*, p. 25.
98   *Totality and Infinity*, p. 40.
99   Ibid., p. 55.
100  Ibid., p. 54.
101  Idem.
102  Ibid., pp. 54–55.
103  Ibid., p. 55.
104  Ibid., pp. 57–58.
105  Ibid., p. 56.
106  Idem.
107  Idem.
108  Idem.
109  Ibid., pp. 56–57.
110  Ibid., p. 241.
111  Ibid., p. 242.
112  Idem.
113  Ibid., p. 244.
114  Idem.
115  Idem.
116  Idem.
117  Ibid., pp. 244–45.
118  Ibid., p. 245.
119  'The Paradox of Morality', p. 174. (This quotation has been altered slightsly, to correct a typographical error in the translation, which substitutes 'face' for 'fact'.) For a detailed analysis of the development of Levinas' understanding of the passage from the ethical relation to justice, see Adriaan Peperzak, *To the Other*, pp. 168–84.
120  Ibid., p. 175.
121  Ibid., p. 170.
122  Idem.
123  Idem.
124  Ibid., p. 175.
125  Idem.
126  Idem.
127  'Rereading', p. 25. I am following Bernasconi in using the terms 'transcendental' and 'empirical' to describe interpretations which respectively take the face-to-face to be the condition for the possibility of justice, or a concrete experience.
128  Ibid., p. 34.
129  *Totality and Infinity*, p. 25.
130  Idem. Similarly, in 'Philosophy and the Idea of Infinity', Levinas writes that the idea of infinity is 'experience in the sole radical sense of the term: a relationship with the exterior, with the other, without this exteriority being able to be integrated into the same'. *Collected Philosophical Papers*, trans. A. Lingis, The Hague, Martinus Nijhoff, 1987, p. 54.
131  Bernasconi, 'Rereading', p. 24.
132  Idem.
133  'Questions et réponses', in *De Dieu qui vient à l'idée*, Paris, Vrin, 1982, p. 141.
134  'Rereading', p. 24.
135  Idem. Bernasconi is here quoting from *Totality and Infinity*, p. 24.
136  Idem.
137  Idem.
138  *Totality and Infinity*, p. 109, following Bernasconi's translation.
139  'Rereading', p. 27.
140  *Totality and Infinity*, p. 125.

141 'Rereading', p. 32.

142 Idem.

143 *Totality and Infinity*, p. 54. 'That there could be a chronological order distinct from the "logical" order, that there could be several moments in the progression—here is separation.'

144 Ibid., pp. 54–55.

145 'Rereading', p. 32.

146 *Totality and Infinity*, p. 147.

147 Peperzak notes that the same structure is exhibited in Levinas' discussion of fraternity. He writes that 'Although it is clear that the concept of such a fraternity presupposes transcendence and the face, some sentences suggest that the latter are also conditioned by the former [...]' ( *To the Other*, p. 199).

148 *Totality and Infinity*, p. 152.

149 Ibid., p. 161.

150 Ibid., pp. 161–2.

151 Ibid., p. 173.

152 Ibid., p. 172.

153 Idem.

154 'Rereading', pp. 33–4.

155 Bernasconi therefore rejects de Boer's argument that the other 'functions as the transcendental foundation of the same'. Ibid., p. 32.

156 *Totality and Infinity*, p. 173. On the meaning of the term 'concretization', see below.

157 'Rereading', p. 33.

158 Idem.

159 'Dialogue with Emmanuel Levinas', in *Face to Face with Levinas*, pp. 32–3. See also 'Questions et Réponses', in *De Dieu qui vient a l'idée*, p. 131.

160 'The metaphysician and the other do not constitute a simple correlation, which would be reversible. The reversibility of a relation where the terms are indifferently read from left to right and from right to left would couple them the *one* to the *other;* they would complete one another in a system visible from the outside.' *Totality and Infinity*, p. 35.

161 'Rereading', p. 34.

162 See for example Greenberg's essay 'Cloud of Smoke, Pillar of Fire: Judaism, Christianity and Modernity After the Holocaust', in *Auschwitz: Beginning of a New Era? Reflections on the Holocaust*, edited by Eva Fleischner, New York, KTAV Publishing House, 1977, pp. 7–55; and Fackenheim's introduction to *Encounters Between Judaism and Western Philosophy A Preface to Future Jewish Thought*, New York, Schocken Books, 1973.

163 *Totality and Infinity,* p. 42.

164 Idem.

165 Idem.

166 Ibid., p. 43.

167 Idem.

168 Ibid., p. 44.

169 Levinas' criticisms of Heidegger will be examined in more detail in Chapter Three.

170 *Totality and Infinity*, p. 44.

171 Idem.

172 Ibid., p. 47.

173 Ibid., pp. 45–46.

174 Ibid., p. 46.

175 Idem.

176 Idem.

177 Ibid., pp. 46–47

178 Ibid., p. 47.

179 *Collected Philosophical Papers*, p. 52

180 Ibid., p. 47.

181 'The Paradox of Morality', p. 175.

182 This point will be discussed in greater detail in Chapter Four.

183 'The Paradox of Morality', pp. 177–78. Nevertheless, some critics have claimed that Levinas is opposed to the modern, liberal state. See, for example, Gillian Rose, *Judaism and Modernity*, pp. 17–18.

184 'The Paradox of Morality', p. 178.

185 *Hermeneutics and the Human Sciences*, Edited and Translated by John B. Thompson, London, Cambridge University Press, 1984, p. 78.

186 Levinas often contrasts 'Hebrew' with 'Greek' or western thought. However, in other contexts he emphasises that western culture has biblical as well as Greek roots. See, for example, 'The Paradox of Morality' in which he states 'I think that Europe is the Bible and Greece' (p. 174).

# Chapter 2

## HUMANISM AND ETHICS

### INTRODUCTION

The previous chapter opened with a discussion of the seemingly out-moded term 'morality'. Similarly, this chapter is concerned with a word that, particularly in the contemporary French context, sounds laughably old-fashioned: 'humanism'. We will see that, in addition to providing the orientation for a critique of traditional humanism, Levinas' ethics also allows for a positive evaluation of the underlying intention of humanism. After looking at the contribution Levinas has made to the debate between humanists and anti-humanists, we will analyse his use of the term to describe his own philosophy as a 'humanism of the other man'. Before doing so, however, it will be helpful to consider the historical background of this debate.

### HUMANISM AND ANTI-HUMANISM

'Humanism' is a word with a long and varied history. As Heidegger points out in his 'Letter on Humanism',[1] the first 'humanism' arose from the encounter of Roman civilisation with late Greek culture.

> *Humanitas*, explicitly so called, was first considered and striven for in the age of the Roman Republic. *Homo humanus* was opposed to *homo barbarus*. *Homo humanus* here means the Romans, who exalted and honored Roman *virtus* throughout the 'embodiment' of the *paideia* [education] taken over from the Greeks. These were the Greeks of the Hellenistic age, whose culture was acquired in the schools of philosophy.[2]

Heidegger explains that the Italian Renaissance consisted in a revival of interest in this romanised Greek culture. Once again, *homo romanus* was being opposed to *homo barbarus*, but in this case 'the inhumane is the supposed barbarism of Gothic Scholasticism in the Middle Ages'.[3]

In addition to referring to the study of classical Greek civilisation, 'humanism' has also, since the Renaissance, been used in a much broader sense. Heidegger defines this broader sense as 'a concern that man become free for his humanity and find his worth in it'.[4] Humanisms, therefore, differ 'according to one's conception of the "freedom" and "nature" of man'.[5]

Kate Soper has argued that when the word 'humanism' is used in this broad sense it functions more as an appeal for approval than an attempt at definition. She remarks that,

[...] despite the very extensive differences of opinion between the self-styled 'humanists' (both past and present) as to what their creed might consist of, none of them has ever been prepared to cede the epithet itself. Indeed [until very recently] 'humanist' doctrine has been so universally regarded as laudable that those who have described themselves as 'humanist' have done so, we must presume, not on account of the definition it lends their thought (a task for which it is, in fact, pre-eminently unsuited), but in order to win approval for it.[6]

Soper points out, however, that much recent continental thought has broken with this tradition and is self-consciously 'anti-humanist'.

Although a detailed analysis of the contemporary debate concerning humanism is beyond the scope of the present study,[7] it will be helpful to consider some of the main features of contemporary anti-humanist thought before examining Levinas' essays on humanism. The writings of such thinkers as Michel Foucault, Jacques Derrida, Gilles Deleuze, Jean-François Lyotard and Louis Althusser are much too diverse to be described as representing a 'school' of thought. However, these thinkers share both a common enemy (traditional notions of subjectivity) and common influences: the works of Marx, Nietzsche, Freud and Heidegger.[8]

The three nineteenth century thinkers named in the above list are jointly credited with instituting a 'hermeneutics of suspicion', or the practice of 'genealogical critique'. Faced with a discourse, the task of the thinker would not be that of analysing its content but of uncovering the underlying conditions of its production, whether these conditions are seen in terms of economic 'infrastructure', *libido* or physiological instinct.[9] Following the lead of Marx, Nietzsche and Freud, the French anti-humanists have treated discourses of consciousness as 'symptoms' to be analysed.[10]

This critical procedure leads to both a dethroning of the traditional subject and a radical revision of the notion of truth. The Nietzschean genealogical critique does not simply displace truth, relocating it in the genealogist's interpretation, but opens the possibility of endless interpretations.[11] The idea that any discourse opens up an infinite number of interpretations can be illustrated in psychoanalytic terms. Although the interpretation of a discourse might be understood to have uncovered the unconscious force behind that discourse, the interpreter is also subject to unconscious influences which must in turn be interpreted.[12]

Even without embracing the Nietzschean argument for infinite possibilities of interpretation, genealogical critique leads to a dethroning of the subject qua consciousness, for it entails that the subject is not the master of his discourse. Indeed, not only is the genealogist not interested in the subject qua consciousness, but genealogical critique involves a certain reification of the conscious subject; the subject is treated as a pure thing, incapable of defending itself against any interpretation.[13] Foucault, for example, writes in 'Nietzsche, Marx, Freud':

> Interpretation, from now on, will always be an interpretation through the 'Who'; one does not interpret what is in the signified; but one interprets in depth: who has proposed the interpretation?[14]

In addition to making the human subject into the object of interpretation, genealogical critique calls for a revised notion of truth. Truth, in the metaphysical tradition, has been understood according to the models of correspondence and coherence. The argument that there is an infinite number of possible interpretations of any discourse does away with the notion of referent which is essential to the first model, and the postulate of unconscious forces is often claimed to render illusory the notion of a self-transparent discourse which is assumed by the second model.[15]

One of the reasons that Heidegger figures so prominently in the writings of the French anti-humanists is that his understanding of truth as unveiling (*aletheia*) meets the needs of the genealogists for a new definition of truth. Heidegger argues that all manifestation is at the same time dissimulation. Ferry and Renaut give the now famous example of a cube: at any one time, three faces of the cube are hidden from the observer's view. Thus, visibility is given only against a background of invisibility and presence against a background of absence.[16] Every discourse would, like the cube, possess 'its hidden face, that is, its outside'.[17]

Such a notion of truth has, however, not been universally adopted by the French anti-humanists. Some currents of Marxist thought in particular have continued to insist on the radical distinction between science and ideology. For example, according to Althusser, the 'science of history' makes possible the scientific discovery of truth, thus providing the background for identifying the errors in ideological thought.[18]

Although Marx has clearly been a major influence on French anti-humanism, it should be noted that, at least in his early writings, he saw his own thought not as anti-humanism, but as a superior form of humanism.[19] Whereas some interpreters of Marx, such as Althusser, see the later works as instituting a radical break with humanism,[20] others insist that Marx was not rejecting humanism per se, but only distancing himself from Feuerbachian humanism.[21] It would therefore be simplistic to label Marx as either a humanist or an anti-humanist. Indeed, as Soper points out, the theoretical opposition between humanism and anti-humanism has been given its most explicit formulation in the debate surrounding Althusser's interpretation of Marx.[22]

Soper defines the technical sense acquired by the terms 'humanism' and 'anti-humanism' in recent continental philosophy as follows:

> *Humanism*: appeals (positively) to the notion of a core humanity or common essential features in terms of which human beings can be defined and understood, thus (negatively) to concepts ('alienation', 'inauthenticity', 'reification', etc.) designating, and intended to explain, the perversion or 'loss' of this common being. Humanism takes history to be a product of human thought and action, and thus claims that the categories of 'consciousness', 'agency', 'choice', 'responsibility', 'moral value' etc. are indispensable to its understanding.
>
> *Anti-humanism*: claims that humanism as outlined above is pre-scientific 'philosophical anthropology'. All humanism is 'ideological'; the ideological status of humanism is to be explained in terms of the systems of thought or 'consciousness' produced in response to particular historical periods. Anthropology, if it is possible at all, is possible only on condition that it rejects the concept of the human subject; 'men' do not make history, nor find their 'truth' or 'purpose' in it; history is a process without a subject.[23]

Although Soper's definitions are largely based on the debate within Marxism, she insists that they are also applicable to non-marxist forms of humanism and anti-humanism. In spite of the major differences between them, Derrida, Foucault, Althusser, Deleuze, and other French anti-humanists have in common that they reject humanism's anthropocentric approach to the human sciences, on the grounds that anthropocentrism 'mythologizes the object—humankind—of which it aspires to provide a rational or scientific understanding'.[24]

## TOWARDS A NEW HUMANISM

### Hebraic Humanism

Levinas offers his own definitions of humanism and anti-humanism in *Difficile liberté*. In the essay 'Antihumanisme et éducation' he identifies two meanings of the word 'humanism'. The first definition incorporates the theoretical elements covered in Soper's definition, as well as including both the notion of humanism as a study of the humanities and the political aspect (guardianship of freedom) mentioned by Heidegger. Humanism, Levinas writes, signifies

> [...] the recognition of an invariable essence called 'man', the affirmation of his central place in the economy of the Real and of his value, which engenders all values: respect for the person, in oneself and in the other, imposing the guardianship of his freedom; blossoming of human nature, of intelligence in Science, of creation in Art, of pleasure in daily life; satisfaction of desires without prejudicing the freedom and

pleasures of other men and, consequently, the institution of a just law, that is, a reasonable and liberal State [...]²⁵

The second sense of humanism that Levinas identifies is a more narrow and less complimentary one: 'humanism' may also signify the reduction of a study of the humanities and of the principles of humanism to *beau langage*. Levinas explains that this process begins, quite innocently, with the homage paid to certain works in which humanist principles and values are presented. Eventually the texts and the articulation of these principles take precedence over action, and as the goal of realising the principles is gradually forgotten, humanism degenerates into rhetoric and ideology.

The *beau langage* of humanism in the second sense has, Levinas argues, been rendered suspect by the inhuman events of the twentieth century. He refers to this mistrust of humanist rhetoric as 'anti-humanism' and insists that such anti-humanism is not necessarily accompanied by an abandonment of the 'human ideal'.

However, even humanism in the first sense is not left untouched by the inhuman events of this century, such as the two world wars, the rise of fascism and Nazism, nuclear bombings and genocide. These events might seem to suggest that the beautiful principles of humanism are based on a naively optimistic view of man.

Levinas argues that humanist ideology has been called into question not only by events, but also by the intellectual developments of this century. Amongst the latter he cites modern science which 'wants to embrace the world and threatens to destroy it' and Heideggerian philosophy which 'subordinates the human to the anonymous games of Being' and, 'despite its "Letter on Humanism", lends understanding to Nazism itself'.²⁶ He asks whether these developments are the result of 'the fragility of humanism in western liberalism' and whether they indicate a 'fundamental inability to safeguard the principles of humanity of which humanism believed itself to be the trustee'.²⁷

Levinas attributes the fragility of humanism not to any external factor, but to its inadequate understanding of the meaning of the human. He argues that the Jews were the first people to become aware of the contemporary 'crisis of the human ideal'. Anti-semitism which, he argues, is in essence 'the hatred of the different man, that is the hatred of the other man' [*la haine de l'homme autre, c'est-à-dire de l'autre homme*], forced this awareness upon them.²⁸ They realised that the meaning of the human in Greco-roman humanism is not 'protected from a shift in meaning which in the beginning is imperceptible and at the end, fatal'.²⁹

As an illustration of the weakness of humanism, Levinas cites the progress of the Nazis and the swastika, applauded by increasingly large and enthusiastic crowds. He insists that the swastika was applauded all the more due to the applause it had already received, success generating greater success. Levinas argues that this behaviour of the masses is a direct reflection of humanism's failure to question success.

> [...] in spite of its generosity, western humanism has never known how to question its triumphs, it has never been able to understand failures, nor to comprehend [*penser*] a history to which the vanquished and persecuted could lend any valid meaning.[30]

Because of this inability to question success western political theory is, on Levinas' view, not sufficient to maintain the equilibrium of humanity. European Jewry's return to its tradition (in the form of a renewed emphasis on 'Jewish education') is not, he argues, a manifestation of masochism; rather it is a 'movement towards a doctrine more capable than [...] humanism of giving meaning to being, to life, and [...] of maintaining in the persecuted his human essence'.[31] Levinas' understanding of how Judaism achieves these ends will be discussed in Chapter Four.

In '*Pour un humanisme hébraïque*',[32] Levinas presents a second criticism of western humanism. He sketches a comparison of Judaism and western thought which draws on the views of Mendelssohn, Spinoza and Maimonides. According to these thinkers, Levinas claims, Judaism is not a revealed religion but a revealed law. Its truth is universal, like reason. The function of its rules and moral institutions is to protect the truth from corruption. According to this view, truths conserved or transmitted as pure abstractions run the risk of being eroded or distorted, and this is the danger faced by western thought. 'The naked intellect rises to the summits, but does not maintain itself there. Reason, sovereign and subject of the true, succumbs to the idolatry of the myths which tempt it, betray it and chain it up.'[33]

Traditional Judaism, however, is seen as being protected from this danger by the Law. Levinas explains that,

> The true, according to Judaism always finds its true symbolism, which protects it from the imagination, only in practical attitudes, in a Law. The great texts of rabbinic Judaism, inseparable from the Bible, expose this law which supports the great truths.[34]

In a footnote to his essay '*Exigeant Judaisme*', Levinas offers a similar argument regarding the attention to concrete detail in the Talmud's exposition of Jewish law.

> It is permitted to think that the interest in the concrete conditions of action which characterise talmudic dialectics teaches the most difficult of arts: that of preserving generous and general ideas from the alienation which threatens them when they are

put in contact with the real; that of distrusting ideologies, discerning in the actions which they inspire the precise moment when the end of a realization is reversed and perversion begins.[35]

Thus the truths of Judaism are protected from corruption, while those of western thought are constantly exposed to the danger of being distorted by the mind that thinks them.

Levinas, then, offers two related explanations of humanism's failure to humanise history. Firstly, he suggests that humanism never achieved an adequate understanding of the meaning of being human. This insufficiency led to the development of philosophies of history which failed to take into account the experience of the conquered and the persecuted. Levinas' second explanation may be construed as a way of accounting for this failure. If the 'naked intellect' is unable to maintain its hold on every truth that it discovers and transmit them in an uncontaminated form, perhaps an understanding of the human which was not prejudiced in favour of the strong has been achieved by some western thinkers, but they were unable either to maintain their idea for long or, more importantly, to achieve its incorporation into the intellectual tradition of western humanism.

Judaism's advantage over western thought, according to Levinas, is that its truths and ideals are not transmitted in abstract form, but are embodied in the concrete commandments of the Law, and thus are less subject to distortion and corruption. Interestingly, the insistence on the importance of law not only provides Levinas with a vantage point from which to criticise humanism, but also differentiates his position from that of radical anti-humanism. As was seen above, Levinas is in agreement with the anti-humanism which rejects the humanism of *beau langage* or rhetoric, without abandoning the ideals of the humanist project. However, he is highly critical of the 'anti-humanism' which celebrates freedom to the point of rejecting all laws.

Levinas outlines his reservations regarding anti-humanism in his essay '*Anti-humanisme et éducation*'. He reiterates that the contemporary crisis of humanism does not simply amount to a rejection of *belles lettres*; rather the anti-humanists' search for the truth behind language's mystifications threatens to disfigure the so-called eternal essence of man.[36] This threat is produced by a line of thought that begins with great respect for man and commitment to the fight for human freedom and autonomy. Respect for man's freedom inspires the fight against economic exploitation. In the course of this battle, however, the law comes to appear as a repressive force:

> But then the law appears to repress the freedom which it makes possible. And beneath its rationality, beneath the rationality of law, one suspects black designs and secrets of clandestine war.[37]

Once the law has become suspect, the battle for economic liberation is no longer perceived as the primary locus of the fight for the liberation of man. Instead, the focus shifts to the freeing of desire from the repressive forces of law.

Levinas sketches the following progression of the anti-humanist idea of freedom:

> From economic liberation to sexual freedom, to sexual education through all the degrees of this liberation; liberation with regard to the obligations to which hetero-sexuality is still naturally attached and as far as the solitary ecstasies of drugs where one no longer has any need for interhuman relations, where at last responsibilities are undone.[...] But there exists yet another level to descend. Everything is permitted, nothing is absolutely forbidden. Perhaps nothing is any longer prohibited with regard to the other man.[38]

Thus, by over-emphasising the importance of freedom and neglecting the value of law, the anti-humanist project, which began out of an ethical concern for the economic exploitation of man, may degenerate into a philosophy of self-centred lawlessness. Levinas insists that the anti-humanist view that 'the happiness and freedom of man demands the suppression of the law, that all law *qua* law is repressive' and the belief that freedom is 'the arbitrary will', amount to a rejection of everything that western culture has stood for until now. Anti-humanism breaks with the West, not only as conceived by the Bible, but also as understood by the 'humanities analogous to the Bible'.[39]

Levinas' objection to the anti-humanist celebration of freedom is not simply that it is revolutionary; his criticism, sketched only briefly in this essay, is substantive. He argues that the pursuit of freedom above all else will lead to the destruction not only of law but also of love.[40] For Levinas, love itself is a law, insofar as it calls for some degree of restraint of the self's will for the sake of the other. The 'ancient divorce between love and law' he argues, is itself questionable. Levinas suggests that this dichotomy, expressed as the supposedly 'biblical' opposition between 'letter' and 'spirit', is not at all biblical in character. It may, rather, have been a concession made to pagan values.

By contrast, the Jewish wisdom of the law and of the 'exterior act' are proposed as the means by which the humanity and personality of man can be preserved. Thus Jewish education, which is the topic of this essay, is seen to be of great importance not only for the Jewish community itself, but for all of western society. However, Levinas is not advocating Jewish proselytisation. 'Judaism', he writes, 'does not take up its responsibilities [...and] right away propose that others share them'.[41] Nevertheless, even without proseslytising, Jews will be of help to non-Jews by holding steadfastly to their Jewish values. Levinas insists that a people who obstinately resist the dissolution of values cannot 'remain indifferent and useless to their contemporaries'. Jewish practice and education can thus help to stem the tide of anti-humanism. Significantly, Levinas refers to Judaism as a 'humanism'.

> The war against Amalek,[42] the symbol according to which Judaism conceives war, draws all of its force from resistance and elevation. But is it Judaism that has perpetuated war in the war made on war? Has its humanism been content with the peace of conquerors? Has it ever ceased to be the humanism of patience?[43]

Levinas' characterisation of Judaism as 'Hebraic Humanism' will be discussed in greater detail in Chapter Four. These two essays have been examined here to show that Levinas agrees with neither side in the humanist versus anti-humanist debate, and that he looks to Judaism, with its respect for law, to criticise each of them. Neither, he claims, is able to safeguard the rights and dignity of the other man. Humanism's over-reliance on abstract thought results in a history that always sides with the conquerors, and a concomitant difficulty in protecting the vanquished, while anti-humanism's pursuit of individual freedom leads to disregard for the other. The alternative which is proposed in these essays is a return to traditional Jewish values and practices, to a Judaism which, despite his reservations about western humanism, Levinas describes as a 'humanism'.

### Beyond Anti-Humanism

The recommendation of traditional Judaism is not the only way in which Levinas responds to the crisis of humanism. His philosophical work also presents both a criticism of humanism and an appreciation of its values and intentions. Whilst in *Difficile liberté* traditional Judaism is advocated as a concrete expression of humanist values, in his philosophical writings Levinas deals with humanism on a conceptual rather than a concrete level. For example, in the essays collected under the title of '*Humanisme de l'autre homme*', he presents a more philosophically sophisticated and much more elaborate critique of western humanism than that offered in *Difficile liberté*. His analyses of humanism and related concepts, such as subjectivity and responsibility, are not simply critical, but lead to a presentation of his own radical understanding of these notions. What emerges is a new way of understanding humanity, one which shares with western humanism its appreciation of the worth of man and the importance of morality, whilst avoiding the errors which Levinas and the anti-humanists have identified in traditional humanism.

In *Humanisme de l'autre homme*,[44] as in *Difficile liberté*, Levinas identifies the inhuman events of the twentieth century as a major cause of the contemporary crisis of humanism.

[...The] unburied dead in wars and extermination camps make one believe the idea of a death without a morning after and render tragic-comic the concern for oneself and illusory the pretension of the rational animal to have a privileged place in the cosmos and the power to dominate and integrate the totality of being in a self-consciousness.[45]

In addition to revealing the extent of man's capacity for evil and thus contradicting humanism's optimistic view of man, the developments and events of the twentieth century call into question the notion of human agency and purpose in history.

That an action could be obstructed by the technology destined to render it efficacious and easy, that a science, born to embrace the world, delivers it over to disintegration, that a politics and an administration guided by the humanist ideal maintain the exploitation of man by man and war—these are singular inversions of rational projects, disqualifying human causality, and thus transcendental subjectivity understood as spontaneity and act also. Everything comes to pass as though the ego, the identity par excellence from which every identifiable identity would derive, were wanting with regard to itself, did not succeed in coinciding with itself.[46]

The traditional humanist notion of the subject is also called into question by psycho-analytic theory which challenges the primacy of consciousness. In place of the Cartesian idea of the ego as a pole of identity, psychology presents us with the model of a consciousness played upon by unconscious forces, passions and influences. Concomitant to this dethroning of the subject by psychology is the abandonment of philosophies and ideologies based on the *cogito*. Truth, Levinas explains, is now sought in being, in an objectivity that would be pure of any ideology, 'without human traces'.[47] Levinas cites structuralism and Heideggerian philosophy as paradigms of this search for truth in the realm of being.

Since 'structuralist', like 'humanist, is a term that has been used to describe very disparate thinkers, it may be useful to look briefly at the history of the movement before considering Levinas' response to it. The structuralist movement was inspired by Saussurean linguistics. Saussure maintained that language (*langue*) was a differential system in which the signs were significant only by virtue of their relations with all other signs of the language. Linguistics is a study of this system and not concerned with particular manifestations of language (which Saussure called *parole*). Meaning is not sought in the intention of the user of language, but arises from the system itself, and it is therefore possible to study language without any reference to 'subjects'.

Structuralist thinkers apply a similar concern with signifying systems not only to linguistics itself but also to the broader realm of social and cultural phenomena. Structuralism is perhaps best known as a loosely-defined method of literary criticism, but it has also been applied to diverse areas of culture by such thinkers as Lacan, Lévi-Strauss, Barthes and Foucault. This application to cultural phenomena of a method devised for studying language is made possible by the premise that these phenomena are governed by language. Soper explains that the diverse branches of structuralist thought are linked by their commitment to semiology and the 'mode of study of human culture which it introduces'. According to the semiologist, she writes, the traditional human sciences have failed because they have treated meanings as though they simply mediated reality. The semiological perspective, on the other hand, reveals that 'meanings are constitutive of human reality itself, not its mediation. There is no ulterior reality prior to and standing "behind" the signs which denote it.'[48]

A structuralist, or semiological, approach to the human sciences thus envisages its object not as human nature, but the existence of the human being qua sign user. Soper explains that, for the structuralists (and post-structuralists),

[...] whether the particular engagement is with the linguistic sign itself (Saussure, Derrida); or with myth (Lévi-Strauss); or with the unconscious (Lacan); or with human communication in literature, dress and gesture—the word and sign created worlds to which Barthes has drawn attention; or (as with Foucault), the mutations in the forms of representation itself, and the specific discourses to which they give rise—in all these cases, the concern is with the universal inscription of humankind within language and systems of codification which regulate all human experience and activity, and therefore lie beyond the control of either individuals or social groups.[49]

It is this denial of human responsibility, and not the emphasis on the importance of language, that Levinas finds objectionable in structuralism. He agrees with structuralism's portrayal of itself as a demythologisation of the idea of man, but his use of the Kantian description of man as an 'end in himself' evokes the ethical difficulties with such demythologisation. Levinas writes that, in the age of structuralism,

We are witnessing the ruin of the myth of man as an end in himself, and the appearance of an order that is neither human nor inhuman, one that is, indeed, ordered across man and across the civilizations he is said to have produced, but ordered in the last analysis by the properly rational force of the dialectical or logico-formal system. To this nonhuman order the name matter—which is anonymousness itself—belongs.[50]

Levinas points out that, like structuralism, Heideggerian philosophy is intent upon destroying the subject of traditional humanism. Heidegger's 1947

'Letter on Humanism', unlike Sartre's essay of 1945, is not an attempt to defend his philosophy as a humanism, but rather a statement of his desire to be done with humanism. As we have seen Heidegger identifies a general meaning of 'humanism' as the 'concern that man become free for his humanity and find his worth in it'.[51] He argues that, in spite of the differences between, for example, Marxist and Christian humanism, in all humanisms 'the *humanitas* of *homo humanus* is determined with regard to an already established interpretation of nature, history, world, and the ground of the world, that is, of beings as a whole'.[52]

In other words, all humanism is a forgetting of the 'question of Being', in that it takes for granted that we know what we mean when we say of something that it 'is'. Moreover, Heidegger insists that humanism not only forgets the question of Being, but impedes it.

> In defining the humanity of man humanism not only does not ask about the relation of Being to the essence of man; because of its metaphysical origin humanism even impedes the question by neither recognizing nor understanding it.[53]

Heidegger argues that every humanism in the history of western philosophy has presupposed that the essence of man is to be the *animal rationale*. Whilst conceding that this is not necessarily a false definition of man, he insists that, by defining man on the basis of *animalitas*, humanism, and all metaphysical thought, fails to 'think in the direction of his *humanitas*'.[54]

According to the author of *Being and Time*, what distinguishes man from other beings and gives him his dignity is his exceptional relation to Being. Man, or Dasein, is distinguished from all other entities in that 'in its very Being, that Being is an issue for it'.[55] Only Dasein is capable of having a relationship to itself and its possibilities. Moreover, Dasein has a relationship not only to its own Being, but also to Being itself. 'Understanding of Being,' Heidegger writes, 'is itself a definite characteristic of Dasein's Being'.[56]

For Heidegger, what is distinctive about Dasein is that it is the entity to which Being discloses itself. In the 'Letter on Humanism', Heidegger writes that he rejects humanism on the grounds that 'it does not set the *humanitas* of man high enough'.[57] Man is not, as the humanists would have it, the 'Subject' or lord and master of being. Instead, he is the 'shepherd of Being', entrusted with guarding its truth.

> Man is [...] 'thrown' from Being itself into the truth of Being, so that ek-sisting in this fashion he might guard the truth of Being, in order that beings might appear in the light of Being as the beings they are. Man does not decide whether and how beings appear, whether and how God and the gods or history and nature come forward into the lighting of Being, come to presence and depart. The advent of being lies in the destiny of Being. But for man it is ever a question of finding what is

fitting in his essence which corresponds to such destiny; for in accord with this destiny man as ek-sisting has to guard the truth of Being. Man is the shepherd of Being.[58]

Heidegger refers to man as 'ek-sisting' in order to emphasise the etymology of the word 'existence', which comes from the Greek root meaning to 'stand out'. As David Krell explains, in *Being and Time*,

> [...] 'ecstatic' (from the Greek *ekstasis)* means the way Dasein 'stands out' in the various moments of the temporality of care, being 'thrown' out of a past and 'projecting' itself toward a future by way of the present. [...] ek-sistence [...] too means the way man 'stands out' into the truth of Being and so is exceptional among beings that are on hand only as things of nature or human production.[59]

By seeing Dasein as in a permanent relation with Being, Heidegger overcomes the difficulties of the subject-object dichotomy raised by the Cartesian model of an interior, sovereign consciousness and an exterior world of objects.[60] Dasein, unlike the subject of modern philosophy from Descartes to Husserl, is always already in the world. As Soper explains, for Heidegger

> [...] all dualisms of subject and object, consciousness and being, humanity and nature, are a secondary and 'inauthentic' derivation from the primary unity of Being (Sein) with human Being (Dasein). Humanity and the world form a whole. In Heidegger's philosophy, therefore, the focus shifts from the role of consciousness 'intending' the object, towards the world as, so to speak, 'already intended'.[61]

After describing Dasein in the 'Letter on Humanism', Heidegger raises the question that is at the heart of his philosophy, 'what is Being?'[62] This, he says, is a question that philosophy has not yet learned to ask, let alone answer.

> Yet Being—what is Being? It is It itself. The thinking that is to come must learn to experience that and to say it. 'Being'—that is not God and not a cosmic ground. Being is farther than all beings and is yet nearer to man than every being [...] Being is the nearest. Yet the near remains farthest from man. Man at first clings always and only to beings. But when thinking represents beings as beings it no doubt relates itself to Being. In truth, however, it always thinks only of beings as such; precisely not, and never, Being as such. The 'question of Being' always remains a question about beings. It is still not at all what its elusive name indicates: the question in the direction of Being.[63]

Without being able to say precisely what Being is, since it is not a being, Heidegger describes the relationship between man and Being.

> [...] how does Being relate to ek-sistence? Being itself is the relation to the extent that It, as the location of the truth of Being amid beings, gathers to itself and embraces ek-sistence in its existential, that is, ecstatic, essence. Because man as the one who ek-sists comes to stand in this relation that Being destines for itself, in that he ecstatically sustains it, that is, in care takes it upon himself, he at first fails to

recognize the nearest and attaches himself to the next nearest. He even thinks that this is the nearest. But nearer than the nearest and at the same time for ordinary thinking farther than the farthest is nearness itself: the truth of Being.[64]

Heidegger argues that man's nearness to Being is primarily enacted through language. Language, for Heidegger, is not just one of the many capacities possessed by man; instead, it is 'the house of Being in which man ek-sists by dwelling, in that he belongs to the truth of Being, guarding it'.[65] This entails that 'in the determination of the humanity of man as ek-sistence *what is essential is not man but Being*—as the dimension of the ecstasis of ek-sistence'.[66]

According to Levinas, this understanding of man as the 'shepherd of Being'[67] is, like structuralism, a subordination of man to 'an order that is neither human nor inhuman', to anonymity. In *Humanisme de l'autre homme*, Levinas sets himself the task of rediscovering man 'in this matter and a name in this anonymity' without re-introducing the transcendental values of the 'one', which would constitute a return to the philosophy of substance and the reification of man. He describes this search for a philosophy which avoids both traditional humanism's reification of 'man' and anti-humanism's destruction of the subject as an attempt to find a meaning in humanism.[68]

The 'humanism of the other man' outlined in this book draws more on the description of subjectivity in *Otherwise than Being* than on the analysis of the face-to-face relation in *Totality and Infinity*. As discussed in Chapter One, one of the major difficulties in interpreting the earlier work is understanding when, if ever, the face-to-face takes place. Bernasconi's analysis of the *anterior posteriori* shows that the descriptions of enjoyment, habitation and the encounter with the other cannot be incorporated into a chronological narrative or a foundational structure. The impossibility of understanding the ethical within time understood as chronology (or 'synchrony') is a recurring theme of *Otherwise than Being*, in which Levinas describes subjectivity as though the call to responsibility for the other has always already taken place, in an 'immemorial past'.

The phrase 'immemorial past' immediately raises difficulties: how can Levinas know and describe what went on in a past inaccessible to memory? Before answering this question, it will be necessary to consider Levinas' analysis of the relationship between Being, time, language and subjectivity.

In order to understand what Levinas means by 'otherwise than Being', it must be noted that, in this phrase, 'Being' does not only stand for the totality of entities, but 'for the whole western philosophical tradition, in particular as it was interpreted and recaptured by Heidegger'.[69] One of the key features of Heidegger's thought is that Being is understood verbally, as a process or deployment, an 'active essence'. Being, therefore, cannot be thought without reference to time. 'Being's essence', Levinas writes, 'is the temporalization of time'.[70]

This understanding of Being's essence implies, Levinas argues, that being somehow differs from itself, gets 'out of phase' with itself.[71] Ontological thought, however, always envisions a recuperation, such that nothing is really lost in the 'getting out of phase of the instant'.[72] Truth, Levinas insists, has traditionally been understood as 'rediscovery, recall, reminiscence, reuniting under the unity of apperception'.[73]

Such recuperation is exemplified by Husserl's analysis of internal time consciousness. According to this account, the awareness of the passing of time is made possible by the variations of sensation. Yet the difference is immediately reabsorbed within the same.

> There is consciousness insofar as the sensible impression differs from itself without differing; it differs without differing, is other within identity. The impression is illuminated by 'opening up' as though it plugged itself up; it undoes that coincidence of self with self in which the 'same' is smothered under itself, as under a candle extinguisher.[74]

The undoing of the 'coincidence of self with self' is, however, only fleeting. Through protention and retention, consciousness maintains its identity.

> Differing within identity, modifying itself without changing, consciousness glows in an impression inasmuch as it diverges from itself, to *still* be expecting itself, or *already* recuperating itself. Still, already—are time, time in which nothing is lost.[75]

Levinas argues that even the Husserlian notion of the *Ur-impression*, which seems to make the notions of origin and creation intelligible, stops short of allowing for a true interruption of the flow of time and the work of consciousness.

> When it turns out that this consciousness in the living present, originally non-objectifying and not objectified, is thematizable and thematizing in retention [...] then we see the non-intentionality of the primal impression fitted back in the normal order to the hither side of the same or of the origin. Nothing enters incognito into the same [...][76]

Levinas' task in *Otherwise than Being* is precisely to consider the implications of the 'hither side', of something that does 'slip into [...] consciousness like a thief',[77] interrupting the flow of time and the mastery of consciousness. In other words, Levinas attempts, in this work as in *Totality and Infinity*, to think transcendence. According to Levinas, transcendence must be thought, firstly, because in the face-to-face relation there is an 'experience' of the infinite and, secondly, because ontological thought, which ignores this 'experience', is 'violent'. The philosophy of transcendence arises from two imperatives: the need for a phenomenological account of human existence that does justice to the 'experience' of encountering the other, and the desire for a philosophy of peace rather than one of war. *Otherwise than Being* similarly answers to both a phenomenological and a critical need, although they are not exactly the same as those of *Totality and Infinity*. As Peperzak points out, whereas in *Totality and Infinity*, 'the central place was taken by the other and his visage', in the later work Levinas is concerned with the '"position" and meaning of the subject'.[78] Moreover, Levinas' criticism of western philosophy is more radical in *Otherwise than Being*. Although Levinas attempted, in *Totality and Infinity*, to 'think beyond the totality of all beings',[79] his formulations were still largely dependent upon the language of ontology.[80] In *Otherwise than Being*, however, Levinas struggles to escape from ontological language; the result of this struggle is the paradoxical and strange use of language which will be discussed in greater detail below.

Although ontology takes many different forms, a characteristic of all ontological description is 'an inner coherence, a systematic unity under the light of Being, within which all beings and all formal elements of Being are gathered'.[81] In *Totality and Infinity*, ontological thought was criticised for its inability to recognize the radical alterity of the other. *Otherwise than Being* highlights another aspect of ontological thought: each entity is conceived of as a *conatus*, existing for itself, and concerned with persevering in being. Since more than one entity exists, the entities' concern for themselves issues in a 'war of all against all'. The only peace possible in such a situation is one that depends on self-interest: violence is repressed for the sake of a secure existence in a community.[82]

Levinas' attempt to think transcendence and produce a philosophy of peace does not consist in contesting the accuracy of philosophy's understanding of being. Levinas does not reject ontology. In *Totality and Infinity*, it is only ontology as first philosophy that is rejected. Similarly, in *Otherwise than Being*, Levinas is concerned not to destroy ontological thought but to uncover its meaning. This meaning will be found in a non-ontological notion of subjectivity, a self that is not a *conatus*, but an existence for the other.

Whereas in *Totality and Infinity* the 'judgment of God', through which I become aware of my infinite responsibility, is described as taking place within the face-to-face relation, in *Otherwise than Being* such responsibility is understood to be the very basis of my identity. Levinas argues that, prior to the self-identification that arises as consciousness, there is a proto-identity which he terms the 'recurrence of the oneself'. The oneself is 'passive', in that it is not the author of its own existence; instead, it is 'provoked', called to responsibility. This responsibility, unlike the projects of consciousness, does not arise from any decision that the oneself has made. Rather, the oneself is 'bound in a knot that cannot be undone in a responsibility for others'.[83] It is responsibility that creates the ipseity of the oneself. In responsibility, he writes, 'the oneself is provoked as irreplaceable, as devoted to the others, without being able to resign, and thus as incarnated in order to offer itself, to suffer and to give'.[84]

Unlike consciousness, the oneself is not self-identical, not an entity, and cannot be named, except with a pronoun.[85] The 'pronoun' metaphor for subjectivity is one that recurs throughout this work. It emphasises the subject's lack of substance. Whereas a name suggests substance and identity, a pronoun has no fixed referent. Just as the meaning of a pronoun arises from the context in which it is used, the oneself, Levinas claims, is not a substance but a function, as it were, of the responsibility for the others.

Levinas not only uses the metaphor of the pronoun to describe the subject, but specifies that it is a pronoun in the accusative case, not 'I' (*Je*) but 'me' ('*moi, me*') or the self ('*soi*'). As John Llewelyn explains,

> The Other is not the object of my concern and solicitude. Beyond what Heidegger means by *Sorge* and *Fürsorge* is my being con-cerned, *con-cerné*, obsessed by the Other. He is not the accusative of my theoretical, practical or affective intentionality or ecstasis. He is the topic of my regard (*il me regarde*) only because I am the accusative of his look (*il me regarde*) (AEAE, p. 147; OBBE, p. 116). The subject is an accusative, *me*, which is not a declension from a nominative, but an accusative absolute like the pronoun *se* for which, Levinas says, Latin grammars acknowledge no nominative (AEAE, p. 143; OBBE, p. 112).[86]

Levinas uses a constellation of seemingly negative terms to describe subjectivity: the oneself is 'under accusation', 'persecuted', 'obsessed' and a 'hostage' to the others. To be a hostage, Levinas writes, is to take on the other's responsibilities and misfortunes, to the point of substituting oneself for the other. Yet substitution does not amount to alienation. It is, rather, 'inspiration'('having-the-other-in-one's-skin'), and it is inspiration that makes human existence meaningful.[87]

> Through substitution for others, the oneself escapes relations. At the limit of passivity, the oneself escapes passivity or the inevitable limitation that the terms within relation undergo. In the incomparable relationship of responsibility, the other no longer limits the same, it is supported by what it limits [...] In this most passive passivity, the self liberates itself ethically from every other and from itself. Its responsibility for the other, the proximity of the neighbour, does not signify a submission to the non-ego; it means an openness in which being's essence is surpassed in inspiration.[88]

The phrase 'the self liberates itself ethically from every other and from itself' requires careful interpretation. The problem lies in understanding the adverb 'ethically'. (The French reads: *Dans cette passivité la plus passive, le soi, éthiquement se libère de tout autre et de soi.*)[89] Levinas is not saying that through substitution the self escapes from ethical responsibility for the other. Rather, through the ethical, the self escapes from limitations, from the determination of beings. Through substitution, the distinction between the self and the other collapses.

> 'Je est un autre.' But this is not the alienation Rimbaud refers to. I am outside of any place, in myself, on the hither side of the autonomy of auto-affection and identity resting on itself. Impassively undergoing the weight of the other, thereby called to uniqueness, subjectivity no longer belongs to the order where the alternative of activity and passivity retains its meaning. *We have to speak here of expiation as uniting identity and alterity.* The ego is not an entity 'capable' of expiating for the others; it is this original expiation.[90]

Substitution not only leads to a unity of self and other, but ('outside of any mysticism')[91] reveals the very unity of the universe. This unity arises from my responsibility for the universe, not as a choice that I would have made, but as what is incumbent upon me.

> The subject is a *sub-jectum*; it is under the weight of the universe, responsible for everything. The unity of the universe is not what my gaze embraces in its unity of apperception, but what is incumbent on me from all sides, regards me in the two senses of the term, accuses me, is my affair.[92]

Levinas emphasises that it is not the ego that makes being meaningful. Instead, being takes on signification through the approach of the other.

> It is not because among beings there exists an ego, a being pursuing ends, that being takes on signification and becomes a universe. It is because in an approach, there is inscribed or written the trace of infinity, the trace of a departure, but trace of what is inordinate, does not enter into the present, and inverts the *arche* into anarchy, that there is forsakenness of the other, obsession by him, responsibility and a self. The non-interchangeable par excellence, the I, the unique one, substitutes itself for others. Nothing is a game. Thus being is transcended.[93]

Whereas in *Totality and Infinity* the encounter with the human other is described as a relationship with the Other who comes from a 'dimension of height', in *Otherwise than Being* the encounter is analysed as an 'approach' of the other, and the relationship with the other is termed 'proximity'. The term, however, is not used to designate nearness in space, but a suppression of the distance of intentional consciousness, or 'consciousness of…'.[94] As in *Totality and Infinity*, the 'way' of the neighbour who commands me 'is a face'.[95] Yet, in the later work, it is as though the commandment that comes from the face has always already been heard. 'In proximity is heard a command come as though from an immemorial past, which was never present, began in no freedom.'[96] The notion of an obligation that is '"older" than the a priori' describes 'a way of being affected which can in no way be invested by spontaneity'.[97] The source of the command can never become a theme of representation. As such, proximity is a 'disturbance of rememberable time', an interruption of the recuperable time of ontological thought.

In essays written after *Totality and Infinity*, Levinas uses the notion of a 'trace' to elaborate on the way in which the face signifies. A face, he writes, is 'abstract' in that it does not settle into 'the horizons of the world', even whilst disturbing immanence.[98] In other words, the face has an effect on the world without becoming part of the world. Levinas describes the face as coming from, and withdrawing to, 'elsewhere'. This elsewhere, however, is not a world behind the world, but 'the absolutely absent'.[99] The face neither indicates nor reveals this absent; yet 'the absent has a meaning in a face'.[100] Levinas argues that 'the relationship which goes from a face to the absent is outside every revelation and dissimulation, a third way excluded by these contradictories'.[101] This third way of signifying is the signifyingness of a trace.

> In the presence of the other do we not respond to an 'order' in which signifyingness remains an irremissible disturbance, an utterly bygone past? Such is the signifyingness of a trace. The beyond from which a face comes signifies as a trace. A face is in the trace of the utterly bygone, utterly passed absent [...][102]

Because my responsibility for the other has been commanded in an immemorial past, I come to the encounter as already guilty of delay. The face 'reclaimed me before I came. [...] I am accused of having delayed.'[103] Thus, to the notion of infinite responsibility—responsibility that increases in the measure it is assumed—is added the idea of an originary delay. I always come too late to assume my responsibility in full. The ethical self is, therefore, forever under accusation.

To be under accusation, a hostage to the others, is, however, to be elected by the Good, if not by God.[104] 'The Good' must be understood without reference to the notion of free will usually associated with the moral terms 'good' and 'bad'. Substitution, as we have seen, occurs prior to any choice that could be made by a will.

> The ego is not an entity 'capable' of expiating for the others; it is this original expiation. This expiation is involuntary,[105] for it is prior to the will's initiative (prior to the origin).[106]

The Good, Levinas insists, is before being.[107] It is the Good that chooses me, assigns me to approach the neighbour in proximity.

> Has not the Good chosen the subject with an election recognizable in the respons-
> ibility of being hostage, to which the subject is destined, which he cannot evade
> without denying himself, and by virtue of which he is unique? A philosopher can
> give to this election only the signification circumscribed by responsibility for the
> other. This antecedence of responsibility to freedom would signify the Goodness of
> the Good: the necessity that the Good choose me first before I can be in a position
> to choose, that is, welcome its choice.[108]

Although Levinas' use of the term 'the Good' has religious overtones, it will
be argued in the next chapter that it is not a theological concept.

Levinas is careful to point out that election by 'the Good' does not amount
to a natural tendency.[109] He does not deny the egoism of human beings and
their capacity for evil. Consciousness can and does forget its infinite responsibility, its election, and become pure egoism.[110] Egoism, however, is 'neither
first nor last'. Alluding to the story of Jonah, the reluctant prophet, Levinas
suggests that it is impossible to escape from the Good (in the biblical story,
represented by God), because the true self is the passivity of responsibility.

> The impossibility of escaping God, the adventure of Jonah,[111] indicates that God is
> at least here not a value among values. [...] The impossibility of escaping God lies in
> the depths of myself as a self, as an absolute passivity. This passivity is not only the
> possibility of death in being, the possibility of impossibility. It is an impossibility
> prior to that possibility, the impossibility of slipping away, absolute susceptibility,
> gravity without any frivolity. It is the birth of a meaning in the obtuseness of being,
> of a 'being able to die' subject to sacrifice.[112]

Levinas' enigmatic references to 'God' will be analysed in Chapter Three.
For the moment, however, let us consider the claim that 'being-able-to-die'
for the other is the 'birth of a meaning in the obtuseness of being'. Levinas
concedes the existentialist claim that mortality renders human existence
absurd, at least insofar as the ego's concern for its own existence is concerned.[113] However, the possibility of dying for the other makes death, and,
consequently, life, meaningful.

> The approach, in as much as it is a sacrifice, confers a sense on death. In it the abso-
> lute singularity of the responsible one encompasses the generality or generalization
> of death. In it life is no longer measured by being, and death can no longer intro-
> duce the absurd into it. [...] No one is so hypocritical as to claim that he has taken
> from death its sting, not even the promisers of religions. But we can have respons-
> ibilities and attachments through which death takes on a meaning. That is because,
> from the start, the other affects us despite ourselves.[114]

Yet, to return to the question raised at the beginning of this discussion, if the
election that makes life meaningful takes place in an immemorial past, how
is it possible for Levinas to know, and to write, about it? In several places,

Levinas offers apparently transcendental arguments in support of his analyses. He argues, for example, that the very existence of pity and compassion
presupposes the subject's election to infinite responsibility.

> It is through the condition of being hostage that there can be in the world pity, com-
> passion, pardon and proximity—even the little there is, even the simple 'After you,
> sir'. The unconditionality of being hostage is not the limit case of solidarity, but the
> condition for all solidarity. Every accusation and persecution, as *all interpersonal
> praise, recompense, and punishment presuppose the subjectivity of the ego, substitu-
> tion, the possibility of putting oneself in the place of the other,* which refers to the
> transference from the 'by the other' into a 'for the other,' and in persecution from
> the outrage inflicted by the other to the expiation for his fault by me.[115]

In addition to describing substitution as the condition of possibility of ethics,
Levinas also writes, in other contexts, as though awareness of responsibility
for the others were part of our everyday experience. He argues, for example,
that

> [...] *the relationship with a past that is on the hither side of every present* and every
> re-presentable, for not belonging to the order of presence, *is included in the ex-
> traordinary and everyday event of my responsibility for the faults or the misfortune
> of others,* in my responsibility that answers for the freedom of another [...][116]

In other words, although the commandment of responsibility proceeds from
a past inaccessible to consciousness, I nevertheless become conscious of this
commandment. Responsibility is, disturbingly, the presence in consciousness
of something that was neither posited, welcomed, intended nor assumed by
consciousness. The commandment, as we saw above, has slipped into consciousness 'like a thief'.[117] Obsession, responsibility for the other, is irreducible to consciousness. However, it is 'betrayed' in consciousness,

> [...] thematized by a said in which it is manifested. Obsession traverses conscious-
> ness countercurrentwise, is inscribed in consciousness as something foreign, a dis-
> equilibrium, a delirium.[118]

In order to appreciate the full significance of this passage, it is necessary to
consider Levinas' use in *Otherwise than Being* of the distinction between 'the
saying' (*le dire*) and 'the said' (*le dit*). In contrast to the saying, the said is the
thematisable meaning of an utterance or discourse. It is the aspect of language
that belongs to ontology. The realm of the said is that of propositions and
assertions, which can be qualified as true or false. Saying, on the other hand,
is the very fact of addressing someone, of speaking (or writing) to the other.[119]
Levinas argues that to address the other is already to express my responsibility. Saying is 'the proximity of one to the other, the commitment of an
approach, the one for the other, the very signifyingness of signification'.[120]

The said, which belongs to the realm of ontology, thus refers to time understood as synchrony. Levinas argues, as we saw above, that being is the temporalisation of time. Following Husserl, Levinas further points out that being is inseparable from its meaning, from its being said. It is language, as the 'already said', which allows an entity to be recognized as such, identical through time.

> Identification is ascription of meaning. Entities show themselves in their meanings to be identical entities. They are not first given and thematized, and then receive a meaning: they are given by the meaning they have. But these rediscoveries by identification occur in an *already said*. The said, the word, is not simply a sign of meaning, nor even only an expression of meaning (contrary to Husserl's analysis in the first Logical Investigation); the word at once proclaims and establishes an identification of this with that in the *already said*.[121]

The said, in other words, performs the task of 'recuperation', of overcoming difference, that Levinas sees as an essential feature of ontology.

Whereas the said, 'the birthplace of ontology',[122] belongs to time understood as synchrony, the saying opens the dimension of diachrony, of the lapse of time that is irrecuperable. Levinas insists, however, that the saying nevertheless calls for philosophy, demands that substitution be analysed by consciousness and become an object of knowledge. The philosopher faces the delicate task of bringing ethics to light, without letting that light 'congeal into essence what is beyond essence'.[123] In other words, the philosopher must write of the Good beyond being and of the responsible subjectivity which is 'otherwise than being' without making them into beings.

Levinas uses the phenomenological term 'reduction' to categorise this task of showing 'the signification proper to the saying on the hither side of the thematization of the said'.[124] However, as Critchley's analysis makes clear, Levinasian reduction is more complicated than the Husserlian procedure.

> The Saying is not the permanent Husserlian *epochē* of the Said; rather, the reduction is the exposure of the Saying by way of a continual contestation of the Said. The Saying shows itself within the said by interrupting it. [...] The Saying is a performative disruption of the Said that is instantly refuted by the language in which it appears.[125]

Since the saying both affirms and retracts the said, the reduction, correspondingly, will be produced 'out of time or in two times without entering into either of them'.[126] In its refusal to enter synchronisable time, the ethical philosophy which carries out this reduction is similar to scepticism.

> [Scepticism...] does not hesitate to affirm the impossibility of statement while venturing to *realize* this impossibility by the very statement of this impossibility. If, after the innumerable 'irrefutable' refutations which logical thought sets against it,

scepticism has the gall to return (and it always returns as philosophy's legitimate child)[127] it is because in the contradiction which logic sees in it the 'at the same time' of the contradictories is missing, because a secret diachrony commands this ambiguous or enigmatic way of speaking, and because in general signification signifies beyond synchrony, beyond essence.[128]

The reduction, Levinas explains, proceeds in a spiralling movement. It is an endless critique which continually destroys 'the conjunction into which its saying and its said [...] enter'.[129] By remaining in two times, the reduction lets the 'unsayable saying' lend itself to the said, without destroying the echo of the 'otherwise' in the saying.

*Otherwise than Being* is an enactment of the reduction of the saying to the said. It is dependent on Levinas' understanding of language as making possible the saying of the unsayable.

> In language qua said, everything is conveyed before us, be it at the price of a betrayal. [...] At this moment language is serving a research conducted in view of disengaging the *otherwise than being* or *being's other* outside of the themes in which they already show themselves, unfaithfully, as being's *essence*—but in which they do show themselves. Language permits us to utter, be it by betrayal, this *outside of being*, this *ex-ception* to being, as though being's other were an event of being.[130]

The argument of *Otherwise than Being* therefore proceeds by a method that alternates saying with unsaying what has been said.[131] The notion of 'unsaying', however, is not identical to that of denying. In a different context, Levinas makes it clear that the sequence of saying and unsaying is not simply equivalent to that of affirmation and negation. Rather, it is a process through which the meaning of the first saying can be clarified. For Levinas, the beauty of 'Greek', that is, of philosophical language, is that the forms of the saying 'do not leave a trace in what has been shown.' It is therefore always possible to unsay 'that to which you were obliged to have recourse in order to show something'.[132]

This process of saying and unsaying is endless when it is a question, as in *Otherwise than Being*, of bringing the saying into the said. As Peperzak explains,

> [...] the discussion or description of the saying changes it into a said, which demands critique in turn. As soon as we have said something about saying, we must take our distance from the said. Saying (*dire*) and recanting (*dédire*) fashion the halting way in which we think back on the preceding saying. Every recantation, however, is necessarily followed by a new saying, which as a repetition indeed wants to say what was brought to the fore and then negated.[133]

The process of saying and unsaying is, therefore, not dialectical. The new saying is not a synthesis of the first saying and its recantation; nor is it the final word. Instead, each new saying is but the latest attempt to bring the otherwise than being into the said.

The method employed by Levinas to undertake this task (without completing it) merits a complete study in itself. For the present, however, we will limit ourselves to a discussion of two important features. Firstly, although Levinas has characterised his method as an 'intentional analysis', he does not follow the rules of Husserlian phenomenology. As we have seen in Chapter One, Levinas not only rejects the notion of the transcendental ego, but also refuses to see philosophy as a search for 'foundations', since the very notion of foundation belongs to ontology. Although, as Peperzak points out, *Otherwise than Being* 'can be read as a series of "intentional analyses" of saying', there is no clear, foundational relation between the various gradations and levels of saying that are analysed.[134] As Levinas himself warns the reader,

> The different concepts that come up in the attempt to state transcendence echo one another. [...The] themes in which these concepts present themselves do not lend themselves to linear exposition, and cannot be really isolated from one another without projecting their shadows and their reflections on one another.[135]

In addition to the inter-connectedness of the various themes, *Otherwise than Being* is also difficult to read[136] because it frequently employs paradoxical expressions. For example, Levinas describes the ethical self as passive. Yet he goes on to add that it is a 'passivity more passive than all passivity'. Although this phrase is paradoxical, it is not meaningless. The characterisation of subjectivity as more passive than all passivity follows from the claim that it is 'otherwise than being'. To escape from being is also to escape from the alternatives of activity and passivity. However, as Llewelyn points out, it is significant that Levinas does not equally refer to the 'passivity beneath all passivity' as an 'activity beneath all activity'.

> That he never does this marks off the superlative emphatic passivity he does refer to not only from Cartesian freedom, the Kantian rational will and Sartrean originative choice; it marks it off too from any respect and *Seinlassen* such as would lend itself to articulation in the middle voice. Levinas' beyond of passivity and activity is beyond being, whether being be expressed by a noun, a verb or by a verbal noun; insofar as it can be expressed by a word, it is more correct to call it a passivity than an activity.[137]

*Otherwise than Being* abounds in similarly paradoxical expressions. Peperzak is particularly interested in the iterative expressions, such as 'denudation of the denudation', 'significance of the signification', 'infinitizing of the infinite', and so forth.[138] He argues that, through these expressions, Levinas formulates 'the structure of the non-identity and of the non-simultaneity of the subject with himself'.[139] The iteration of the expression betrays 'an inner duplication of the subject'; this duplication can be thought of as the subject's differing from itself 'in a quasi-time'.[140]

Although a thorough analysis of the style of *Otherwise than Being* lies beyond the scope of the present study, the few elements of style that we have highlighted indicate that the content of the work cannot be detached easily from the language used to convey it. Since Levinas struggles, in this work, to discover a new way of writing, one which can overcome the limitations of the language of ontology, the reader must also struggle to adapt to this new use of language. The novelty of Levinas' writing entails two difficulties for the reader: firstly that of comprehending what is written; and secondly, that of evaluating it. As we have seen in Chapter Two, Bernasconi argues that in *Totality and Infinity*, Levinas tries to find a third way between the language of empiricism and that of transcendental philosophy; however, his interpreters have mostly understood this work as one of either transcendental or empirical philosophy.[141] To a philosophical community which finds the language of *Totality and Infinity* difficult, *Otherwise than Being,* with its attempt to leave ontological language behind, must pose even greater problems. Moreover, Levinas himself is not particularly illuminating concerning his method. For example, after discussing the role of emphasis in his work, he states:

> I don't know any more about it. I do not think that transparency of method is possible nor that philosophy is possible as transparence. Those who have spent their lives doing methodology have written a lot of books which have taken the place of the more interesting books that they could have written.[142]

However, in spite of the challenges presented to the reader by Levinas' attempt to escape ontological language, the foregoing exposition of *Otherwise than Being* has shown that Levinas sides neither with the anti-humanists nor with the humanists in the contemporary debate on subjectivity. His description of the self as 'otherwise than being', as a superlative responsibility for the other, even to the point of substitution and self-sacrifice, is completely unlike the self-identical subject of traditional humanism which is attacked by the anti-humanists. Whilst welcoming the anti-humanist attack on the reified subject, Levinas claims that modern anti-humanism 'is true over and beyond the reasons it gives itself'.[143] Anti-humanism, he writes,

> [...] clears the place for subjectivity positing itself in abnegation, in sacrifice, in a substitution which precedes the will. Its inspired intuition is to have abandoned the idea of person, goal and origin of itself, in which the ego is still a thing because it is still a being.[144]

However, the anti-humanist 'de-reification' of the subject does not go far enough, because it does not uncover the passive subject which is the true self.

Already the position of the subject is a deposition, not a *conatus essendi*. It is from the first a substitution by a hostage expiating for the violence of the persecution itself. We have to conceive in such terms the de-substantiation of the subject, its de-reification, its disinterestedness, its subjection, its subjectivity. It is a pure self, in the accusative, responsible before there is freedom.[145]

Levinas concludes that humanism 'has to be denounced only because it is not sufficiently human'.[146]

This denouncement of humanism resembles Heidegger's criticism that humanism 'does not set the *humanitas* of man high enough'.[147] However, there is a profound difference between the two philosophers' understanding of the truly human. In Heidegger's philosophy, Dasein's dignity consists in its task of guarding the truth of Being, acting as the shepherd of Being, its messenger and poet. For Levinas, on the other hand, what distinguishes the human from all other beings is the ability to break with the *conatus essendi*, by consciously choosing to sacrifice one's own needs for the sake of the other.

Jean-François Lyotard has noted that Being in Heidegger's philosophy plays the same role as the Other in Levinas' ethics. Like the Other, Being cannot be thamatized by the knowing subject; rather, it puts us in question, calls us to responsibility.[148] Although Levinas dismisses this resemblance between the two philosophies as 'merely formal',[149] it may provide us with a broad characterisation of both the similarities between the two philosophies, and the decisive difference. Each philosopher points the way to answers to profound questions of human existence: how are we to understand language, subjectivity, the meaning of human existence itself? Heidegger argues that the responses are to be found through the analysis of Dasein's relation to Being. Levinas argues that the answers lie in an understanding of the subject's relation to the Other. Both Being and the Other (and, in Levinas' later work, the otherwise than being) are, ultimately, unsayable.

In addition to the 'formal' similarity between the two thinkers' philosophical systems, Levinas' work resembles Heidegger's early philosophy in its use of the phenomenological method. Indeed, Levinas has frequently remarked that he has the greatest admiration for Heidegger *qua* phenomenologist.[150] However, in spite of Levinas' obvious indebtedness to Heidegger, he often disagrees with the latter as to the significance of particular phenomena. For example, in 'No Identity',[151] Levinas opposes Heidegger's interpretation of the human experience of foreignness.

Levinas begins by offering a brief sketch of the philosophy of *Being and Time* and the 'Letter on Humanism'. Heidegger, he explains, 'connects the notion of transcendental subjectivity with a certain orientation of European philosophy, metaphysics', and thinks that this philosophy is at its term.

Notions such as the ego, psyche, consciousness and the subject, being metaphysical, are suspect. Heidegger rejects the view of history as 'the movement of reason itself, transfiguring being by art, science, the State and industry'.[152] Heideggerian philosophy, Levinas explains, understands the process of Being, 'Being's essence', as 'the unfolding of a certain meaning, a certain light, a certain peace that borrow nothing from a subject, express nothing that would be inside a soul'.[153] Rather, the process of being would be 'manifestation, that is, expansion into a site, a world, hospitality.' Manifestation, however, requires man, 'it entrusts itself to man as a secret and as a task.' Man's role is to express being, not himself. Heidegger claims that it is only in 'forgetting being' that man makes himself into a soul or consciousness by closing himself up like a monad. European metaphysics would be the expression of the history of this monadic closure. But this metaphysics and this history are, according to Heidegger, at an end. Levinas emphasises that, according to Heidegger, man is estranged from the world and this estrangement results from metaphysics. 'The foreignness of man in the world, his stateless condition, is taken to attest to the last spasms of metaphysics and the humanism it sustains.' With the end of metaphysics, man will be able to return to rootedness in Being and fulfil his task as the 'messenger and poet' of Being.[154]

Although Levinas makes it clear that he sees the Hegelian and Marxist understandings of alienation as insufficient explanations of man's sense of foreignness, his main concern is to show that performing the role of 'the shepherd of being' will not overcome this feeling of otherness. The Bible, he argues, presents a notion of estrangement which is a foreignness that the end of metaphysics will not dissipate and which, unlike alienation, is not a negative phenomenon, because it leads to ethical behaviour. Levinas' intention in appealing to the Bible is not to offer scriptural verses as proofs, but to look at them as witnesses to a tradition and an experience. As such, he argues, they are as worth of being cited as are the poetry of Hölderlin and Trakl, which Heidegger quotes.

Levinas cites Psalm 119, 'I am a stranger on the earth: do not hide thy commandments from me' (verse 19) and Leviticus 25:23 'The land shall not be sold forever: for the land is mine; for you are strangers and sojourners with me.' The foreignness in question in these verses is, he points out, neither the Platonic soul 'exiled among the passing shadows', nor the Heideggerian 'displaced state which the building of a house and the possession of land will enable one to overcome by bringing forth, through building, the hospitality of sites which the earth envelopes'.[155] According to the biblical view, the difference between the ego and the world is increased by obligations towards others, as is suggested by the call for commandments in Psalm 119. Levinas insists that the verses he has cited express an idea that is present throughout the Bible: the condition (or 'noncondition') of being slaves in Egypt brings men closer to their neighbours. 'In their noncondition of being strangers men seek one another. No one is at home.'[156] The non-coinciding of self with self that is described negatively by other philosophers as 'alienation', amounts positively, Levinas asserts, to concern for other people. 'The difference that opens between the ego and itself, the non-coincidence of the identical, is a fundamental non-indifference with regard to men.'[157]

Levinas illustrates the biblical view that 'no one can save himself without the others' with a verse from the story of Noah: 'And they that went in, went in male and female of all flesh, as God had commanded him: and the Lord shut him in.'[158] The implication of this verse, Levinas suggests, is that Noah could not close himself off from a humanity in peril.

> The closed domain of the soul cannot be closed from the inside. It is 'the Eternal that closed the door of the Ark behind Noah', a text of Genesis tells us, with wonderful precision. How could it be shut at the hour in which humanity is perishing? And are there hours in which the deluge is not threatening?[159]

Levinas argues that the story of Noah illustrates the impossibility of interiority, that is, of a subject closed off from others. He stresses that we needed neither metaphysics nor the end of metaphysics to learn of this impossibility, for the very 'humanity of man' is 'responsibility for the others'.[160]

This responsibility singles out the ego in its uniqueness, a uniqueness which is not that of a self-identical *cogito*, but that of the one who is always responsible for the others. Levinas' subject is, as noted above,

> A stranger to itself, obsessed by the others, dis-quiet, [...] a hostage in its very recurrence as an ego ceaselessly missing itself. [...] It is a passivity no 'healthy' will can will; it is thus expelled, apart, not collecting the merit of its virtues and talents, incapable of recollecting itself so as to accumulate itself and inflate itself with being. It is the non-essence of man, possibly less than nothing.[161]

The subject which is 'less than nothing' is, however, unique.

> But this responsibility undergone beyond all passivity, from which no one can release me by taking from me my inability to shut myself up, this responsibility which the ego cannot escape (I for whom another cannot be substituted) designates the uniqueness of the irreplaceable. A uniqueness without inwardness, an ego without rest in itself, a hostage for everyone, turned away from itself in each movement of its return to itself—man is without identity.[162]

In the final paragraph of this section, Levinas summarises his position vis-à-vis humanism's understanding of man. Once again he concedes the anti-humanists' argument that 'Man understood as the individual of a genus or as an entity situated in an ontological region, persevering in being like all substances, does not have any privilege that would establish him as the goal of reality.'[163] However, Levinas insists that it is necessary to understand man as a responsibility prior to being *conatus*. This responsibility for everyone entails that I am not of the same genus as other people, since I am responsible for the others and do not consider their responsibility for me, because ultimately I am responsible even for their responsibility for me. It is 'by virtue of this supplementary responsibility', Levinas remarks, that 'subjectivity is not the ego, but me'.[164]

Levinas' notion of subjectivity as the accusative 'me', which is 'less than nothing' and at the same time unique and responsible for the whole of humanity, is a far cry from being the self-identical, reified, substantial *cogito* that anti-humanism, in its various forms, denounces. Why, then, does Levinas use the humanist language of subjectivity to describe his understanding of man? Although, as Soper has pointed out, the word 'humanist' could once be used as an appeal for approval, Levinas is well aware that, in the contemporary context, the word is more likely to have the opposite effect. He acknowledges this difficulty in the final section of 'No Identity'.

> Do these considerations belong to 'thoughts out of season' despite their starting point in the intellectual situation of our time? Will they not shock by their outdated, idealist and humanist vocabulary?[165]

Levinas' answer to these questions, which forms the conclusion of 'No Identity', takes shape through a consideration of the meaning of 'youth'. He has in mind the 'anti-humanism' of the youth of 1968 and identifies, in their critique of humanism, the concern for the other that he calls 'subjectivity'.

> The idea of a subjectivity incapable of shutting itself up, to the point of substitution, responsible for all the others, and, consequently, the idea of a defense of man understood as a defense of the man other than me, presides over what in our day is called the critique of humanism. It rejects the responsibility congealed into 'belles lettres' in which the saying reduced to the said enters into conjunction with its own conditions, forms a structure with its contexts and loses its youth as a saying. This youth is the break in a context, the trenchant, Nietzschean, prophetic word, without status in being. Yet it is not arbitrary, for it has come from sincerity, that is, from responsibility for the other. This unlimited responsibility is not felt as a state of the soul, but signifies in the oneself of the self, consuming itself, the subjectivity of the subject, as embers covered with ashes—and blazing up into a living torch.[166]

Levinas sees in certain 'privileged moments' of 1968 the rejection not only of the *belles lettres* of humanism, but of anti-humanism's own rhetoric.

In the fulguration of some privileged moments of 1968, quickly extinguished by a language as conformist and garrulous as that it was to replace, youth consisted in contesting a world long since denounced. But the denunciation had long since become a literature and a way of speaking. Certain voices of certain outcries gave back to it its own unexceptionable signification. [...] *Able to find responsibilities again under the thick stratum of literature that undo them (one can no longer say 'if only youth knew'), youth ceased to be the age of transition and passage ('youth must pass'), and is shown to be man's humanity.*[167]

In 'No Identity', then, Levinas reaches the same conclusions regarding anti-humanism that were reached regarding humanism in *Difficile liberté*: although it easily (indeed, inevitably) degenerates into the 'said', 'rhetoric' and *'belles lettres'*, its underlying sense is the responsibility of the self for the others. Levinas' assertion that this responsibility is 'man's humanity'[168] indicates the meaning he attributes to the word 'humanism', but is not an adequate answer to the question he himself has raised: why does he retain the humanist language of subjectivity?

CONCLUSION

This question regarding the use of the words 'humanism' and 'anti-humanism' can be answered by returning to Levinas' own definitions. As noted earlier, he understands the word 'humanism' to signify

> [...] the recognition of an invariable essence called 'man', the affirmation of his central place in the economy of the Real and of his value, which engenders all values: respect for the person, in oneself and in the other, imposing the guardianship of his freedom; blossoming of human nature, of intelligence in Science, of creation in Art, of pleasure in daily life; satisfaction of desires without prejudicing the freedom and pleasures of other men and, consequently, the institution of a just law, that is, a reasonable and liberal State [...][169]

With the exception of the first element of this definition, this description of humanism is in accord with Levinas' philosophy. He rejects the Heideggerian and structuralist removal of Man from the centre of meaning, and insists that values are to be taken seriously. Despite his argument that western thought fails to recognise the transcendence of the Other, he is equally insistent on the importance of the 'humanities', especially philosophy, and the need for a liberal state. In a footnote to 'No Identity', Levinas writes

> [...] unless we renounce society [...] one can avoid neither the said, letters, *belles lettres*, the comprehension of being, nor philosophy. One cannot do without them if one means to manifest to thought, even if one thus deforms it, what is beyond being itself. This manifestation takes place at the price of a betrayal, but it is necessary

for justice, which resigns itself to tradition, continuity and institutions, despite their very infidelity. To not care about them is to play with nihilism.[170]

Levinas' philosophy, then, amounts to a restatement of humanist values with a radically different theoretical foundation from that of traditional humanism. Although man still occupies centre stage, humanism has been displaced. As the title *Humanisme de l'autre homme* indicates, man is to be thought starting from the other rather than the self.

This displacement of humanism on the theoretical level should, however, have practical consequences. Levinas has argued that humanism's failure to humanise history is not simply attributable to the failure of human beings to live up to their ideals. Rather, the theoretical basis of humanism is itself inadequate. Because the other is always thought starting from the same, humanism ultimately fails to recognize obligations to the human other *qua* other. Its ideals, which on Levinas' view arise from the same 'pre-philosophical experience' as his 'humanism of the other man', are therefore subject to distortion. In *Difficile liberté*, Levinas argued that abstract truths are always at risk of being eroded or distorted by the one who thinks them. A striking example of the fragility of western thought's concept 'human' is provided by Nazism, which succeeded in eroding the concept so that it no longer included Jews, Gypsies or homosexuals. By contrast, a humanism which does not think the meaning of the human on the basis of the self, but sees the self as the locus of an infinite responsibility for the other, must be better suited to protecting terms such as 'human' from 'fatal shifts of meaning'.[171]

The footnote from 'No Identity' we have cited indicates the way in which Levinas' philosophy is better suited than traditional humanism to protecting ideas from corruption: it is a philosophy of vigilance. One must constantly try to bring the 'otherwise than being' into the said (into literature, philosophy, institutions), knowing all the while that it will thereby be betrayed and that what has been said must be unsaid. The alternation between saying and unsaying what has been said calls for an extreme attention to the degree of success achieved in bringing the otherwise than being to thought. Whereas the traditional humanist, comfortable with his 'truths', might inadvertently distort them, the Levinasian humanist is always aware of both the inadequacy of his attempt to bring the 'otherwise than being' into the said, and the ethical imperative to continue trying to do so.

Levinas' ethical philosophy, his 'humanism of the other man', could therefore appropriately be described with the same phrase he uses in *Difficile liberté* to describe Judaism. It is a philosophy 'more capable than [...western] humanism of giving meaning to being, to life, and [...] of maintaining in the persecuted his human essence'.[172]

1   Martin Heidegger: *Basic Writings, From Being and Time to the Task of Thinking*, translated by David Farrel Krell, New York, Harper & Row, 1976, pp. 190–242. Hereafter cited as 'Letter on Humanism'.

2   'Letter on Humanism', p. 200.

3   Ibid., p. 201.

4   Idem.

5   Idem.

6   Kate Soper, *Humanism and Anti-Humanism*, London, Hutchinson, 1986, p. 10.

7   My concern here is more hermeneutical than philosophical, in that I am trying to establish what Levinas means by humanism. In doing so, I certainly do not claim to have resolved all the philosophical difficulties inherent in the notion of humanism. I hope rather to indicate some of the ways in which Levinas' notion of a 'humanism of the other man' re-orients the debate in an ethical direction.

8   The following characterisation of contemporary French anti-humanism is largely based on the analysis given by Luc Ferry and Alain Renaut in the introductory chapters of *La pensée 68* (Paris, Gallimard, 1988). It should be noted that this analysis is based on an 'ideal type', a model of philosophy, rather than a compilation of themes from the various philosophers under consideration. (See pp. 39–40.) Thus, in what follows, not all statements will apply equally to each of the contemporary philosophers named in our text; for example, the influence of Marx, Nietzsche and Freud, appears to varying degrees in the French thinkers. We have, however, pointed to this influence as a common feature of the French thinkers because the three German thinkers are the source of the 'genealogical critique' (see below) that has been such a major influence on contemporary French thought.

9   *La pensée 68*, pp. 43–6.

10   Ibid., p. 43.

11   See Nietzsche, *The Gay Science*, par. 374. 'Rather the world has become "infinite" for us all over again inasmuch as we cannot reject the possibility that *it may include infinite interpretations*' (translated by Walter Kaufmann, New York, Vintage, 1974, p. 336). Ferry and Renaut point out, however, that the French anti-humanists have not all abandoned the notion of scientific truth in favour of Nietzsche's 'new infinity'. Marxists, Althusser in particular, have been tempted to maintain the notion that truth can be located in the scientific interpretation of a discourse (p. 48).

12   *La pensée 68*, p. 45.

13   Ibid., p. 56. The authors even suggest that such reification is 'intrinsiquement terroriste' (p. 55).

14   In *Nietzsche, Actes du Colloque de Royaumont*, Paris, Minuit, 1967, p. 189. My translation.

15   *La pensée 68*, pp. 46–7.

16   Although the example of the cube is helpful as an image, two points should be noted. Firstly, if the cube happened to be made of translucent glass, all six sides would be visible simultaneously. Secondly, and more importantly, discussions of the perception of the cube tend to treat vision as if it were the only form of perception. Vincent Descombes, for example, writes, 'The six-sided cube is the cube as an object of predicative statements. As for the perceived cube, it can never have six sides at once'. (*Modern French Philosophy*, translated by L. Scott-Fox and J.M. Harding, Cambridge, Cambridge University Press, 1979, p. 64.) Although it is not possible to see all six sides of an opaque cube at the same time, it is possible to feel them.

17   *La pensée 68*, p. 47

18   Ibid., p. 48. The authors point out that the currents of Marxism which maintain the notion of scientific truth are the heirs of a different form of genealogical critique, the Hegelian (pp. 45–6).

19   *Humanism and Anti-Humanism*, pp. 35–8.

20   See *La pensée 68*, pp. 64–8.

21   *Humanism and Anti-Humanism*, p. 38.

22   Ibid., p. 12.

23   Ibid., pp. 11–12.

24   Ibid., p. 11.

25   *Difficile liberté*, p. 385.

26  Ibid., p. 39. For a discussion of Levinas' claim that Heideggerian philosophy is inherently 'violent', see Chapter One.
27  Idem.
28  Ibid., p. 391.
29  Idem.
30  Ibid., p. 392.
31  Idem.
32  *Difficile liberté* pp. 380–84.
33  Ibid., p. 382.
34  Idem.
35  *L'Au-delà du verset*, p. 21.
36  *Difficile liberté*, p. 394.
37  Ibid., p. 396.
38  Idem.
39  Ibid., p. 397.
40  Idem.
41  Ibid., p. 398.
42  See Glossary.
43  Ibid., p. 399.
44  Paris, Fata Morgana, 1973. The essays which make up this book have been translated by Alphonso Lingis and included in *Collected Philosophical Papers.*, The Hague, Martinus Nijhoff, 1987.
45  *Collected Philosophical Papers*, p. 127.
46  Ibid., p. 142.
47  Ibid., p. 143.
48  *Humanism and Anti-Humanism*, p. 96.
49  Ibid., p. 97.
50  *Collected Philosophical Papers*, p. 130.
51  'Letter on Humanism', p. 201.
52  Ibid., p. 202.
53  Idem.
54  Ibid., p. 204.
55  *Being and Time,* translated by John Macquarrie and Edward Robinson, Oxford, Basil Blackwell, 1962. p. 32.
56  Idem.
57  'Letter on Humanism', p. 210.
58  Ibid.
59  Translator's footnote to 'Letter on Humanism', p. 204.
60  For a discussion of the history of the subject-object dichotomy in relation to the philosophies of Heidegger and Levinas, see Manning, *Interpreting Otherwise* pp. 168–88.
61  *Humanism and Anti-Humanism,* p. 57.
62  'Letter on Humanism', p. 210.
63  Ibid., pp. 210–11.
64  Ibid., pp. 211–12.
65  Idem.
66  Idem. Emphasis added
67  Some of the general differences between Heidegger and Levinas will be discussed in the course of our exposition of *Humanisme de l'autre homme*, below.
68  *Collected Philosophical Papers*, pp. 131–132.
69  Adriaan Peperzak, 'Beyond Being', *Research in Phenomenology*, No. 8, 1978, p. 243.
70  *Otherwise than Being*, p. 29.
71  Ibid., p. 28.
72  Idem.
73  Ibid., p. 29.
74  Ibid., p. 32.

75  Idem.
76  Ibid., p. 33.
77  Ibid., p. 13.
78  'Beyond Being', p. 242.
79  Idem.
80  Levinas himself makes this point in many places, including 'The Paradox of Morality', p. 171 and his preface to the German edition of *Totality and Infinity*, which is included in Emmanuel Levinas, *Entre Nous: Essais sur le penser-à-l'autre*, Paris, Editions Grasset, 1991, pp. 249–252.
81  'Beyond Being', p. 242.
82  Ibid., p. 246.
83  *Otherwise than Being*, p. 105.
84  Ibid., p. 105.
85  Idem, p. 107.
86  'Levinas, Derrida and Others Vis-à-vis', in *The Provocation of Levinas*, p. 140. Llewelyn's abbreviations AEAE and OBBE stand for *Autrement qu'être* and *Otherwise than Being*.
87  *Otherwise than Being*, pp. 114–15.
88  Ibid., p. 115.
89  *Autrement qu'être*, p. 146.
90  *Otherwise than Being*, p. 118. Emphasis added.
91  Ibid., p. 115.
92  Ibid., p. 116.
93  Ibid., pp. 116–17.
94  Ibid., p. 89.
95  Ibid., p. 88.
96  Idem.
97  Ibid., p. 101
98  'The Trace of the Other', translated by A. Lingis, in *Deconstruction in Context*, edited by Mark Taylor, Chicago, University of Chicago Press, 1986, p. 354.
99  Ibid., p. 355.
100  Idem.
101  Idem.
102  Idem. The notion of the trace, and the related concept of 'illeity' will be discussed further in Chapter Three.
103  *Otherwise than Being*, p. 89.
104  Whether or not notions such as 'election' should be understood theologically will be discussed in Chapter Three.
105  There is an error in the translation, rendering '*involontaire*' as 'voluntary'.
106  *Otherwise than Being*, p. 118.
107  Ibid., p. 122.
108  Idem.
109  Ibid., p. 124.
110  Ibid., p. 128.
111  Lingis' translation retains the French spelling '*Jonas*'.
112  *Otherwise than Being*, p. 128.
113  'No doubt nothing is more comical than the concern that a being has for an existence it could not save from its destruction, as in Tolstoi's tale where an order for enough boots for 25 years is sent by one that will die the very evening he gives his order. That is indeed as absurd as questioning, in view of action, the stars whose verdict would be without appeal.' *Otherwise than Being*, p. 129.
114  *Otherwise than Being*, p. 129.
115  Ibid., pp. 117–18. Emphasis added.
116  Ibid., p. 10. Emphasis added.
117  Ibid., p. 13.
118  Ibid., p. 101.

119  See Simon Critchley's analysis of the distinction between the saying and the said in *The Ethics of Deconstruction*, p. 7.
120  *Otherwise than Being*, p. 5.
121  Ibid., p. 37.
122  Ibid., p. 42.
123  Ibid., p. 44.
124  Ibid., p. 43.
125  *The Ethics of Deconstruction*, p. 164.
126  *Otherwise than Being*, p. 43.
127  It should be noted that Lingis here mistranslates '*légitime*' as 'illegitimate'.
128  *Otherwise than Being*, p. 7.
129  Ibid., p. 44.
130  Ibid., p. 6.
131  Ibid., p. 7.
132  'The Paradox of Morality', pp. 178–79.
133  'Beyond Being', p. 248.
134  Ibid., p. 249.
135  *Otherwise than Being*, p. 19.
136  The difficulty in reading this work arises, as Peperzak points out, from 'our need for an architectonic, which is characteristic for [sic] the investigating, grounding and constructing thinking of ontology'. 'Beyond Being', p. 249.
137  'Levinas, Derrida and Others *Vis-à-vis*' in *The Provocation of Levinas*, p. 141.
138  'Beyond Being', pp. 260–61.
139  Ibid., p. 261.
140  Idem.
141  'Rereading', p. 34.
142  *De Dieu qui vient à l'idée*, Paris, Vrin, 1986, p. 143.
143  *Otherwise than Being*, p. 127.
144  Ibid., pp. 127–28.
145  Ibid., p. 127.
146  Ibid., p. 128.
147  'Letter on Humanism', p. 210.
148  *Autrement Que Savoir*, Paris, Osiris, 1988, p. 31.
149  Ibid., p. 32.
150  Levinas' 1949 work *En découvrant l'existence avec Husserl et Heidegger* (Paris, Vrin) played an important role in introducing Heidegger's thought into France. Although Levinas has subsequently adopted a much more critical stance towards Heidegger, he continues to acknowledge his indebtedness to Heidegger and his admiration for the latter's work *qua* phenomenologist. See for example *Autrement que savoir*, p. 86.
151  *Collected Philosophical Papers*, pp. 141–52.
152  Ibid., p. 143.
153  Ibid., pp. 143–44.
154  Ibid., p. 144. Although Levinas does not refer to specific texts, the outline of Heideggerian thought given in this essay (and in other contexts) seems to be limited to Heidegger's earlier works, in particular *Being and Time* and the 'Letter on Humanism'. It is, of course, important to ask why Levinas limits himself to these works. However, a discussion of the issue is beyond the scope of the present study.
155  *Collected Philosophical Papers*, pp. 148–49
156  Ibid., p. 149. Translation slightly altered.
157  Idem.
158  Genesis 7:16.
159  *Collected Philosophical Papers*, p. 149.
160  Idem.
161  Idem.

162   Ibid., p. 150.
163   Idem.
164   Idem.
165   Idem.
166   Ibid., pp. 150–51.
167   Ibid., p. 151. Emphasis added.
168   Idem.
169   *Difficile liberté*, p. 385.
170   *Collected Philosophical Papers*, note 11, p. 151.
171   *Difficile liberté*, p. 391.
172   Ibid., p. 392.

# Chapter 3

## IS LEVINAS' ETHICS THEOLOGICAL?

### INTRODUCTION

In the previous chapters, we have shown how Levinas' descriptions of the 'face-to-face relation' and the 'otherwise than being' both provide a quasi-phenomenological account of ethics and form the basis of a far-reaching critique of western philosophy. The next chapter will show that this account of ethics can be combined with Levinas' understanding of Scripture as 'ethical saying' to describe a non-theological interpretation of Jewish texts and teaching. Before doing so, however, we must pause to consider the meaning of the word 'God' in Levinas' philosophical writings.

Levinas has always insisted that he writes philosophy, not theology. However, some readers continue to think of Levinas' writings on the ethical relation as theological. The claim that Levinas' work is 'theological' can be understood in various ways. The most obvious, perhaps, is to understand it as asserting that his thought either takes the existence of God as a presupposition, or reaches it as a conclusion.[1] We will see that Levinas insists that God is 'otherwise than being' or 'beyond being' and therefore cannot properly be said to 'exist'. However, this is only a partial argument against the characterisation of Levinas' ethics as theological, since the epithet 'theological' can be more broadly understood as referring to a pre-occupation with 'God', whether conceived as a 'being' or as 'beyond being'. We will therefore also ask whether Levinas' description of the ethical relation can be understood without reference to 'God'.

### TOTALITY AND INFINITY

The characterisation of *Totality and Infinity* as a theological work is sometimes based on a reading in which 'the Other' (*autrui*) is identified with God. The *prima facie* case for this identification consists in Levinas' insistence that the Other is 'wholly other', his comparison of the idea of the Other with the Cartesian 'idea of Infinity', and the description of the Other as transcendent and commanding. As Jan de Greef points out, it is as almost as though there were an absence of distinction between 'the other in his dimension of height' and 'a transcendent God' in *Totality and Infinity*; for example, the prohibition of murder that is revealed in the face-to-face relation is not a Kantian categorical imperative, but seems to be the commandment of the Torah.[2] However, de Greef argues that the Other is not

God but 'the only way, for me, towards the alterity—the holiness (*saintété*)—of God'.[3]

There is ample textual support for de Greef's refusal to identify the Other with God. Firstly, since the pronoun *'autrui'*[4] is normally used to designate other people, it is doubtful that Levinas would use it to refer to God without specifically stating that he was doing so. Moreover, he uses the word 'God' in this text without any indication that it is being used interchangeably with 'the Other'. The distinction between the two terms is made clear in the section entitled 'the Metaphysical and the Human'.

> The Other is not the incarnation of God, but precisely by his face, in which he is disincarnate, is the manifestation of the height in which God is revealed. It is our relations with men, which describe a field of research hardly glimpsed at […] that give to theological concepts the sole signification they admit of.[5]

For Levinas, then, the relation with God is distinct from, but dependent on, the social relation.

Having argued that 'God' and 'the Other' are not to be identified, we must ask what is meant by 'God'. In the section referred to above, the meaning that Levinas attributes to the word 'God' does not emerge with any clarity. Rather than presenting Levinas' own ideas about God, the section reads as a critique of 'positive religion', in which the believer aspires toward 'a union with the transcendent through participation'. Such religions, he argues, are 'violent' in that the encounter with the 'sacred' is meant to destroy or replace the identity of the believer.[6] Moreover, there is a danger that in seeking the sacred man will ignore his ethical duties towards others.

Levinas, however, insists that man can relate to God only by maintaining his identity as a separated being, and encountering the human other.

> The dimension of the divine opens forth from the human face. A relation with the transcendent free from all captivation from the Transcendent is a social relation. It is here that the Transcendent, infinitely other, solicits us and appeals to us. […] The atheism of the Metaphysician means positively that our relation with the Metaphysical is an ethical behaviour and not theology, not a thematization, be it a knowledge by analogy, of the attributes of God. […] It is our relations with men […] that give to theological concepts the sole signification they admit of.[7]

Levinas is not simply arguing that in order to please God and enter into relationship with Him we must first establish ethical relationships with other people. Rather, he insists that the relationship with God can only be enacted through social relations.

> The work of justice is necessary in order that the breach that leads to God be produced—and 'vision' here coincides with the work of justice. Hence metaphysics is

enacted where the social relation is enacted—in our relations with men. *There can be no 'knowledge' of God separated from the relationship with men. The Other is the very locus of metaphysical truth, and is indispensable for my relation with God.*[8]

The claim that the relationship with God is only enacted in the social relation might, if taken in isolation, lend credence to the view that the Other is God. Yet the statement, quoted above, that 'the Other is not the incarnation of God but precisely by his face [...] is the manifestation of the height in which God is revealed', makes it clear that this identification is contrary to Levinas' meaning. The statement also suggests the possibility that not every encounter with the Other is necessarily a moment of divine revelation: what is made manifest in the face of the Other is not God *per se*, but the 'height in which God is revealed'. We can similarly understand that the 'breach' which is produced in justice may not always 'lead to God', or at least that this way to God may not always be followed.

This ambiguity, together with the lack of a clear indication of the meaning of 'God' in this section, serves to emphasise the critical nature of Levinas' discussion of the relationship between the metaphysical and human. As was pointed out above, the function of this section is to criticise a certain religious outlook which Levinas considers primitive, and to stress the fundamental differences between this outlook and his own view of the relationship between the metaphysical and the human. The aspects of Levinas' view of this relationship which emerge from the description are largely negative, in that he does not attempt to describe God or the precise nature of the divine-human encounter, but rather states what they are not. God, he insists, 'is not only a being superlatively being, a sublimation of the objective, or, in the solitude of love, a sublimation of a Thou'.[9] Our relation with God is 'not theology, not a thematization [...] of the attributes of God'.[10] The only positive statement that Levinas makes about the divine-human relation is that it is enacted where social relations are enacted.

In 'The Metaphysical and the Human', then, Levinas uses the word 'God', but the role of this term appears to be extremely limited. It is the Other, not God, who commands, and it is not the relationship with God that governs one's relations with people, but the ethical relation itself which makes possible the relation with God. No positive meaning or role is ascribed to the word 'God' and it is difficult to see how Levinas could say anything positive about God, given his insistence that 'the direct comprehension of God is impossible' and his rejection of theological discourse.

The other passages in *Totality and Infinity* in which the word 'God' appears are equally silent about the precise meaning of the term and the nature of the divine-human encounter. The term appears most frequently in the context of discussions of Descartes' 'idea of the Infinite'. In these discussions, Levinas is not interested in Descartes' idea of God *per se*, but in presenting the Cartesian idea of the Infinite as a model of transcendence through which to understand the relation between the I and the Other. Levinas explicitly states that he is not interested in Descartes' attempt at proving the existence of God.

> [...] without holding to the Cartesian argumentation that proves the separated existence of the Infinite by the finitude of the being have an idea of infinity [...] it is of importance to emphasize that the transcendence of the Infinite with respect to the I which is separated from it and which thinks it measures (so to speak) its very infinitude.[11]

Whereas Descartes was interested in the way that the idea of God overflows the thought which thinks it, Levinas is primarily interested in the similar impossibility of conceiving an adequate idea of the human Other.

> To approach the Other in conversation is to welcome his expression, in which at each instant he overflows the idea a thought would carry away from it. It is therefore to *receive* from the Other beyond the capacity of the I, which means exactly: to have the idea of infinity.[12]

As we saw in Chapter One, Levinas describes the encounter with the Other as leading to judgment, in which the self discovers that its freedom is 'murderous in its very exercise'.[13]

> To discover the unjustified facticity of power and freedom one must not consider it as an object, nor consider the Other as an object; one must measure oneself against infinity, that is desire him. It is necessary to have the idea of infinity, the idea of the perfect as Descartes would say, in order to know one's own imperfection. The idea of the perfect is not an idea but desire; it is the welcoming of the Other, the commencement of moral consciousness, which calls in question my freedom.[14]

The idea that the encounter with the Infinite culminates in judgment has religious overtones, which are even more pronounced in Levinas' discussion of the ' judgment of God'. We noted earlier that Levinas contrasts the judgment of God with the 'virile judgment of history' which he describes as cruel.[15] The judgment of history is inevitably violent, in that it does not recognise the singularity of the 'I', does not address it but speaks of it in the third person. 'The judgment of history is always pronounced in absentia.'[16] Subjectivity is present, however and thus able to defend itself, at the judgment of God, for 'God sees the invisible.'[17]

The claim that 'God sees the invisible', if taken in isolation, would appear to be a blatantly theological statement. However, immediately after making the claim, Levinas asks '[...] how is that situation which we can call judgment of God [...] concretely brought about?'[18] His answer does not refer to God at all, but describes the infinite responsibility of the will, 'a responsibility increasing in the measure that it is assumed'.[19] 'Judgment of God' does not describe a particular relationship between the self and an omniscient being; instead, the will's 'coming under judgment' consists in 'a new orientation of the inner life, called to infinite responsibilities'.[20] It consists in 'goodness'.

> To place oneself beyond the judgment of history, under the judgment of truth, is not to suppose behind the apparent history another history called judgment of God [... It] is to exalt the subjectivity, called to moral overstepping beyond laws, which is henceforth in truth because it surpasses the limits of its being. The judgment of God that judges me at the same time confirms me. But it confirms me precisely in my interiority, whose justice is more severe than the judgment of history. Concretely to be an I presenting itself at a trial—which requires all the resources of subjectivity—means for it to be able to see, beyond the universal judgments of history, that offence of the offended which is inevitably produced in the very judgment issued from universal principles. [...] To be I and not only an incarnation of a reason is precisely to be capable of seeing the offence of the offended, or the face. [...] Beyond the justice of universal laws, the I enters judgment by the fact of being good. Goodness consists in taking up a position in being such that the Other counts more than myself.[21]

We have quoted this passage at length in order to show that the analysis of 'judgment of God' is not a discussion of God's relations with people, but a description of subjectivity in terms of responsibility and goodness. Levinas conceivably could have analysed the self's coming to judgment as an infinite responsibility without using the term 'judgment of God'. In Chapter Five, we will consider the reasons for Levinas' use of theological language. For the present however, let us simply consider the methodology at work in this description. Beginning with the apparently theological notion of 'judgment of God', Levinas proceeds to a phenomenological analysis of goodness.[22] This movement from apparently theological statements to phenomenological analyses can be discerned at other points in the text. For example, Olmedo Gaviria Alvarez has devoted an entire article to analysing the phenomenological significance of the idea of creation in Levinas' work. He writes that Levinas follows the phenomenological method of Husserl insofar as he begins by 'bracketing' the dogmatic and philosophical significations suggested by notions such as the idea of creation. This bracketing

> permits him to grasp the intentionality of this idea, that at which it aims, its *eidos*, which he describes 'formally' according to the teaching of monotheistic religions but which he justifies philosophically, either by categories borrowed from Plato and Descartes, or, and this is the 'return to things in themselves', by an original experience which gives to the idea of creation [...] the only signification which it admits of in his work.[23]

That Levinas' interest in religious notions such as creation *ex nihilo* or judgment is phenomenological[24] rather than theological is indicated in the text by phrases such as 'concretely this is produced as ...' or 'this means ...', as in the passage quoted above where Levinas writes that 'concretely to be an I presenting itself at a trial [...] means for it to be able to see [...] that offence of the offended which is inevitably produced in the very judgment issued from universal principles'. In the preface to *Totality and Infinity*, Levinas informs the reader that phenomenological deductions are signalled by such expressions.

> The break-up of the formal structure of thought (the noema of a noesis) into events which this structure dissimulates, but which sustain it and restore its concrete significance, constitutes a *deduction*—necessary and yet non-analytical. In our exposition it is indicated by expressions such as 'that is', or 'precisely', or 'this accomplishes that', or 'this is produced as that'.[25]

However, *Totality and Infinity* lacks the systematic character that would consistently make clear Levinas' intention in appealing to theological notions.[26] The text sometimes reads as though Levinas were uncritically accepting religious dogma. For example, in describing separation he writes, 'One lives outside of God, at home with oneself; one is an I, an egoism.'[27] He then describes the separated being as 'atheist' and exclaims, 'It is certainly a great glory for the creator to have set up a being capable of atheism, a being which, without having been *causa sui*, has an independent view and word and is at home with itself.'[28] Although these remarks, read in isolation, would seem to imply that Levinas is taking for granted the existence of God the creator, his discussion of creation *ex nihilo* is phenomenological rather than cosmological or theological. As Gaviria Alvarez explains, Levinas is interested in this notion because 'the idea of creation [...] is the only witness in the history of thought to an exceptional relation with the Other'.[29] To be created from nothing means to be totally dependent for one's very existence on the creator. Yet man experiences himself as free. Monotheism, however, as Levinas understands it, sees in this paradoxical relationship the investiture of man's freedom: 'man is free because he is dependent.'[30]

Levinas takes up this idea of creation *ex nihilo* to argue against the 'primitive' understanding of the relationship between the human and the transcendent which was discussed above. The believers of myths and 'positive religions' place too much emphasis on man's dependence while denying his freedom, thus envisaging the relationship with transcendence as that of participation or unity, or viewing human history fatalistically, as a drama written and directed by God. For Levinas, however, the monotheistic notion of man as creature is the thought of a being that is both 'atheist', separated from the infinite, and at the same time 'capable of receiving a revelation, learning that it is created, and putting itself in question'.[31]

Similarly, Gaviria Alvarez points out that Levinas is not interested in the cosmology of Descartes' *Meditations*, but in the search for the foundation of truth. 'The relation with the Infinite', he writes, 'appears to the subject in the context of a critical science [*savoir critique*] which is seeking its foundation.' As such, the notion of creation 'does not express the problem of the origin beginning with a cause but, to put it in contemporary language, *the problem of the foundation of meaning*.'[32] Gaviria Alvarez cites Levinas' essay 'Liberté et commandement', in which Levinas clearly defines creation in terms of intelligibility. 'Creation,' Levinas writes, 'is the fact that intelligibility precedes me. [...] This is not a theological thesis; we reach the idea of creation out of the experience of a face.'[33]

Before examining the way in which the experience of the face leads to the idea of creation, Gaviria Alvarez presents Levinas' 'formal' description of this notion, which draws on both Descartes and Plato. He explains that the God recognised in the third Meditation is, as we have seen, the Infinite which overflows any idea of it. Gaviria Alvarez points out that in escaping thematisation by the *cogito*, the infinite also rescues the *cogito* from solipsism: 'it is the discovery of a true Alterity, of a true Transcendence'.[34] Levinas appeals to Plato's notion of the Good to argue that this idea of transcendence is not theological, but philosophical. The significance for Levinas of the notion of a Good beyond being is that the Good 'does not participate in a system. It is able to enter into relation without losing its transcendence, and without competing with man's freedom'.[35] Levinas uses Descartes' *Meditations* and Plato's notion of the Good to argue that

> the critical knowledge through which the Cogito discovers its status as a creature is not of the order of thematization but of ethics. 'Creaturality' is not derived from the *lumen naturale* of the Cogito, it is revealed to moral consciousness by the Infinite, by the Good, which overflows it in the face of the neighbour [...].[36]

Gaviria Alvarez's reference to the face of the neighbour leads him to the second part of his analysis of the idea of creation in Levinas' work. Having presented the 'formal' description of creation, supported by Descartes and Plato, he turns to the experience which provides its justification, the face-to-face relation. The face of the Other reveals the prohibition of murder, and creates moral consciousness. The structures which were described 'formally' through the Idea of the Infinite and the notion of the Good Beyond Being, are concretised in the face-to-face relationship.

> In this revelation [...] which gives birth to moral consciousness, the formal structure of the Cogito is concretized; it discovers a signification which precedes it, which escapes thematization: the Infinite which overflows its idea, a Transcendence which must be approached as Majesty. Because the Other invites to goodness, the relationship of subjectivity with the beyond being—with the Good—is concretized.[37]

Gaviria Alvarez's essay, then, points the way towards a non-theological understanding of *Totality and Infinity*: The dogmatic content of theological notions is to be 'bracketed', while we attempt to discern the 'intention' of these notions, as understood by Levinas, and seek the concrete experiences which he argues correspond to them. For example, following Gaviria Alvarez, Levinas' references to 'God' in 'The Metaphysical and the Human', which we discussed above, can be understood to indicate not that he is presupposing the existence of God, but that he is describing 'formally' the relationship between the self and the other according to monotheism. Levinas' use of biblical idiom in this section—such as the description of God as 'invisible', and of the other as 'the Stranger, the widow and the orphan'[38]—is not an appeal to the Bible as proof of his ideas, but belongs to the description of a monotheistic understanding of the relationship between the self and the transcendent Other. As we will see in Chapter Four, the description given here of the relationship between the 'metaphysician' and the 'Metaphysical' is similar to Levinas' description of the relationship between man and God according to Judaism. The Metaphysical, or God, is 'invisible'. The relationship with Him is not one of comprehension, but of 'ethical behaviour'. No direct relation with God is possible; rather 'the Other is the very locus of metaphysical truth, and is indispensable for my relation with God'.[39]

More importantly for our present purposes, the description of the relationship between the self and God which is given in 'The Metaphysical and the Human' corresponds to aspects of the face-to-face relation which are described concretely in other sections of the work. For example, the 'atheism' of the metaphysician corresponds to the 'separated' existence of the self, which makes possible a relationship with the absolutely other. Similarly, the biblical notion of hearing a divine commandment is explicitly correlated with the concrete experience of entering into discourse with the human other, a 'relation with a substance overflowing its own idea in me'.[40]

Although some aspects of the monotheistic account of the relationship between man and God can thus be directly correlated with Levinas' descriptions of the self-other relationship, other aspects of the description present greater difficulty. For example, we may ask whether there is a concrete correlate of the notion of a 'breach that leads to God' which is said to be opened up through the social relation. We will see below that the notion of the Good in Levinas' later work might be said to fill this role. However, Gaviria Alvarez makes two points that are of special significance to the discussion of 'The Metaphysical and the Human'. Firstly, as we saw above, he acknowledges that Levinas' phenomenological analysis of monotheistic beliefs is not carried out in a systematic way. There is thus no reason to assume (as the above analysis may seem to suggest) that every aspect of the relationship between man and God which Levinas describes can be directly correlated with his description of the face-to-face relation, and our failure to identify a concrete experience which corresponds to 'the breach which leads to God', without implying the existence of God, does not therefore constitute a refutal of Gaviria Alvarez's argument.

A remark that he makes in the context of his discussion of Levinas' later work is also relevant to our understanding of the notion of a 'breach that leads to God'. We argued above that Levinas' description of the face of the other as 'the manifestation of the height in which God is revealed' left open the possibility that not every encounter with the Other was necessarily a moment of divine revelation. In other words, God may be revealed in the encounter with the human other, but He might not be. Commenting on Levinas' description, in *En découvrant l'existence avec Husserl et Heidegger*, of the face as 'carrying, perhaps, the trace of the Infinite', Gaviria Alvarez highlights the importance of the 'perhaps'.

> It is necessary to say 'perhaps' [*peut-être*] because the appeal which is formulated does not let itself be converted into evidence in a philosophical discourse, it always remains in the dimension of 'the enigma': it is nothing in the world of objective significations.[41]

Similarly, the understanding that God is not always revealed in the encounter with the human other prevents Levinas' use of the term 'God' from being interpreted as evidence or proof. If Levinas had argued that God is always revealed in the face of the other, his description of the face-to-face might be understood as somehow offering evidence for belief in God. However, as he has pointed out in *Difficile liberté*, 'the idea of a personal God, a unique God, does not reveal itself like an image in a dark room.'[42]

In fact, the idea of a unique God is not developed in *Totality and Infinity* either. We have seen that although Levinas uses apparently theological notions, such as 'judgment of God' and 'creation *ex nihilo*', he is not interested in their dogmatic content, but in a phenomenological analysis of their underlying intention. Moreover, even where his reference to God cannot be directly correlated with an aspect of the relationship between the self and the human other, God does not serve as a proof of any thesis. We have argued that the section on the metaphysical and the human does not present any positive description or definition of God, but functions negatively, as a critique of 'positive religion'. Although Levinas writes of the 'height in which God is revealed' it is not clear how this is any different from 'height' *tout court*. As Gaviria Alvarez points out, in *Totality and Infinity* 'everything seems to unroll between the subject and the Other in a relationship *à deux*; even if it is said that the Other "resembles God" [...],[43]this resemblance is far from being specified'.[44] In *Totality and Infinity* then, the question of God is fairly marginal, and it is possible to understand the face-to-face relation without either positing the existence of God or assigning any positive meaning to this term.

LEVINAS' LATER WORK

In Levinas' later work, the question of God becomes more central. We will examine below the role of God in *Otherwise than Being*. Before doing so, however, it will be helpful to look at the essay 'God and Philosophy', in which Levinas specifically addresses the problem of the meaning of 'God' for philosophical thought.

### *'God and Philosophy'*

Levinas opens the discussion by quoting the Greek claim that 'Not to philosophize is still to philosophize'.[45] Although, as Derrida points out, Levinas has elsewhere indicated his awareness of the difficulty of escaping from philosophical discourse,[46] in this essay he argues that there is meaning outside of philosophy. Western philosophy, he explains, understands meaning as belonging to the realm of being, to 'being's move'.[47] 'Meaningful thought' and 'thought about being', according to this view, are equivalent notions; it is thus impossible for western philosophy to treat the biblical notion of a truly transcendent God, a God 'beyond being', as meaningful. To thematise God in philosophical discourse is necessarily to destroy his transcendence. Moreover, Levinas insists that it is not sufficient to assign belief in God to the realm of opinion or faith, for 'faith and opinion speak the language of being'.[48] Opinion is itself an ontological thought which does not allow for appreciation of the meaning of transcendence. Levinas also argues that thought about God which is based on 'religious experiences allegedly independent of philosophy'[49] does not escape the ontologising of philosophical thought. This is so because the very notion of 'experience' refers to the *cogito* and thus to philosophy.

The 'narration' of religious experience does not shake philosophy and cannot break with presence and immanence, of which philosophy is the emphatic completion. [...] From the start then a religious being interprets what he lived through as an experience. In spite of himself he already interprets God, of whom he claims to have an experience, in terms of being, presence and immanence.[50]

Levinas sets out to show that 'God' does not signify as 'the theme of the religious discourse which names God' but as 'the discourse which, at least to begin with, does not name him, but says him with another form of address than denomination or evocation'.[51] Once again, he draws on the Cartesian 'Idea of the Infinite', which is an idea of God that 'overflows every capacity', and 'breaks up the thought which is an investment, a synopsis and a synthesis'.[52] Levinas emphasises , however, that although the idea of the Infinite cannot be contained in consciousness, it is yet 'in me', as though 'the *in* of the Infinite were to signify both the *non* and the *within*'.[53] He highlights Descartes' claim in the third Meditation that 'in some way I have in me the notion of the infinite earlier than the finite—to wit, the notion of God before that of myself'.[54] Consciousness thus discovers the idea of the Infinite as an idea which was not welcomed by it, but put in it in an inaccessible past. The idea of the Infinite is thus the passivity of the self, 'a passivity more passive still than any passivity'.[55] It is also a challenge to consciousness.

The putting into us of an unincludable idea overturns that presence to self which consciousness is, forcing its way through the barrier and checkpoint, eluding the obligation to accept or adopt all that enters from the outside. It is then an idea signifying with a signifyingness prior to presence, to all presence, prior to every origin in consciousness and thus an-archical, accessible in its trace.[56]

Levinas emphasises the unbreachable gap between the signifyingness of the idea of the Infinite and its exhibition or manifestation. The idea of the Infinite, he writes,

[...] signifies with a signifyingness from the first older than its exhibition, not exhausting itself in exhibiting itself, not drawing its meaning from its manifestation, and thus breaking with the coinciding of being with appearance in which, for Western philosophy, meaning or rationality lie [...].[57]

Levinas then suggests that the meaning of this 'antiquity of a signification' is an awakening of consciousness.

The Infinite affects thought by devastating it and at the same time calls upon it; in a 'putting back in its place' it puts thought into place. It awakens it. The awakening of thought is not a welcoming of the infinite, is not a recollecting, not an assuming, which are necessary and sufficient for experience. The idea of the Infinite puts these in question.[58]

As in *Totality and Infinity*, the relationship with the Infinite is described as arousing an insatiable desire, 'desire for the Good'.

> The negativity of the in of the Infinite [...] hollows out a desire which cannot be filled, nourishes itself with its very augmentation, and is exalted as desire, withdraws from its satisfaction in the measure that it approaches the desirable. It is a desire that is beyond satisfaction, and, unlike a need, does not identify a term or an end. This endless desire for what is beyond being is dis-inter*estedness*, transcendence—desire for the Good.[59]

Levinas denies that desire for the Good necessarily destroys the transcendence of the Good by reducing it to immanence. As long as the desirable remains 'separated in the desire' it is not absorbed in immanence'.[60] In the desire for the Good, God, or the desirable, is 'near but different: holy'.[61] God remains separated by ordering me to the human other, who is described as 'the non-desirable, the undesirable par excellence'.[62] This description represents a marked departure from the thought of *Totality and Infinity*, in which it is desire for the human other that issues in goodness. Whereas in the 'face-to-face relation' the other is himself the source of ethical commandment, the relationship described in 'God and Philosophy' involves the detour of 'illeity', whereby 'the Infinite, or God', while being desired by the self, refers the self to the 'non-desirable' human other.[63] Through this detour, God retains his transcendence, and the desire remains unfulfilled:

> The desirable is intangible and separates itself from the relationship with desire which it calls for; through this separation or holiness it remains a third person, the *he* in the depth of the you. He is good in just this eminent sense; He does not fill me up with goods, but compels me to goodness, which is better than goods received.[64]

The notion of 'illeity', together with that of trace, was introduced in the essay 'The Trace of the Other', which was written between the publication of *Totality and Infinity* and that of *Otherwise than Being*. As we have seen in the previous chapter, Levinas argues that the face comes from a 'beyond', an 'utterly bygone past', and that this beyond signifies as a 'trace'.[65] 'A trace,' Levinas explains, 'is a presence of that which properly speaking has never been there, of what is always past.'[66] The being that is always past can only be a transcendent being, which is 'somehow outside the distinction between being and entities'.[67] The encounter with the face, Levinas argues, takes place in the 'trace' of this transcendence, in 'illeity'. Both the idea of the 'trace' and that of illeity are therefore closely connected to the notion of an 'immemorial past', from which the commandment of responsibility comes. The 'He' [*Il*] of illeity is he who is never present in the assemblable present of 'my life'. It is He who 'has already passed'.[68]

Levinas does not hesitate to associate the *Il* of illeity with the God of the Bible. The God of Judeo-Christian tradition, he writes,

maintains all the infinity of his absence, which is in the personal order itself. He shows himself only by his trace, as is said in Exodus 33.[69] To go toward Him is not to follow this trace which is not a sign; it is to go toward the others who stand in the trace of illeity.[70]

Like the God of the Bible, the He of illeity can never become present; illeity, like God, orders us to responsibility for the neighbour. Moreover, the God of the Bible is a personal God, and Levinas has derived the term 'illeity' from a personal pronoun;[71] the source of the commandment of responsibility is neither Being, nor an impersonal Good Beyond Being, but He.[72]

Given these similarities, it may be tempting to see 'illeity' as simply another name for the biblical God. However, it should be noted that the 'he' of illeity does not become the subject of a theological discourse. Unlike the God of biblical narrative, the 'he' of illeity is neither described, as if he were a being, nor identified as the Creator. Instead, 'illeity' remains a phenomenological term, employed to describe the self's experience of the call to responsibility. Let us, therefore, consider what is added to Levinas' account of ethical responsibility by the introduction of the term 'illeity'.

We can begin by asking why Levinas was not satisfied with the account of the face-to-face relation given in *Totality and Infinity*. Levinas' attempt, in *Otherwise than Being*, to break with the ontological language of that book has been discussed in the previous chapter, and will not be considered here. Instead, let us focus on the differences between the face-to-face and the description of the ethical in *Otherwise than Being*. In the earlier work, the call to responsibility seemed more straightforward: the 'I' of enjoyment is called into question by the encounter with the other. In the face-to-face, the self's infinite responsibility for the other is revealed. However, this does not entail that the self becomes a self-sacrificing altruist, completely devoted to the service of the other. Instead, two conflicts arise, that between the self's duties to the other and his duties to the third (because there are always more than two people in the world) and that between responsibility for the other(s) and the natural inclination to be concerned with one's own being. The first conflict gives rise to the thought of justice; the second, to a struggle between conscience and the instinct for self-preservation.

The question that guides Levinas' enquiry in *Totality and Infinity* is whether or not we are 'duped by morality'. His answer, which takes the form of a phenomenological account of the possibility of ethics, is that we are not duped. However, the account of the face-to-face relation does not touch on the question of why the awareness of ethical responsibility is sometimes translated into ethical behaviour, and sometimes not. Although *Otherwise than Being* does not deal with this question explicitly, its description of the self makes ethical behaviour more understandable. This is, firstly, because the later work establishes responsibility as part of the very definition of human selfhood and, secondly, because the commandment is described as coming from elsewhere, from an immemorial past, rather than directly from the human other.

As we have seen in Chapter One, the face-to-face is understood empirically by some readers of Levinas, and transcendentally by others. If the encounter with the other is understood as an experience, we must ask what happens after that experience, i.e. when the other is no longer facing me. Levinas emphasises the ease with which the intrusion of alterity into the order of the same can be integrated into the same, or forgotten. The disturbance of the same, he writes,

> is a movement that does not propose any stable order in conflict or in accord with a given order; it is a movement that already carries away the signification it brought [...] It enters in so subtle a way that unless we retain it, it has already withdrawn. [...] It remains only for him who would like to take it up. Otherwise, it has already restored the order it troubled—Someone rang, and there is no one at the door: did anyone ring? [...] A God was revealed on a mountain or in a burning bush, or was attested to in Scriptures. And what if it were a storm! And what if the Scriptures came to us from dreamers! Dismiss the illusory call from our minds![73]

If the face-to-face relation is an empirical experience, its significance can be subsequently dismissed or forgotten. If, however, when encountering the other I discover a responsibility in myself, or discover myself *as responsible*, the significance of the commandment is more difficult to dismiss.

In other words, we might say that one weakness of the account of the face-to-face in *Totality and Infinity* [74] is that it is modelled on revelation. Just as, after the event, one can raise doubts about the true nature of 'religious experiences', so one might come to question the revelation of the face, the commandment 'thou shalt not kill'. Although this would not detract from the value of the face-to-face as an account of the possibility of ethical awareness, or conscience, it is less helpful in accounting for actual ethical behaviour.

The description of subjectivity in *Otherwise than Being*, however, makes ethical behaviour more understandable, because it makes my responsibility, as it were, an internal rather than an external truth. The commandment is not revealed to me by the other; instead, when I encounter the other I discover myself as already committed to him. Indeed, I discover my responsibility for the others as the underlying source of my selfhood. The call to responsibility is, therefore, more difficult to evade since it is part of my self.

Moreover, the commandment that is issued in the 'trace of illeity' might be said to carry more authority than the commandment issued directly from the face. Illeity, the fact that the commandment comes from elsewhere, from the immemorial past, introduces a new dimension of meaning into human existence. To be sure, the face, which *qua* face is transcendent, was said to open up the dimension of height. Yet the meaning of this opening was not clear, and as noted above, this lack of clarity has led to readers identifying God with the Other in *Totality and Infinity*. In *Otherwise than Being*, however, as noted in the previous chapter, responsibility reveals the very unity and meaning of the universe—the universe is that which is my responsibility, and I am chosen for this inescapable responsibility by the Good. In the earlier work, too, my life is made meaningful by responsibility for the Other; but, because we are never alone in the world with the Other, this source of meaning is always in conflict with another source, another commanding face. Moreover, with the appearance of the third party, the Other becomes subject to comparison and calculation, and it is no longer possible to relate to him as absolutely other. My election by the Good Beyond Being, however, brings me into relation with an absolute transcendence that always remains transcendent, the source of an incontestable meaning.

By identifying illeity, rather than the face of the other, as the source of the commandment to responsibility, Levinas' may seem to be contradicting the arguments put forward in *Totality and Infinity*. In the earlier work, the face-to-face seemed to be, to use the language of transcendental philosophy, the condition of possibility of the relation with the divine.[75] In 'The Trace of the Other', however, Levinas seems to make illeity the condition of possibility of the face. He writes, for example, that 'a face, wholly open, can at the same time be in itself because it is in the trace of illeity. Illeity is the origin of the alterity of being in which the in itself of objectivity participates, while also betraying it'.[76] Yet this is not a straight-forward reversal of the position argued in *Totality and Infinity*. Levinas makes it clear that the ethical remains the only possible form of relation to the divine.

> To be in the image of God does not mean to be an icon of God, but to find oneself in his trace. [...] He [God] shows himself only by his trace, as is said in Exodus 33. To go toward Him is not to follow this trace which is not a sign; it is to go toward the others who stand in the trace of illeity.[77]

Levinas would seem, then, to be arguing both that the ethical is the condition of possibility for the relation with the divine, and that the divine is the condition of possibility of the ethical. The presence of such a paradoxical claim should not surprise us, given our discussion in the Chapter One of the inability of the language of either transcendental or empirical philosophy to express the ideas that Levinas struggles to convey. As we have seen, Bernasconi regards Levinas' use of the '*anterior posteriori*' structure and the notion of a double origin as one of the keys to understanding the method of *Totality and Infinity*. It may be helpful to keep in mind Bernasconi's thesis that 'Levinas follows the transcendental method to the point where it is halted and in order to sustain itself must draw on that which is radically exterior to it'.[78] In the case of 'The Trace of the Other' and *Otherwise than Being*, the transcendental method is halted by the discovery that the face and illeity are each the condition of possibility of the other. This abrupt halt prevents either the alterity of the other person or that of the He of illeity from being integrated into a system. The other person is neither identical with He who commands me, nor merely the recipient of my ethical gesture. At the same time, He who commands can neither be reduced to the subject of a theological discourse, nor be ignored.

By presenting this double transcendental argument, Levinas shows that the ethical cannot have a beginning in time understood as synchrony, that is, in being. If the ethical relation refers us to the alterity of illeity which in turn refers us to the ethical, we cannot identify a point at which the ethical can begin. Levinas therefore describes the ethical as an 'interruption'[79] in being, and revelation as an 'irruption'.[80] Since philosophy is, according to Levinas, the language of being, it should not surprise us that in describing the ethical which interrupts being, Levinas defies the law of non-contradiction which is essential to philosophy.[81]

However, what is of greater concern to many readers of Levinas than the paradoxical nature of his claims is his introduction of seemingly theological notions in his later work. Whereas readers of *Totality and Infinity* are tempted to identify the Other with God, the temptation in Levinas' later work is to identify the one who chooses me for responsibility as the God of Jewish, or biblical, religion. Levinas himself, however, insists that the notions of election, illeity, and the Good are to be understood without reference to the question of God's existence. Instead, he argues that the empirical experience of responsibility for the others can lead us to an understanding of the ethical significance of transcendence. As we have seen, Levinas describes this responsibility as infinite, increasing in the measure that it is assumed, and as coming from a time prior to my freedom (or to the distinction between freedom and non-freedom). The subject is a hostage to the other, substitutes itself for the other and thus empties itself of its identity as an ego. Just as the responsibility is infinite and can never be fulfilled, so the emptying of the self is without end. Levinas argues that in taking on responsibility for the other, and continually 'exhausting' itself, the self as hostage bears witness to the Infinite. He insists however that the subject as a hostage does not experience the Infinite, nor does it provide a proof of the Infinite. Rather, the hostage is 'a witness borne of the Infinite [...] a testimony that no disclosure has preceded'.[82]

Levinas terms the excessive, unfulfillable demand of the Infinite its 'glory' and argues that in 'saying' the self bears witness to it. As we have seen in Chapter Two, he distinguishes two aspects of language, the 'saying' and the 'said'. The 'said' is the thematisable content of what is signified, whereas the 'saying' is not a content. 'Saying makes signs to the other, but in this sign signifies the very giving of signs.'[83] The 'saying' signifies my openness to the other, my proximity to, and responsibility for, him. It is like silence, in that it is without words, but not with 'empty hands'. Instead, it speaks silently 'through the hyperbolic passivity of giving, which is prior to all willing and thematization'.[84] As such, 'saying' bears witness to the Infinite which orders the passive self to give to the other.

Since the order comes from an immemorial past, outside the realm of experience, the 'saying' does not depend on any 'religious experience'. Rather, it is 'pure testimony' which testifies to 'the Infinite which is not accessible to the unity of apperception, non-appearing and disproportionate to the present'.[85] This testimony is given not as an announcement of belief in God, but as the statement 'here I am', ready to serve the other.

> The infinite is not 'in front of me'; I express it, but precisely by giving a sign of the giving of signs, of the 'for-the-other' in which I am dis-interested; here I am (me voici)! The accusative (me voici!) here is remarkable: here I am under your eyes, at your service, your obedient servant. In the name of God. But this is without thematization; the sentence in which God gets mixed in with words is not 'I believe in God.' The religious discourse that precedes all religious discourse is not dialogue. It is the 'here I am' said to a neighbour to whom I am given over, by which I announce peace, that is, my responsibility for the other.[86]

In insisting that prophecy, bearing witness to the Infinite, is not about belief in God, but consists in my responsibility for the other, Levinas again indicates that the question of God's existence is not relevant to the question of ethics. Although we said above that the term 'God' is more central in Levinas' later work than in *Totality and Infinity*, even in the later works 'God' has no positive meaning independent of the ethical relation. In ordering the approach to the other, Levinas writes, God is

> [...] drawn out of objectivity, presence and being. He is neither an object nor an interlocutor. His absolute remoteness, his transcendence, turns into my responsibility [...] for the other. And this analysis implies that God is not simply the 'first other', the 'other par excellence', or the 'absolutely other', but other than the other (*autre qu'autrui*), other otherwise, other with an alterity prior to the alterity of the other,

prior to the ethical bond with another and different from every neighbour, transcendent to the point of absence [...][87]

The claim that the alterity of God is 'prior to the ethical bond with another' does not amount to a statement of the greater importance of God, but belongs to the description of the inescapable nature of my responsibility for the other. God or the Infinite is in me as an order, directing me to the other, which has not been heard in any present, but has always already entered my consciousness.

> The Infinite transcends itself in the finite, it *passes* the finite, in that it directs the neighbour to me without exposing itself to me. This order steals into me like a thief, despite the outstretched nets of consciousness, a trauma which surprises me absolutely, always already *passed* in a past which was never present and remains unrepresentable.[88]

It should be noted, however, that Levinas is not claiming that there is an awareness of the commandment which directs me towards my neighbour prior to the encounter with the neighbour. In *Otherwise than Being* he writes that whilst the Infinite 'orders me to the neighbor as a face', this order is not 'the cause of my response, nor even a question that would have preceded it in a dialogue.' Instead, 'I find the order in my response itself.'[89] This formulation seems to make God redundant: if the order is found in the response, why describe it as coming from God? The answer to this question lies in the excerpt from 'God and Philosophy' quoted above: I become aware of the order as something that has always already been in me, which was not freely accepted by consciousness, but somehow placed in me prior to my awareness of it. The order 'steals into me like a thief'. It has come from elsewhere, in an immemorial past. When I encounter the other and become aware of his needs, I realise that I am already committed to responsibility for him. Although some readers may find Levinas' use of 'God' an unfortunate choice of word, it should be realised that he is not attributing any precise meaning to this term apart from what appears in his descriptions of illeity, glory and the ethical relation. He insists that the witness borne to the Infinite cannot be reduced to 'the relationship that leads from an index to the indicated'.[90] Thus prophecy does not refer us to the 'God of Abraham, Isaac and Jacob', does not lead us to theological discourse about God or the Infinite, but is 'the *passing itself* of the Infinite'.[91] God, in other words, has no place, or meaning, outside of the ethical relation, and the insistence in *Totality and Infinity* that 'it is our relations with men that give to theological concepts the sole signification they admit of'[92] appears to be true of *Otherwise than Being* as well.

## Otherwise than Being

However, in addition to the characterisation of God as the enigmatic source of the commandment which directs me to the neighbour, God is also described as making possible the 'turning of the I into "like the others"'[93] which occurs in justice. In both *Totality and Infinity* and *Otherwise than Being*, the ethical relation with the unique other, the 'face-to-face' or the relationship of 'proximity', is said to be interrupted by the third party. The entry of the third party, another other, necessitates the comparison of the incomparable which leads to the institutions of justice.[94] Within the rationality of justice, I become a member of society, like everyone else, subject to the same logic of rights and obligations. However, whereas in other contexts this passage from the unique I, responsible for the other, to a member of society like the others seems to belong unproblematically to the logic of justice, here Levinas insists that 'it is only thanks to God that, as a subject incomparable with the other, I am approached as another by the others'.[95] This claim appears strange not only because it introduces God in a context where in other essays the logic of justice seems to suffice, but also because it seems to contradict the notion of the glory of the Infinite that we have just described. How can we reconcile the claim that the I bears witness to the Infinite through its inescapable responsibility for the other, with the claim that God makes possible the escape from this same responsibility?

It is worth noting that, when introducing the notion that God is somehow necessary for the 'reverting of the incomparable subject into a member of society', Levinas first writes not of the self's way of conceiving itself, but of the way it is treated by others: 'I am approached as an other by the others, that is, "for myself"'.[96] Although the paragraph in which this sentence appears has been described as 'liturgical' in tone,[97] the references to God do not evoke the language of Jewish prayer as much as the idiomatic expressions used by those who discern divine providence in the events of daily life. The phrases 'thanks to God' and 'with the help of God'[98] which Levinas uses, enclosed in quotation marks, in this context, evoke the *'baruch Hashem'* ('Blessed is God') and *'b'ezrat Hashem'* ('with God's help') which punctuate the speech of observant Jews. Moreover, an analogy can be drawn between the relationship of divine providence to natural laws, and that of 'divine intervention' with the relationship between ethics and justice. A Jew who thanks God for present successes and appeals for divine aid for future plans does not thereby deny the functioning of natural laws. Thanking God for one's recovery from an illness does not necessarily entail that one disregards the effects of medical treatment; instead, it may reflect one's belief that divine providence is somehow at work through the agency of nature. More importantly for our present purposes, it reflects the subjective feeling that the natural explanation of the phenomenon is in some way incomplete. Similarly, the person who is treated as an equal member of society by others knows that he is a person 'like the others', belonging to the genus human and to a certain society. He knows that as a member of that society he has certain rights, and logically there is no reason why he should not expect to be treated like the others. However, if we are to believe Levinas, the self's very selfhood consists in his feeling that he is not like the others, but responsible for them, even to the point of responsibility for their responsibility for him. Subjectively, therefore, if not logically, the experience of being treated 'like the others' is miraculous for subjectivity, just as a narrow escape from death or injury is miraculous for a religious person, who nevertheless knows that the escape can be explained purely by reference to natural laws.

However, in addition to describing the turning of the responsible self into a member of society like the others in terms of my experience of other people's treatment of me, Levinas also describes my own concern for myself as bound up with the Infinite. He asks, 'is not the Infinite which enigmatically commands me, commanding and not commanding, from the other, also the turning of the I into "like the others", for which it is important to concern oneself and take care?'[99] The suggestion that God somehow sanctions my concern for myself might appear to contradict the claim that the self bears witness to God through its unlimited and selfless responsibility for the other. How can God be both the call to such responsibility and the justification of escape from it? The tension between these two claims can be lessened somewhat by viewing the second statement as a sort of corollary of the first. To experience (authentically) one's concern for oneself as somehow approved by God is to acknowledge that this concern is not justified in itself, because one has an infinite responsibility, commanded by God, for the others. Hence, paradoxically, to experience my concern for myself as sanctioned by God is at the same time to experience myself as uniquely responsible for the others; the lapse from responsibility is bound up with that responsibility. Seen in this perspective, concern for myself can itself be understood as part of my concern for the others. If I do not stop serving the others in order to eat and sleep, and otherwise attend to my own needs, I will not be able to continue serving them. Levinas writes that 'my lot is important. But it is still out of my responsibility that my salvation has meaning.'[100]

On the other hand, Levinas acknowledges the risks involved in claiming that God sanctions my concern for myself. Such a claim puts responsibility in danger; concern for my own salvation may

[...] encompass and swallow up [my responsibility], just as the State issued from the proximity of the neighbor is always on the verge of integrating him into a we, which congeals both me and the neighbor. The act of consciousness would thus be [...] in reference to God, to a God always subject to repudiation and in permanent danger of turning into a protector of all the egoisms.[101]

Indeed, our own way of describing God as sanctioning concern for the self could contribute to the process whereby God becomes 'the protector of all the egoisms'. Whereas Levinas studiously avoids writing about God as if he were a being capable of acting in one way or another, our unfortunate use of language has contributed to the view of God as a being sitting on high, observing human actions and approving or disapproving of them. Whereas we have described God's sanctioning of concern for oneself, Levinas has equated 'the turning of the I into "like the others"' with 'the Infinite'.[102] In evoking the notion of divine providence through expressions such as 'with the help of God' or 'thanks to God', he has also distanced himself from this notion by placing the expressions in quotation marks. Rather than writing about God issuing commandments, Levinas, as we have seen, describes the 'passing' of the Infinite.

> The Infinite transcends itself in the finite, it *passes* the finite, in that it directs the neighbour to me without exposing itself to me. This order steals into me like a thief, [...] always already *passed* in a past which was never present and remains unrepresentable.[103]

Even more importantly, Levinas frequently insists that we can speak of God only in terms of the glory of responsibility or the grace through which the I becomes another. Prophecy bears witness to God without pointing to him as in a relationship that 'leads from an index to the indicated'.[104] Similarly, after announcing that '"Thanks to God" I am another for the others', Levinas insists that I can speak of God 'only by reference to this aid or this grace'.[105]

In addition to writing of 'God' only in this indirect manner, Levinas also assigns 'God' a role that is plainly redundant. God commands me to assume responsibility for the other, but this commandment is not the cause of my response; I am only aware of it after the fact. 'With the help of God' I become another for the others; but this passage from ethics to justice, from my unlimited responsibility for the others to status as a member of society like the others, has elsewhere been explained by Levinas without reference to God.

The redundancy of the role of God in *Otherwise than Being* has important consequences for our reading of the text. Firstly, it means that a reader who not only does not believe in the existence of God, but also refuses to allow any reference to 'God' as a meaningful term, can still accept Levinas' account of the ethical relation and justice.[106] The question which Levinas poses in the

Preface to *Totality and Infinity*, and which we have understood as one of the major preoccupations of his entire corpus, i.e. 'are we not duped by morality', can be answered in a Levinasian fashion without reference to God. Ethics, justice and morality are meaningful terms because I experience myself as responsible for the others. If, like Levinas, I recognise that this responsibility is somehow commanded by God, this recognition adds an extra dimension to my understanding and experience of the ethical. If not, my understanding of the ethical lacks this added dimension, but I nevertheless see morality as meaningful.

The redundancy of God is also necessary to protect the transcendence of the Infinite. If God could be directly deduced from the ethical experience, as the necessary source of the commandment directing me to the other, this would constitute a proof of God and make the 'otherwise than being' into a cause acting within being. As noted above, Gaviria Alvarez points out the importance of Levinas' indirect formulations of the relationship between ethics and a commandment coming from God. He emphasises that Levinas characterises the face as 'perhaps' carrying the trace of the Infinite; the 'perhaps' is significant because 'the appeal which is formulated does not let itself be converted into evidence in a philosophical discourse'.[107] In *Otherwise than Being*, Levinas similarly insists that

> The Infinite would be belied in the proof that the finite would like to give of its transcendence; entering into conjunction with the subject that would make it appear, it would lose its glory. Transcendence owes it to itself to interrupt its own demonstration.[108]

Levinas' insistence on the 'enigmatic' way in which the Infinite passes, together with the redundancy of the term God and the refusal to assign any meaning to the word beyond that which 'passes' in ethics and justice, supports his explicit denials that his work is in anyway theological. However, we must ask why Levinas uses the word 'God' if he does not wish to evoke any theological presuppositions.

One way of answering this question is to return to the critique of 'positive religions' which Levinas presents in *Totality and Infinity*. Two deplorable features of such religions which he highlights are the turning away from social relations in the belief that a relationship with God can be 'accomplished in the ignorance of men and things',[109] and the denial of human freedom through a view of history as 'a drama of salvation or damnation that would be enacted in spite of me'.[110] Levinas' insistence that the Infinite is beyond the reaches of theological discourse, and that God only 'comes to pass' in ethics and justice, can be understood as a continuation of his attack on positive religion and the perversions to which they can give rise.

In addition to this negative reason for using the word 'God' in order to emphasize what God is not, Levinas also indicates that he has positive reasons for this choice. 'The word God', he writes, 'is an overwhelming semantic event that subdues the subversion worked by illeity.'[111] Although in uttering the word 'God' we bring the Infinite into the said, Levinas argues that this word 'unsays' itself without, however, 'vanishing into nothingness'. It gets its meaning from the witness borne of the Infinite. This witness is thematised in theological discourse, but the thematisation itself is immediately perceived as 'forbidden'. Although the interdiction of thematisation of the Infinite evokes negative theology, Levinas emphasises that there is a positive aspect to this refusal of thematisation. He writes:

> Infinity is beyond the scope of the unity of transcendental apperception, cannot be assembled into a present, and refuses being collected. This negation of the present and of representation finds its positive form in proximity, responsibility and substitution. [...] The refusal of presence is converted into my presence as present, that is, as a hostage delivered over as a gift to the other. In proximity, in signification, in my giving of signs, already the Infinite speaks through the witness I bear of it [...] Its signification has let itself be betrayed in the logos only to convey itself before us. It is a word already stated as a kerygma in prayer or blasphemy. It thus retains in its statement the trace of the excession of transcendence, of the beyond.[112]

We have quoted at length from this paragraph in order to show that even when describing the extraordinarily evocative power of the word 'God', Levinas' analysis does not draw on theology or mysticism, but always returns to the meaning attested to in ethical relations. The word 'God' only 'retains the trace of the beyond' because the beyond is attested to in the ethical relationship of proximity.

CONCLUSION

Neither *Totality and Infinity* nor *Otherwise than Being* should be interpreted as theological texts. On the contrary, these texts are explicitly critical of the theology of 'positive religions', and frequently emphasise that the Infinite is refractory to the thematising discourse of theology. The apparently theological claims in *Totality and Infinity* can be understood phenomenologically as belonging to the description of the relationship between the self and a transcendent other.

Although the term 'God' plays a more central role in *Otherwise than Being* than in *Totality and Infinity*, 'God' and 'the Infinite' are not theological terms in the later work. The God in question is not an infinite being who exists independently of the relations between men, but the 'Infinite' which is 'in' the finite and 'comes to pass' in proximity. A God 'transcendent to the point of absence', the Infinite has meaning only as its turning into my responsibility for the other. Moreover, even a reader who is uncomfortable with any reference to God could accept Levinas' analysis of the relationship between the self and the others, whilst refusing the dimension of meaning which is added by recognising the commandment of God in one's response to the face of the neighbour. Because the commandment coming from God is redundant, as is His role in establishing justice, the reader can extract Levinas' descriptions of ethical relations from his descriptions of the glory of the Infinite to which they are said to bear witness. It has been our contention, however, that this surgical approach is not required for a reading of Levinas as providing a non-theological justification of the meaningfulness of morality.

Given Levinas' critical approach towards theology, his interest, *qua* philosopher, in Jewish teaching might appear surprising. However, we will see in the next two chapters that Levinas' understanding of Judaism itself is not theological.

1   Andrius Valevicius, for example, acknowledges that Levinas 'wants to purify the heavens of the divine images by showing that God's existence can neither be demonstrated by ontology nor described by anthropomorphisms.' However, Valevicius continues, 'he is also conscious of the fact that man needs to discover some kind of system which will give him an unalterable certainty with regards to the existence of God. [...] This certainty is contained in ethics'. (*From The Other to the Totally Other; The Religious Philosophy of Emmanuel Levinas*, Peter Lang, New York, 1988, p. 6.) As will be shown in this chapter, the characterisation of Levinas' project as a search for certainty about the 'existence' of God is entirely inaccurate.

2   'Ethique et religion chez Levinas', *Revue de théologie et de philosophie*, 1970, vol. 103, part 1, p. 37.

3   Ibid., p. 40.

4   '*Autrui*' is translated by Lingis as 'the Other', while '*l'autre*' is translated as 'the other'.

5   *Totality and Infinity*, p. 79.

6   Ibid., p. 77.

7   Ibid., pp. 78–79.

8   Ibid., p. 78, our emphasis.

9   Idem.

10   Idem.

11   Ibid., p. 49.

12   Ibid., p. 51.

13   Ibid., p. 84.

14   Ibid., pp. 83–84.

15   Ibid., p. 243.

16   Ibid., p. 242.

17   Ibid., p. 244.

18   Idem.

19   Idem.

20   Ibid., p. 246.

21   Ibid., pp. 246–47.

22   The differences between Levinas' method and Husserlian phenomenology, which were outlined in Chapter One, should of course be borne in mind throughout this discussion.

23   Olmedo Gaviria Alvarez, 'L'idée de création chez Levinas: une archéologie du sens', *Revue philosophique de Louvain*, Vol. 72, 1974, p. 512. Hereafter cited as 'L'idée de création'.

24 For the reasons discussed in Chapter One, the term 'quasi-phenomenological' is more accurate in describing Levinas' method of 'deduction'. However, for the sake of readability, we will retain the term 'phenomenological.'

25 *Totality and Infinity*, p. 28.

26 'L'idée de création', p. 512.

27 *Totality and Infinity*, p. 58.

28 Ibid., pp. 58–9.

29 'L'idée de création', p. 513.

30 Idem.

31 *Totality and Infinity*, p. 89.

32 'L'idée de création', p. 521.

33 'Freedom and Command', *Collected Philosophical Papers*, p. 22.

34 Idem.

35 Idem.

36 Idem.

37 'L'idée de création', p. 526.

38 *Totality and Infinity,* p. 78.

39 Idem.

40 Ibid., p. 77.

41 'L'idée de création', p. 535.

42 *Difficile liberté*, pp. 175–76.

43 The quotation is from *Totality and Infinity,* p. 269.

44 'L'idée de création', p. 532. Gaviria Alvarez is here not denying the importance of 'the third', 'all of humanity', but stressing that the role of God in *Totality and Infinity* is extremely limited.

45 'God and Philosophy', translated by Richard A. Cohen and Alphonso Lingis, in *The Levinas Reader*, p. 167.

46 'Violence and Metaphysics', p. 152.

47 'God and Philosophy', p. 167.

48 Ibid., p. 169.

49 Ibid., p. 172.

50 Ibid., p. 172–73.

51 Ibid., p. 173.

52 Idem.

53 Ibid., p. 174.

54 Idem.

55 Idem.

56 Ibid., p. 175.

57 Idem.

58 Ibid., p. 176.

59 Ibid., p. 177. Levinas' italics.

60 Ibid., p. 178.

61 Idem.

62 Idem.

63 We will examine the notion of illeity in more detail below.

64 Ibid., pp. 178–79.

65 'The Trace of the Other', p. 354.

66 Ibid., p. 358.

67 Idem.

68 Ibid., pp 358–59.

69 Levinas is referring to Exodus 33:17–23, in which Moses asks to sees God's glory, and God responds 'Behold, there is a place by me, and thou shalt stand upon a rock: and it shall come to pass, while my glory passes by, that I will put thee in a cleft of the rock, and will cover thee with my hand while I pass by: and I will take away my hand and thou shalt see my back: but my face shall not be seen.'

70  'The Trace of the Other', p. 359.

71  'Illeity' is a neologism formed from the Latin third person pronoun *ille*.

72  '[...] the signifyingness of a trace [...] establishes a relationship with illeity, a relationship which is personal and ethical', 'The Trace of the Other', p. 356.

73  'Phenomenon and Enigma', *Collected Philosophical Papers*, p. 66.

74  If this account is understood empirically.

75  See our discussion of 'The Metaphysical and the Human', above.

76  'The Trace of the Other', p. 359. Similarly, earlier in the essay Levinas writes, 'The supreme presence of a face is inseparable from this supreme and irreversible absence [of illeity] which founds the eminence of visitation' (p. 356). The use of the verb 'to found' suggests a transcendental argument.

77  'The Trace of the Other', p. 356.

78  'Rereading', p. 24.

79  *Otherwise than Being*, p. 43 ff.

80  See our discussion, in the next chapter, of Levinas' essay 'Revelation in the Jewish Tradition'.

81  One could certainly argue that, having abandoned the strictures of philosophical logic, Levinas is no longer writing philosophy. However, our concern in this chapter is not to decide to what discipline, if any, his work most properly belongs, but whether or not his writings make use of theological premises.

82  'God and Philosophy', p. 182.

83  Ibid., p. 183.

84  Idem.

85  Idem.

86  Ibid., p. 184.

87  Ibid., p. 179.

88  Ibid., p. 184.

89  *Otherwise than Being*, p. 150.

90  Ibid., p. 151.

91  Ibid., p. 150.

92  *Totality and Infinity*, p. 79.

93  *Otherwise than Being*, p. 161.

94  It should be noted, however, that Levinas insists that the entry of the third party is not an empirical event. See *Otherwise than Being*, p. 158.

95  Ibid., p. 158.

96  Idem.

97  Peter Carey Atterton, 'Ethics and Justice; The Problem of Kantian Rationality in the Philosophy of Emmanuel Levinas', PhD thesis, submitted to the Dept. of Philosophy, University of Essex, May 1990. Appendix, p. 286.

98  *Otherwise than Being*, p. 158 and p. 161.

99  Ibid., p. 161.

100  Idem.

101  Idem.

102  Idem.

103  'God and Philosophy', p. 184.

104  *Otherwise than Being*, p. 151.

105  Ibid., p. 158.

106  For an excellent example of an atheistic reading of Levinas' ethics which sensibly deals with the question of God in Levinas by ignoring it (except in an Appendix in which he defends this leaving aside of the question of God), see Peter Atterton's PhD thesis, cited above.

107  'L'idée de création', p. 535.

108  *Otherwise than Being*, p. 152.

109  *Totality and Infinity*, p. 78.

110  Ibid., p. 79.

111  *Otherwise than Being*, p. 151.

112  Idem.

# Chapter 4

## POST-HOLOCAUST JUDAISM

### INTRODUCTION

Our enquiry into Levinas' ethical philosophy began with the question as to whether we are not 'duped by morality'. An analogous question could be asked about Judaism: has it not been definitively falsified by the *Shoah*? Should we not conclude, with Richard Rubenstein, that 'God is dead' and that 'we stand in a cold, silent, unfeeling cosmos, unaided by any purposeful power beyond our own resources'?[1] Or, as Levinas phrases the question, 'Did not the word of Nietzsche on the death of God take on, in the extermination camps, the signification of a quasi-empirical fact?'[2]

The most famous Jewish response to the challenges raised by the *Shoah* is Emil Fackenheim's '614th commandment': 'Jews are forbidden to hand Hitler posthumous victories.'[3] Since Fackenheim is the post-Holocaust philosopher par excellence, the thinker who has assessed the implications of the *Shoah* for both Judaism and philosophy in the most relentless and rigorous manner, our discussion of Levinas' contribution to post-Holocaust Jewish thought, his conception of Judaism as a 'Hebraic Humanism', will begin with a comparison of Levinas' approach with that of Fackenheim.

### ETHICS AND THE '614TH COMMANDMENT'

#### Intertextuality in Fackenheim and Levinas

A thorough comparison of these two thinkers is of course beyond the scope of the present study. Instead, we will focus on key aspects of their respective understandings of Judaism, especially *vis-à-vis* the *Shoah*. We will begin by looking at two moments of intertextuality within their writings on this subject: firstly, a text which both cite as an exemplary Jewish response to the Holocaust, and secondly, Levinas' reading of Fackenheim in his essay 'Useless Suffering'.

The first text is commented on at length by Levinas in his essay '*Aimer la Torah plus que Dieu*'[4] and quoted at length, but with only the briefest of comments, by Fackenheim. We will therefore begin with an account of Levinas' essay.

The essay takes the form of a commentary on an anonymous[5] monologue entitled 'Yossel Ben Yossel of Rakover Speaks to God'. The monologue is set in the last hours of the Warsaw Ghetto Uprising. Levinas' approbation of the text is evident throughout the commentary; he refers to it as a 'wonderful and true text, true as only fiction can be' and asserts that it 'conveys a Jewish science [...] and translates an experience of profound and authentic spiritual life'.[6]

The narrator of the text, Yossel ben Yossel of Rakover, is the last surviving member of his family. Overwhelmed by what he has experienced, he has come to the recognition that if any God exists, it is one who has withdrawn from the world and hidden His face. In so doing, Yossel says, 'He has sacrificed men to their ferocious instincts [...] and since it is these instincts which dominate the world, it is natural that those who preserve the divine and the pure are the first victims of this domination.'[7] Rather than inferring God's non-existence from His absence, the narrator chooses to believe that God, for reasons unknown to him, has chosen to hide His face. As the monologue develops, it becomes apparent that this belief is not based on blind faith. Paradoxically, Yossel's experience of the absence of God is lived as revelation. The inhumanity he has witnessed makes him more appreciative of the ethical principles of the Torah, thus intensifying his pride in being Jewish and his commitment to Judaism. Through this strong identification with the Torah, he experiences an intimacy with the otherwise distant God. 'Now I know that you really are my God,' he says, 'because you could not be the God of those whose acts are [...] the most horrible expression of an absence of God.'[8] This intimacy with the Divine in no way diminishes the centrality of the Torah. Echoing an expression of the Talmud,[9] Yossel exclaims 'I love Him, but I love his Torah even more [...] and even if I were disappointed by Him and downtrodden, I would nonetheless observe the precepts of the Torah.'[10]

Some of Levinas' comments on this text appear to be moving towards a type of theodicy. Having stated that 'true monotheism must devote itself to answering the legitimate exigencies of atheism', he suggests that some atheists unfairly arrive at their position by beginning with a conception of God as a being who 'distributed rewards, imposed penalties or pardoned faults and, in His goodness, treated men as eternal children'.[11] Against this approach he asserts that 'an adult's God manifests Himself precisely through the emptiness of a childish heaven' and argues that 'suffering reveals a God who, in renouncing all helpful manifestations, appeals to the maturity of an entirely responsible man.'[12] However, Levinas does not develop these ideas along the lines of a theodicy which would justify God's tolerance of evil by claiming that the possibility of man maturing to an 'adult faith' is somehow more important than the suffering generated along the way.[13] Instead, Levinas presents the relationship between man and God as that of creditor and debtor, suggesting that man need not resignedly accept everything that happens as

God's will and therefore 'for the good'. 'The creditor', he writes, '[...] possesses faith above all, but he is also the one who does not resign himself to the evasions of the debtor.'[14] Yossel accepts the challenge God has presented by absenting Himself from a consequently evil world: he will continue to believe in God, even to love Him and, above all, to observe the precepts of the Torah. But he knows full well that he is the creditor and God the debtor, and that he is justified in reproaching God for His excessive demands, in crying out 'do not strain the ark too much'.[15]

Yossel succeeds in maintaining faith in God in spite of his experience of radical evil. Levinas stresses that there is nothing mystical or blind about this faith. The divine-human relationship, he asserts, is one mediated by a teaching, by the Torah. Since God does not reveal Himself through any terrestrial authority, faith in Him can only rest 'on the inner evidence and the value of a teaching'. He is made real 'not through incarnation, but through the Law'. The Jew's faith is 'born of the Torah'.[16]

It is this emphasis on the 'inner evidence of the Torah' that constitutes the most striking difference between Levinas' approach and that of some other post-Holocaust thinkers. For the latter, the issue appears to be clear: either a way of reconciling belief in God with the reality of radical evil must be found, or intellectual integrity would dictate that traditional Judaism must be abandoned.

The logic of this argument appears incontestable if one concedes that a life dedicated to fulfilment of the commandments is senseless without grounds for belief in the existence of the Giver of those commandments. For Levinas, however, it is commitment to the principles of the Torah which has priority over faith in God. Yossel's pride in being part of the Jewish people, 'the people for whom the Torah represents the most elevated and beautiful of laws and moral principles'[17] is, in the first instance, completely independent of any consideration of his relationship to God. Nor does appreciation of the ethical teachings of Judaism fade into the background once a sense of relationship with the Divine has been established; rather, the Torah remains the focus of the Jew's life, as expressed in Yossel's exclamation, 'I love Him, but I love His Torah even more'.[18]

Although 'To Love the Torah More than God' is one of Levinas' early essays on Judaism, the story of Yossel ben Yossel of Rakover contains many of the ideas that he develops in his later writings. The title itself still summarises his approach to Judaism: rather than viewing the Jewish religion as a set of propositions about God, Levinas sees it primarily as a relationship to a text, the Torah. Moreover, like Yossel ben Yossel, he understands the Torah as essentially an ethical teaching, and insists that no relationship with God is possible without the mediation of this teaching and the ethical relation to the other.

Fackenheim, on the other hand, quotes the monologue not in support of an ethical interpretation of Judaism, but to illustrate the thesis, which he had only recently adopted, that Jewish theology cannot be immune to history.[19] For Fackenheim, the price of such immunity is 'an essential indifference to all history between Sinai and the messianic days'.[20] He insists that Jewish theology cannot pay that price, 'for *its* God of history (whose work is as yet incomplete) must be capable of continued presence in history, not merely at its messianic end'.[21]

Fackenheim's reference to God's presence in history evokes, of course, the title of his first book on post-Holocaust theology.[22] Although this insistence on the centrality of God's presence is somewhat at odds with Levinas' own emphasis on a God who has always already passed, who can be approached only by going 'toward the others who stand in the trace of illeity',[23] Levinas was clearly impressed by *God's Presence in History*, particularly the notion of a '614th commandment'.[24] Shortly after the publication of a French translation of this work,[25] Levinas wrote 'Useless Suffering', an essay in which Fackenheim's ideas play a key role. Levinas cites Fackenheim's argument that the Holocaust was a unique evil, in that the Nazi murder was 'annihilation for the sake of annihilation, murder for the sake of murder, evil for the sake of evil'.[26] He then goes on to cite the claim that Jews are obliged to survive and to remain Jewish.

> According to [Fackenheim], Auschwitz would paradoxically entail a revelation of the very God who nevertheless was silent at Auschwitz: a commandment of faithfulness. To renounce after Auschwitz this God absent from Auschwitz—no longer to assure the continuation of Israel—would amount to finishing the criminal enterprise of National-Socialism, which aimed at the annihilation of Israel and the forgetting of the ethical message of the Bible, which Judaism bears, and whose multimillenial history is concretely prolonged by Israel's existence as a people. For if God was absent in the extermination camps, the devil was very obviously present in them. From whence, for Emil Fackenheim, comes the obligation for Jews to live and remain Jews, in order not to be made the accomplices of a diabolical project.[27]

It should be noted that Levinas' summary of Fackenheim's position is not entirely accurate. As Fackenheim points out,[28] he avoided identifying the source of the commandment when discussing the commanding voice of Auschwitz in *God's Presence in History*.[29] Nevertheless, this does not seriously detract from Levinas' analysis. 'Useless Suffering' is not an essay in Jewish theology, but a philosophical discussion of what for Levinas must characterise the intellectual climate of the late 20th century—an abandonment of 'theodicy' in all its forms. By theodicy Levinas does not simply mean religious doctrines that justify God's role in creating evil and allowing it to flourish, but also any ideology that sees suffering as necessary for, or insignificant in comparison to, some over-riding greater 'Good'. He argues that theodicy in this broader sense has been a component of western thought up until this century,[30] and suggests that the most revolutionary aspect of contemporary consciousness is the destruction of this sense that suffering is somehow meaningful or necessary for the greater good.

The abandonment of theodicy is not the result of abstract philosophical thought but, according to Levinas, a response to the concrete historical conditions of our time. He cites the familiar inventory of human slaughter and genocide, from the first world war to Auschwitz and Cambodia.[31] The suffering of the innocent on such a scale, has, he argues, lead to a revolution in contemporary consciousness, due to 'the destruction of all balance between the explicit and implicit theodicy of Western thought and the forms which suffering and its evil take in the very unfolding of this century'.[32]

Fackenheim too insists that western thought must be fundamentally altered by exposure to historical events, particularly the *Shoah*. If we substitute the term 'Platonism' for 'theodicy', which Levinas uses in a highly idiosyncratic way, the similarities between the two positions become clear. Fackenheim insists that after the Holocaust, philosophers can no longer be 'platonists', serenely contemplating timeless metaphysical truths.[33]

Although Levinas includes the Holocaust in a long list of inhuman events, he sees it as the most powerful example of contemporary historical events that radically challenge theodicy. Levinas describes the *Shoah* as 'the paradigm of gratuitous human suffering'.[34] Like Fackenheim, he rejects any explanation of the Holocaust as punishment for sin. For Levinas, the morally necessary end to theodicy also reveals the immorality of any attempt to justify the suffering of others.

> But does not this end of theodicy, which obtrudes itself in the face of this century's inordinate distress, at the same time in a more general way reveal the unjustifiable character of suffering in the other person, the scandal which would occur by my justifying my neighbour's suffering? [....] For an ethical sensibility—confirming itself, in the inhumanity of our time, against this inhumanity—the justification of the neighbour's pain is certainly the source of all immorality.[35]

Levinas argues that Fackenheim's analysis of the Jewish situation after Auschwitz, his insistence that Jewish survival is now a divine imperative,[36] is of universal significance. He finds in Fackenheim's '614th commandment' not just a Jewish response to the Jewish crisis of faith, but a way for humanity to respond to the inhuman events of the twentieth century. Fackenheim has described the Jewish people as facing a choice between remaining faithful to their Jewishness or allowing evil to flourish; Levinas sees all of contemporary humanity as facing a similar choice between accepting the self's responsibility for the suffering of the other, or abandoning the world 'to the political fatality—or the drifting—of the blind forces which inflict misfortune on the weak and conquered'.[37]

> Is humanity, in its indifference, going to abandon the world to useless suffering, [... or ...] must not humanity now, in a faith more difficult than ever, in a faith without theodicy, continue Sacred History; a history which now demands even more of the resources of the self in each one, and appeals to its suffering inspired by the suffering of the other person, to its compassion which is a non-useless suffering (or love) [...]. *At the end of the twentieth century and after the useless and unjustifiable pain which is exposed and displayed therein without any shadow of a consoling theodicy, are we not all pledged—like the Jewish people to their faithfulness—to the second term of this alternative?*[38]

Levinas' references to 'Sacred History' will be explained below. For the moment, however, let us focus on his interpretation of Fackenheim. In the same year that Levinas published 'Useless Suffering', *To Mend the World* appeared. Although Fackenheim's '*magnum opus* in Jewish philosophy'[39] constitutes a much more rigorous and systematic exploration of the significance of the *Shoah* and the relationship between Judaism and western thought than anything he had previously published, the insights that lead him to formulate the '614th commandment' continue to dominate his thought. He still insists that the *Shoah* was a *novum* in human history, and that, as such, it provides a radical challenge to all western thought, whether Christian, Jewish or philosophical. Western thought must either face up to the Holocaust, or lapse into inauthenticity. Moreover, Fackenheim argues that the responses demanded of the philosopher, the Christian and the Jew are different. The Jew's response, in particular, must be a concrete commitment to the continuing existence of the Jewish people.[40]

Although Fackenheim has been arguing this case for a quarter of a century, much of what he has written has been misunderstood, even, in his opinion, by close friends and colleagues.[41] Often the stumbling block to comprehension is Fackenheim's emphasis on the particular and concrete. Gregory Baum, for example, displays unease at the lack of universality in Fackenheim's response to the Holocaust.[42] He criticises Fackenheim for claiming that the 'Commanding Voice of Auschwitz' calls upon Jews to survive but does not call upon them 'to help make visible the history of suffering of other humiliated peoples and extend solidarity to them'. He then distorts Fackenheim's arguments by claiming that the commandment calls for a 'theological suspension of the ethical'.[43] 'Whatever their ethical feelings and ideas,' Baum writes, 'Jews must obey the 614th commandment by giving all their strength to the struggle for their own survival.'[44]

Fackenheim, of course, has never sanctioned a 'suspension' of ethical considerations in order to guarantee the survival of Jews.[45] Nor has he argued that Jews must give 'all their strength' to their own struggle—only that this struggle must be their first priority.[46] But let us concentrate on the aspect of the '614th commandment' that Baum does not misunderstand: it is radically particular. Jews are commanded to survive *as Jews*. In *God's Presence in History*, Fackenheim gave the following answer to the question 'what does the Voice of Auschwitz command?'

> Jews are forbidden to hand Hitler posthumous victories. They are commanded to survive as Jews, lest the Jewish people perish. They are commanded to remember the victims of Auschwitz, lest their memory perish. They are forbidden to despair of man and his world, and to escape into either cynicism or otherworldliness, lest they cooperate in delivering the world over to the forces of Auschwitz. Finally, they are forbidden to despair of the God of Israel, lest Judaism perish. A secularist Jew cannot make himself believe by a mere act of will, nor can he be commanded to do so … And a religious Jew who has stayed with his God may be forced into new, possibly revolutionary relationships with Him. One possibility, however, is wholly unthinkable. A Jew may not respond to Hitler's attempt to destroy Judaism by himself cooperating in its destruction. In ancient times, the unthinkable Jewish sin was idolatry. Today, it is to respond to Hitler by doing his work.[47]

Although, according to both Fackenheim and Levinas, the '614th commandment' has implications of universal significance, the obligation upon Jews is not expressed in terms of universality. Baum, as we have seen, would have been happier if the commandment had ordered not only a commitment to Jewish survival, but a commitment to work for other suffering and persecuted peoples; if, in other words, Jews could be seen, and see themselves, as members of the genus 'suffering people'. The Jewish theology that he would prefer, 'holds that the words "never again," which the Jewish people are commanded to utter after the Holocaust, commits them to struggle against any new humiliation inflicted on them—and on any other humiliated people'.[48]

This sounds like a laudable theological position. However, Baum's preference for a more universal version of the '614th commandment' reveals the shortcomings of his reading of Fackenheim. Firstly, he has failed to grasp that the commandment is not a statement of general moral principles ('it is good to work on behalf of suffering peoples') but an articulation of the concrete response on the part of a particular people to an attempt to destroy them. Fackenheim sees his writings on the commandment as descriptive rather than prescriptive. He claims to have been instructed by the actions of what he likes to refer to as 'amcha', that is 'ordinary Jewish folk'. In *God's Presence in History*, Fackenheim writes that he has been able to speak of the '614th commandment' only 'because it no more than articulates what is being heard by Jews the world over—rich and poor, learned and ignorant, believing and secularist'.[49]

Secondly, for Fackenheim there is a crucial distinction to be made between the commitment of Jews to help other suffering people and the commitment of Jews to Jewishness. The first is moral, but after the Holocaust, the second is nothing short of miraculous. In a speech delivered in 1970, shortly after a pilgrimage to Bergen-Belsen, Fackenheim made a comparison between the patriarch Abraham and European Jewry of the nineteenth century. Like Abraham, those Jews 'brought a child sacrifice, by obeying the mere minimum commandment of the Jewish faith of raising Jewish children; only unlike Abraham, they did not know what they were doing'.[50] To continue to affirm one's Jewishness after the Holocaust, he stated, was an incomparable act of faith and faithfulness.

> Where are witnesses comparable to the Jew who is committed to his Jewishness, who in this very act says No! to the demons of Auschwitz, and who stakes on this No! his own life, the lives of his children, and the lives of his children's children?[51]

Like Baum, Levinas recognises that there is a need for a universal '614th commandment'; but he understands this commandment as being addressed to humanity as a whole. On a purely pragmatic level, Levinas' universalisation of the commandment is clearly more sensible. Baum's preferred theology is laudable but unrealistic. How can we expect the Jewish people—small in number, dispersed and so recently delivered from the threat of total annihilation[52]—to devote themselves to the struggle on behalf of *all* oppressed peoples? Levinas at least realises that if the scope of the '614th commandment' is to be universalised, it must similarly be addressed to a universal audience. The 'we' who must say 'never again, for any people' is all of humanity.

However, both Fackenheim and Levinas are well aware of the dangers inherent in such broad and general commitments. Fackenheim has emphasised the risk of denying the particularity of Jewish experience by focusing too much on universal ideas. In *God's Presence in History*, he states that the '614th commandment' includes the negative imperative neither to despair of the world nor to flee into other-wordliness. He explains that

> the commanding voice of Auschwitz bids Jews, religious and secularist, not to abandon the world to the forces of Auschwitz, but rather to continue to work and hope

for it. Two possibilities are equally ruled out: to despair of the world on account of Auschwitz, abandoning the age-old Jewish identification with poor and persecuted humanity; and to abuse such identification as a means of flight from Jewish destiny. It is precisely *because* of the uniqueness of Auschwitz, and *in* his Jewish particularity, that a Jew must be at one with humanity.[53]

For Fackenheim, Jewishness certainly entails identification with 'poor and persecuted humanity' but is not reducible to such identification.

Levinas is similarly wary of attempts to express the meaning of Jewishness in high-sounding universal moral principles. For Levinas, however, the fear is not so much that these principles will be employed as an excuse for fleeing the Jewish condition, but that the ideas themselves require the protection of the structures of Jewish life and teaching. He stresses that Judaism teaches ethics not through abstract ideas but through the particular, concrete structure of the *Halakha* and the rabbinic writings on Jewish law.[54] The embeddedness of moral ideas in concrete actions and texts that require careful interpretation lends them some protection from the contamination to which 'generous and general ideas' are subject when they are transmitted solely as ideas.[55]

Although Levinas does not develop this argument in great detail, it is useful for understanding his own approach to Judaism. In his talmudic commentaries and essays on Judaism, Levinas writes philosophically about the Jewish religion. If, like the potential convert who asked Hillel to explain Judaism to him while he stood on one foot, we sought a succinct formulation of Levinas' understanding of Judaism, it would be something like 'Judaism teaches the self's inescapable responsibility for the others.' But, just as Hillel's answer had two components ('That which is hateful to you do not unto your fellow. The rest is commentary—go and learn.')[56] so Levinas' work both extracts an ethical principle from Jewish texts and practices and refuses to reduce Judaism to this principle.

The ethical lesson is universal. But the particular way in which that lesson is lived concretely as Judaism is not just a matter of cultural or ethnic specificity. Instead, for Levinas, the particular Jewish obligation to study and observe the law is of service to the universal meaning. As discussed above Levinas argues that by enshrining its 'great truths' in the law, Judaism protects them from corruption. One of the ways in which it does this is through the system of *mitzvot*. For Levinas, even the ritual laws have an ethical significance. The discipline of observing the law in all matters of daily life is the 'severe discipline' which provides the training in the self-sacrifice and control needed to sacrifice one's needs or desires for the sake of another, that is, to act ethically.[57]

Levinas, therefore, unlike Baum, is not in the least troubled by the concrete and particular commitments to Jewish existence expressed in the '614th commandment'. Rather, his own reflections on the relation between the universal and the particular in Judaism accord fully with Fackenheim's insistence that it is 'precisely *because* of the uniqueness of Auschwitz, and *in* his Jewish particularity, that a Jew must be at one with humanity'.

Levinas, whose primary philosophical interest is 'the ethical', writes favourably of the '614th commandment', whereas Baum criticises it on ethical grounds. Although one might be inclined to dismiss this difference as due to the Jewish thinker's natural sympathy for the cause of Jewish survival, it might be better explained as arising from their differing conceptions of the ethical and its relation to the universal. For Baum, as indeed for most western thinkers, the realm of the ethical appears to be that of generalisable moral principles, which are valid for all people at all times. (Hence his misreading of the '614th commandment' as something like a moral principle and his insistence that it can be improved by making it command concern for all persecuted people.) For Levinas, as we have seen, the 'ethical' is the realm of the radically particular.[58]

Levinas' understanding of the relationship between the universal and particular aspects of Judaism will be discussed in more detail below. For the moment, however, it will be helpful to extend our analysis of the relationship between Levinas' ethics and the '614th commandment'. Levinas reads Fackenheim's description of the post-Holocaust Jew's obligation to survive as a Jew as a paradigm of the ethical self's obligation to persist in its commitment to the Good despite the apparent failure of morality. Levinasian ethics, with its emphasis on radical particularity and the asymmetry of ethical obligation, facilitates a sympathetic reading of Fackenheim, free from the suspicion that the lack of universality makes a Jewish commitment to Jewish survival less than moral, if not immoral.

Levinas' account of the ethical can illuminate both Fackenheim's understanding of the commandment and Baum's critique of it. Firstly, we can look at the obligation of Jewish survival as a simple commitment on the part of one Jew to help other Jews. Baum seems to imply that for a Jew to limit his endeavours to helping only fellow Jews is somehow less, or other, than ethical.[59] Paradoxically, Levinasian ethics both supports and contradicts this view. On the one hand, in focusing only on my responsibilities towards fellow Jews, I neglect my responsibilities towards the rest of humanity. Hence, the more responsibly I behave towards fellow Jews, the guiltier I am *vis-à-vis* non-Jews.[60] On the other hand, helping my fellow Jew is clearly ethical, insofar as he is no less 'other' than any other person.[61]

Whom should I help? To which face should I respond first? Levinas' articulation of the ethical relation does not issue any guidelines for resolving these difficulties, nor does his discussion of 'justice' provide the answers. Rather, his ethical philosophy shows that, however hard I try, I can never adequately fulfil my responsibility towards the others.

Is the Jewish commitment to Jewish survival, as expressed in the '614th commandment', therefore morally neutral from the perspective of Levinas' philosophy? Considered as the action of one individual helping another, there seems to be nothing to recommend such commitment in the place of commitment to other good causes. However, for both Levinas and Fackenheim, such a commitment has to be viewed from a very different perspective, that of history.

For both thinkers, Jewish particularity (or, in Levinas' word, 'singularity') consists in the fact of being 'singled out'. Levinas explains the theme of 'election' in Judaism as that of being singled out not for extra privileges, but for extra responsibility.[62] The notion that Jewish existence is characterised by being 'singled out' is also one of the main themes of Fackenheim's *God's Presence in History*. Fackenheim argues that throughout Jewish history Jews have been singled out either by God, as recipients of revelation, or by man, as victims of anti-semitic persecution.

To argue, as Fackenheim does, that anti-semitism, particularly Nazi anti-semitism, should not be subsumed under general categories such as persecution, fascism, or suffering of the innocent, is not to argue that the suffering of Jews is somehow more important than the suffering of others.[63] It is instead to insist on seeing anti-semitism in its historical context and seeking meaning in—or at least, learning from—this history.

Although Fackenheim insists that the Holocaust was a unique event, without precedent either within or outside of Jewish history, he is equally adamant that the historical background of anti-semitism must be taken into account when formulating a response to the *Shoah*. It is interesting in this respect to consider Fackenheim's reply to Michael Wyschogrod's critique of the 614th commandment. Wyschogrod claims that the logic of Fackenheim's argument can be clarified, and criticised, through a fictional analogy. Let us suppose, he suggests, that a wicked tyrant sets out to exterminate all the stamp collectors in the world, and indeed manages to murder a large proportion of the world's philatelists before being made harmless. Although it would clearly be the duty of every decent person to do everything in his power to frustrate this diabolical scheme, once the tyrant had been stopped, there would, according to Wyschogrod, be no further obligations.

Does it now follow that subsequent to the tyrant's demise it becomes the duty of the remaining stamp collectors not to lose interest in their stamp collecting so as not to hand the tyrant a posthumous victory? Isn't there all the difference in the world between exterminating persons who wish to be stamp collectors just because they wish to be stamp collectors and the right of individuals or groups to lose interest in something they no longer wish to remain interested in?[64]

Fackenheim's reply to this critique, in his recent 'testament of thought', is terse. 'The learned professor', he writes, 'forgot what *amcha*—ordinary Jewish folk—would never forget: there has been no bimillenial history of dictators murdering stamp collectors.'[65] Levinas is similarly insistent on seeing the Holocaust not as an isolated event, but as part of the drama of 'Sacred History'. He asks:

> Is it necessary to be surprised, then, that this drama of Sacred History [i.e. the Holocaust] has had among its principal actors a people which, since forever, has been associated with this history, whose collective soul and destiny would be wrongly understood as limited to any sort of nationalism, and whose *gesture*, in certain circumstances, still belongs to Revelation—be it as apocalypse—which 'provokes thought' from philosophers or which impedes them from thinking?[66]

For Levinas, the Holocaust, and the Jewish role in history, call for philosophical thought not just *qua* particular examples of phenomena such as persecution, but as subjects for reflection in their own right. Although Levinas does not explain the phrase in this essay, his association of 'Sacred History' with 'Revelation' provides us with an indication of his meaning. As we shall see below, Revelation, for Levinas, is not a theological concept, but consists in 'ethical saying'. Similarly, the Jewish experience of persecution does not have to be seen as somehow part of a divine historical plan, but can be understood as the negative mode of revelation, in which the ethical is revealed through the suffering of the other. The Jewish people would then be doubly bound to the process of Revelation or 'Sacred History' as both bearers of the Torah, the positive mode of revelation, and as victims of persecution, which is the negative mode.

### Biblical Hermeneutics

Despite the affinity between Levinasian ethics and Fackenheim's '614th commandment', the two thinkers differ profoundly in their approach to biblical hermeneutics. For Fackenheim, Judaism is characterised by the insistence that God is, at least potentially, present in history. Jewish faith is a commitment to revelation, and revelation, for Fackenheim, is not 'propositions or laws backed by divine sanction, but rather, at least primordially, the *event* of divine presence'.[67] This understanding of revelation is largely dependent on Buber, as is Fackenheim's insistence on reading the 'naked' text of the Bible rather than approaching Scripture in the traditional Jewish manner, via the commentaries.[68] Fackenheim argues that Scripture must be read without reference to rabbinic tradition because, after the Holocaust, our hermeneutical situation is radically altered. An abyss separates our 'here and now' from the 'then and there' both of the Bible and of its rabbinic interpreters.[69]

Levinas agrees that there is a lack of continuity between the world of the Bible and our own. However, he points to a certain 'modernity', rather than the *Shoah*, as the source of this discontinuity. In the Introduction to *Quatre lectures talmudiques*, his first collection of talmudic commentaries, he writes:

> It is legitimate to distinguish two regions within the past. One belongs resolutely to history and does not become intelligible without the scholarly and critical intervention of the historian. It inevitably contains a mythological dimension. The other belongs to a more recent period and is defined by the fact of being linked in an immediate way to the present and to the present's understanding.[70]

Biblical narratives would belong to the first region; we can have immediate access to them only through faith. But, according to Levinas, however paradoxical it may seem, because of the uninterrupted tradition of talmudic study, the Talmud (and, by implication, rabbinic interpretation of the Bible) belongs to 'the modern history of Judaism'.[71]

Fackenheim would probably want to counter this claim with his own insistence that the rabbinic world-view has been ruptured by the Holocaust, by the fact that this time salvation 'came too late'.[72] For Levinas, however, the rabbinic world-view has less to do with promises of physical salvation than with ethics. The Talmud, and indeed all of the oral Torah, extract from the written Torah 'ethical meaning as the ultimate intelligibility of the human and even of the cosmic'.[73]

JUDAISM AS ETHICAL TEACHING: LEVINAS' HEBRAIC HUMANISM

### *'Revelation in the Jewish Tradition'*

Levinas expands upon his understanding of biblical hermeneutics in his essay 'Revelation in the Jewish Tradition',[74] in which he asks how Revelation, 'the abrupt invasion of truths from outside',[75] is possible. Whilst respectfully acknowledging the existence of many Orthodox Jews for whom revelation does not constitute a philosophical problem, but consists in a 'communication between Heaven and Earth', corresponding to the obvious meaning of the Biblical narrative, Levinas insists that most Jews today do not live outside History, but are concerned with the 'intellectual destiny of the West'.[76]

These modern Jews find that belief in Revelation is challenged by the same intellectual developments which have transformed the word 'humanism' from a term of approbation to one of abuse;[77] a 'modern person' is troubled by

> [...] the news of the end of metaphysics, by the triumphs of psychoanalysis, sociology and political economy; [a modern person is] someone who has learnt from linguistics that meaning is produced by signs without signifieds and who, confronted with all these intellectual splendours—or shadows—sometimes wonders if he is not witnessing the magnificent funeral celebrations held in honour of a dead god.[78]

For such a person, Levinas argues, the 'ontological status' of Revelation is a major concern, even more pressing than the need to examine the contents of the Revelation.

Before dealing directly with the question of the ontological status of the biblical Revelation, however, Levinas describes the structure of its content. He points out that the traditional Jewish way of reading the Bible differs significantly from the Christian approach. 'Prescriptive lessons', he explains, 'occupy a privileged position within Jewish consciousness, as far as the relationship with God is concerned.'[79] This pre-occupation with commandments leads Jewish exegetes to uncover allusions to commandments in every scriptural text, regardless of its 'genre'.

> Every text is asked to produce such [prescriptive] lessons; the psalms may allude to characters and events, but they also refer to prescriptions: Psalm 119:19 says, notably, 'I am a sojourner on earth: hide not thy commandments from me!' The texts of the Wisdom literature are prophetic and prescriptive. Cutting across the 'genres' in all directions, then, are allusions and references which are visible to the naked eye.[80]

In addition to its prescriptive bias, the Jewish reading of the Bible also differs from the Christian in its insistence on using the Hebrew text rather than a translation. This insistence is due neither to pedantry nor to simple piety, but to an awareness of the ambiguity and polysemy of the Hebrew text. Levinas explains that in the Hebrew syntax 'the words co-exist, rather than falling immediately into structures of co-ordination and sub-ordination, unlike the dominant tendency in the "developed" or functional languages'.[81] This inherent ambiguity has important consequences. Firstly, it entails that it can be extremely difficult to determine the 'obvious' meaning of a verse or book of Scripture; secondly, it means that the text is open to a multitude of interpretations; and, thirdly, the openness of the text is an invitation to the reader to become actively involved in the production of meaning. 'The reader', Levinas maintains, is 'in his own fashion, a scribe.'[82]

The need for the individual to interpret Scripture points out the paradoxical structure of revelation; although revelation 'comes from elsewhere, from outside' it 'lives within the person receiving it'.[83] Levinas goes further, and maintains that the 'uniqueness of the self' is the necessary condition for revelation, for the breach of totality which revelation constitutes.

> The Revelation has a particular way of producing meaning, which lies in its calling upon the unique within me. It is as if a multiplicity of persons—and it is this multiplicity, surely, that gives the notion of 'person' its sense—were the condition for the plenitude of 'absolute truth', as if each person, by virtue of his own uniqueness, were able to guarantee the revelation of one unique aspect of the truth, so that some of its facets would never have been revealed if certain people had been absent from mankind.[84]

Levinas is not simply saying that the Revelation 'adopts the measure of the people listening to it'.[85] Instead, each individual's understanding of the Revelation is itself part of the Revelation. 'The multiplicity of people, each one of them indispensable, is necessary to produce all the dimensions of meaning; the multiplicity of meanings is due to the multiplicity of people.'[86]

Levinas argues that the appeal to the individual that is essential to Revelation means that Revelation is not static, but requires History. It also entails that God is a personal God, for 'surely the first characteristic of any God calling upon persons must be that he is personal?'[87] He points out a difficulty raised by this conception of the relationship between man and God: if the relationship to the Revelation is a personal one, how can one guard against the 'arbitrariness of subjectivism' in interpreting the Revelation? Suggesting that it may be necessary for the truth to take 'a certain risk of subjectivism, in the pejorative sense of the term', Levinas at the same time argues that the community of readers provides some protection from subjectivism.

> There is, moreover, a means of discriminating between personal originality brought to bear upon the reading of the Book and the play of the fantasms of amateurs (or even charlatans): this is provided by the necessity of referring subjective findings to the continuity of readings through history, the tradition of commentaries which no excuse of direct inspiration from the text allows one to ignore. No 'renewal' worthy of the name can dispense with these references; nor, equally, can it fail to refer to what is known as the Oral Law.[88]

The Oral Law, Levinas emphasises, is an essential part of the Revelation; it is not simply a later commentary on the written law, but, according to Jewish teaching, was also revealed at Sinai. The Talmud, which is the written form of the Oral Law, claims for itself an authority which is 'at least equal'[89] to that of the Bible, and was accepted as such by the medieval Jewish philosophers. It should be noted that in pointing out the Talmud's alleged status as revelation, Levinas is not making any claim about historical events, but simply describing the relationship between oral and written law as it is understood by the tradition. He goes on to explain that although the Oral Law claims an independent authority, its teachings are nevertheless inseparable from the Bible. The Talmud

> [...] is a guide to the interpretation of the Old Testament. Its way of reading, scrutinizing the text [...] defines the entire Talmudic approach. All the prescriptive part of the Torah is 'reworked' by the rabbinical doctors, and the narrative part is amplified and placed in a particular light. Thus it is the Talmud which allows us to distinguish the Jewish reading of the Bible from the Christian or 'scientific' reading of historians or philosophers. *Judaism is indeed the Old Testament, but read through the Talmud.*[90]

Although the traditional Jewish reading of the Bible is often described as 'literal', Levinas argues that it is more accurate to understand the 'guiding spirit' of this reading as an attempt to 'keep each particular text within the context of the whole'.[91] This aim, he argues, helps us to understand the true significance of the comparisons between texts which are made on the basis of seemingly trivial similarities or differences in the language used. These comparisons '[...] which can seem merely verbal, to depend upon the letter of the text, actually demonstrate this attempt to make the "harmonics" of a particular verse resound within other verses'.[92] The importance of this 'harmonising' is that it can help to bring to light the significance of Biblical passages which seem to us harsh or unspiritual.

> The aim is also to keep the passages which are entirely to our taste—in their talk of spiritualization and interiorization—in contact with the tougher texts, in order to extract from these, too, their own truth. And, by developing those remarks which seem most severe to us, we may also bring the most generous moments of the text closer to its hardest realities.[93]

Although Levinas does not develop these ideas at this stage of the essay, he does point out that the apparent 'harshness' of the Old Testament reflects the nature of man and the world.

> The language of the Old Testament is so suspicious of any rhetoric which never stammers that it has as its chief prophet [i.e. Moses] a man 'slow of speech and of tongue'. In this disability we can see more than the simple admission of a limitation; it also acknowledges the nature of this kerygma, one which does not forget the weight of the world, the inertia of men, the dullness of their understanding.[94]

For Levinas then, Revelation, although it comes from the 'outside', is never expressed in a 'pure' form; living 'within' people, it is shaped by their limitations. Moreover, he argues that the 'miraculous' origin of the Scriptures is not by itself the source of their influence; instead, it is the 'confluence' of the texts which keeps them alive.

Tradition is the expression, perhaps, of a way of life thousands of years old, which conferred unity upon a collection of texts, however disparate historians say they were in their origins. The miracle of this confluence is as great as the miracle of the common origin attributed to the texts—and it is the miracle of that life. Just as the strings of a violin are stretched across its wood, so is the text stretched across all the amplifications brought by tradition. *The Scriptures are therefore far from being a source of exercises for grammarians, in complete submission to the philologists; rather, their mode of being is such that the history of each piece of writing is less important than the lessons it contains, and its inspiration is measured in terms of what it has inspired.*[95]

The 'miracle of confluence', Levinas argues, also helps to account for the survival of Judaism as a unity, throughout centuries of crisis. At such times, the findings of historians and critics have no spiritual significance. Instead, 'the voice which speaks out' at times of crisis 'belongs to [...] the miracle of confluence and the thought and sensibility through which it reverberates understand it at once, just as if they were already expecting it.'[96]

Like the Scriptures, the Oral Law also calls for interpretation and the active participation of the reader. Although the Oral Law was written down, for contingent historical reasons, the Talmud retains the style of oral teaching. Rather than simply presenting the conclusions of debates between the sages, it reproduces the discussions themselves, thus inviting the reader to participate in the on-going task of interpretation.[97]

In addition to recording divergent opinions, the Talmud also lacks any systematic expression of doctrine which could unify Jewish religious thought. Levinas explains that it was not until the Middle Ages that attempts were made to formulate 'articles of faith' such as the 'Thirteen Principles' of Maimonides. By this time, Jewish religious life 'had already been ordered and was two thousand years old (if we believe historical research)'.[98]

Rather than being unified through doctrine, Judaism is unified by *Halakha,* the law. Levinas points out that within the Oral Tradition, there is a distinction to be made between *Aggada* and *Halakha.* He defines the former as the body of 'texts and teachings of homiletic origin which, in the form of apologues, parables and amplifications of Biblical tales represent the theological and philosophical part of the tradition'.[99] The *Aggada,* Levinas continues, 'constitutes the metaphysics and philosophical anthropology of Judaism'.[100] By contrast, halakhic texts and teachings are defined as those which 'relate to conduct and formulate practical laws, which constitute the real Torah, and are recognizably "prescriptive" in Ricoeur's sense [...]'.[101]

Levinas notes that halakhic and aggadic texts co-exist side by side within the Talmud. Discussions of halakhic problems frequently lead to 'more intellectual issues',[102] such as the reasons for a particular *mitzvah.* Levinas emphasises the importance of the linkage, stressing that 'the thought generated by prescriptive problems goes beyond the question of which material act should be carried out'.[103] However, the determination of the *halakha* remains of paramount concern, since it is precisely the body of decisions regarding material actions which unifies Judaism.

Having discussed 'the four compass points' of Judaism (Oral Law, Written Law, *Halakha*, *Aggada*), Levinas makes some general remarks about the contents of the Revelation. He insists that the Revelation does not simply invite man to have faith in God, but also asks him to accept responsibility for his neighbour.[104] Levinas understands the story of the enslavement of the Israelites, and their subsequent Exodus from Egypt, as a description of the very essence of man's humanity.

> The traumatism of my enslavement in Egypt constitutes my very humanity, that which draws me closer to the problems of the wretched of the earth, to all persecuted people. It is as if I were praying in my suffering as a slave, but with a pre-oratorial prayer; as if the love of the stranger were a response already given to me in my actual heart.[105]

Levinas' description of the self's relationship to Revelation echoes his description of the responsible self in *Otherwise than Being*. The uniqueness of the self is identified as 'my responsibility for the other' and Levinas insists that no one can take my place.[106]

Man, Levinas continues, is 'the irruption of God within Being, or the bursting out of Being towards God'.[107] It is the act of giving, breaking with the *conatus essendi* of beings which constitutes this 'irruption' and is the true meaning of being chosen.[108] In taking up this position of responsibility, man enters into a relationship with the Infinite, a relationship which Levinas characterises as 'waiting for God'.

> Man can what he must; he shall master the hostile forces of History and bring into being the messianic reign foretold by the prophets. The awaiting of the Messiah is the duration of time itself—waiting for God—but here the waiting no longer attests to the absence of Godot, who will never come, but rather to a relationship with that which is not able to enter the present, since the present is too small to contain the Infinite.[109]

In characterising the relationship between man and God as one with 'that which is not able to enter the present' Levinas reaches the crux of the problem of Revelation: how is a relationship with the Infinite possible, if the present is too small to contain it? How can a Jew '"explain" to himself the very fact of the Revelation, in all its extraordinariness, which tradition [...] presents as coming from outside this world, and belonging to another order?'[110] Levinas points out that the Bible both indicates that its origin is supernatural, and issues warnings against the dangers of heeding false prophets. Thus Revelation 'does not leave worry behind'; rather, an essential part of the Revelation is its call to be 'vigilant', to distinguish true prophecy from false. Moreover, Levinas argues that, in principle, prophecy is not limited to a few exceptional individuals; instead, man is 'inherently able to become a prophet!'[111] In support of this argument, he cites Deuteronomy 5:4, 'The Lord God spoke with you face-to-face', which refers to the Israelites who were present at Sinai. Everyone who was at Sinai experienced an unmediated relationship with God. However, Levinas claims that the possibility for prophecy on such a wide scale did not end at Sinai. He cites a verse from Amos—'The Lord God has spoken; who can but prophesy?' (3:8) to suggest that the 'receptivity of the prophet already lies within the human soul'.[112]

Levinas emphasises that what the prophet receives is not an image, but, more often than not, a commandment. This was certainly the case at Sinai, regarding which it is written 'Therefore take good heed to yourselves. Since you saw no form on the day that the Lord spoke to you at Horeb out of the midst of the fire' (Deut. 4:15). Revelation is a 'saying':

> Revelation is of words and offers no image to the eyes. And if the words which describe the Revelation in the Scriptures borrow from the vocabulary of visual perception, what you perceive of God is a divine verbal message (*devar elohim*) which is, more often than not, an order.[113]

The idea that what one perceives of God is a 'divine verbal message', rather than an image, is well illustrated by a verse in Exodus that Levinas does not cite. The verse, according to Rashi,[114] describes part of the experience of the Revelation at Sinai as 'seeing that which should be heard'.

> And all the people *saw the thunderings* and the flaming torches, *and the voice of the cornet*, and the mountain smoking: and when the people saw it, they moved, and stood afar off. (Exodus 20:15)[115]

Rather than translating the first phrase as 'and all the people saw the thunderings', Rashi understands it as meaning that they saw 'the sounds which issued from the mouth of the Almighty'. The word which Rosenbaum and Silbermann have translated as 'thunderings' is *kolot*. The singular, *kol*, can be used generically to mean 'sound', or more specifically to indicate 'voice' or other particular sounds, such as that of a musical instrument. (For example, the phrase in this verse which has been translated as 'the voice of the cornet' is *kol hashofar*.) In the plural, *kolot* can mean thunder, as well as the plural form of these other meanings. Rashi's decision to understand *kolot* here as referring to the voice of God is supported by the context. The verse is immediately preceded by the pronouncement of the Ten Commandments. Thus, if we accept Rashi's translation, what was 'seen' was indeed a 'divine verbal message' and, as Levinas indicates was usually the case, the message took the form of commandment.

Rashi remarks that in seeing what should be heard, the Israelites saw 'something which is impossible to see on any other occasion'; he thus emphasises the extraordinary nature of the experience of Revelation. Levinas argues, however, that the medieval Jewish philosophers, such as Maimonides, failed to appreciate the full significance of the rupture of nature brought about by the Revelation.

> The Jewish philosophers of the Middle Ages, notably Maimonides, do trace back the Revelation to the prophetic gifts. But, rather than thinking of these in terms of a heteronomous inspiration, they assimilate them—to various degrees—to the intellectual faculties described by Aristotle. The Maimonidean man, like the Aristotelian man, is a 'being' situated *in his place* in the cosmos; he is a part of being which never leaves being behind, in which there never occurs any fracture of the same (même), that radical transcendence which the idea of inspiration and the whole traumatism of prophecy seem to involve in the Biblical texts.[116]

Levinas attempts to explain the 'fracture of the same' which occurs in prophecy, without simply claiming that the experience of transcendence is refractory to rational thought.

> The problem lies in the possibility of a fracture or opening in the closed order of totality, of the world, or equally in the self-sufficiency of reason which is its correlative. This fracture would be produced by a movement from outside but, paradoxically, it would not entail the loss of that rational self-sufficiency.[117]

Levinas argues that our difficulty in conceiving such a fracture of the same arises from 'our habit of thinking of reason as the correlative of the possibility of the world, the counterpart to its stability and identity'.[118] In order to arrive at a conception of rationality or intelligibility that leaves room for the transcendence of Revelation, we would have to abandon the equation of rationality with possibility, and consider the structure of practical reason.

> Could we account for intelligibility in terms of a traumatic upheaval in experience, which confronts intelligence with something far beyond its capacity, and thereby causes it to break? Surely not. Unless, perhaps, we consider the possibility of a command, a 'you must', which takes no account of what 'you can'. In this case, the exceeding of one's capacity does make sense. In other words, the type of reason corresponding to the fracture we have spoken of is practical reason.[119]

Although the use of the phrase 'practical reason' evokes Kantian ethics, Levinas wishes to distance himself from the notion of a 'categorical imperative', in which the will is directed by a universalisable maxim. Instead, he sees the 'fracture' of the totality as occurring through the attitude of obedience, which derives either from 'love of one's neighbour, a love without eros' or from 'fraternity', 'responsibility for one's neighbour'.[120] In either case, 'the relationship with the other is placed right at the beginning.'[121] Levinas suggests that the second formulation of the categorical imperative moves closer to this type of ethics, in which the person has priority over the universality of the maxim.[122]

The break-up of the totality through ethics, or 'practical reasoning', should constitute, Levinas argues, our model of revelation. In support of this argument he cites the 'primordial importance in Judaism of the prescription' which was described above, as well as the 'attitude of obedience' in which the Revelation is received.[123] Levinas sees this attitude as being exemplified in the Israelites' response to revelation in Exodus 24:7: 'All that the Eternal has said, we will do and hear' (my translation).[124] In Hebrew, the verb 'to hear', *lishmo'a*, also means 'to understand'; Levinas interprets the order of the two expressions as an indication that obedience here takes precedence over understanding.[125]

In this reversal of the normal, logical order of understanding and then doing, Levinas sees a departure from Greek rationality; this, however, does not mean that the 'attitude of obedience' is irrational. Rather, it arises from the 'radical passivity' of the self that Levinas describes in *Otherwise than Being* as responsibility for the Other, the 'responsibility of a hostage'.[126] He does not claim that the content of Scripture can in any way be deduced from this responsibility. However, he wishes to show that the attitude of obedience which characterises the response to revelation is not simply irrational.

> We are concerned, rather, to formulate the possibility of a heteronomy which does not involve servitude, a receptive ear which still retains its reason, an obedience which does not alienate the person listening, and to recognize, in the ethical model of the Bible, the transcendence of understanding.[127]

Levinas reiterates the problem he posed at the beginning of the essay: the Revelation establishes a relationship with exteriority, in which the exteriority 'cannot be transformed into a content within interiority; it remains "uncontainable", infinite (infinie), and yet the relation is maintained'.[128] He proposes that, 'in solving the paradox of the Revelation', we make use of the model of relationship with exteriority established in his descriptions of the ethical relationship of responsibility. 'Ethics', he argues, 'provides the model worthy of transcendence and it is as an ethical kerygma that the Bible is Revelation.'[129]

In understanding Revelation as an ethical 'saying', Levinas rejects rational theology which 'equates the rational with the identity of the Same'.[130] Like western philosophy, rational theology is an ontology which attempts to reduce all alterity to sameness and, always seeking repose, understands its opposites as privation. For Levinas, however, the opposites of repose—'worry, questioning, seeking, Desire'—do not simply arise from unfulfilled needs, but represent the 'idea of the Infinite' and 'demonstrate a psyche which is more alert than that of intentionality, or a knowledge adequate to its object'.[131] A reason satisfied with such knowledge has only reached a certain level of intelligence where 'it is prone to become *embourgeoisé* and fall asleep, satisfied with its own presence'. It has 'already resigned from life'.[132] Levinas argues that we should regard a consciousness equal to itself not as the primordial self, but as a mode or modification of the self awakened by the idea of the Infinite. The form of this awakening, he suggests, is 'obedience' and the Revelation should be understood 'not in terms of received wisdom, but as this awakening'.[133]

Without providing an exhaustive analysis of the meaning of revelation in Judaism, this essay elaborates the idea of post-Holocaust faith outlined in 'To Love the Torah more than God'. Levinas has shown that, through its form, the Torah (both written and oral) cries out for interpretation, and lends itself to a multiplicity of readings, thus allowing for readers at all epochs to find it relevant to their situation. Moreover, the unity of the texts and teachings from different eras, which Levinas terms 'the miracle of confluence', allows one to enter into a relationship with the tradition as a whole, rather than always interpreting specific texts. His interpretation of the content of the tradition as 'ethical kerygma' also helps us to understand Yossel's fervent decision to adhere to the ethical precepts of the Torah: Yossel was relating to the Revelation in the 'attitude of obedience' that Levinas attributes to the Israelites at Mount Sinai. However, unlike the Israelites, Yossel's attitude was not elicited by the unmediated presence of God, but by the face(s) of the other(s) suffering near him. We might say that, in the proximity of human others, he responded to the same call to obedience that is the 'Saying' of the Revelation.

### The Purpose of Mitzvot

One might wonder, however, whether there really is a need for Revelation, understood as 'ethical saying', if the proximity of the other already commands obedience. Levinas' emphasis on the importance of Jewish law might seem problematic, particularly since so much of it is concerned with ritual practices. Edith Wyschogrod formulates the question as follows:

> What is the justification for Jewish ritual if ethical action is founded in the upsurge of the other and if such action is the way in which Judaism appears in the world? What, in short, accounts for the necessity of Jewish ritual *praxis*?[134]

In 'Revelation in the Jewish Tradition', Levinas touches only briefly upon the question of the purpose of the *mitzvot*, the body of commandments that form the basis of Jewish law. He notes that the 'real motivation' of the *halakha* is 'still under debate',[135] but suggests that an essential feature of ritual observance is the establishment of a certain distance between man and nature.

> There is nothing numinous about ritual, no element of idolatry; in ritual a distance is taken up within nature, towards nature, which constitutes perhaps the very act of awaiting the Most High.[136]

Although Levinas does not develop this idea in 'Revelation in the Jewish Tradition', he has done so in earlier essays in *Difficile liberté* and *Quatre lectures talmudiques*. In the essay 'Une religion d'adultes' to which Wyschogrod refers, Levinas characterises the *halakha* as a 'severe discipline' which 'tends towards justice'. After describing the centrality of justice in the Jewish religion, Levinas writes, 'Jewish ritual law constitutes the severe discipline which tends towards this justice'.[137] Wyschogrod, however, examines the argument that ritual practice 'tends towards justice' by training us to obey the Other (in this case God) and finds it inadequate as an explanation of the need for ritual.

> [... If] ritual is merely a discipline and if the appearance of the other in and of itself commands obedience the question must be raised why, from Levinas' point of view, is ritual law necessary? If transcendence is experienced in the very upsurge of the one who is near, ritual seems superfluous [...] Given Levinas' emphasis upon the upsurge of alterity as the pre-requisite for *religio*, both as its necessary and sufficient condition, it is difficult to understand his stress upon the necessity for ritual *praxis*.[138]

Wyschogrod's question loses its force when we focus on the difference between recognising a commandment and obeying it. The 'upsurge of alterity' may be a sufficient condition for recognising my responsibility to the Other, but there is no guarantee that I will act in accordance with this responsibility. Levinas makes it very clear in other contexts that to hear a commandment is not necessarily to obey it. To argue otherwise would obviously make him an altruist of the utmost naivety. In *Totality and Infinity* and other essays, Levinas has stressed the difference between moral authority and force. We saw in Chapter Two that he describes the *ethical* impossibility of murder, while recognising that actual murders do take place.[139] Moreover, in 'The Paradox of Morality' he clearly states the importance of the distinction between force and authority to his understanding of the face.

> When I said that the face is authority, that there is authority in the face, this may undoubtedly seem contradictory: it is a request and it is an authority. You have a

question later on in which you ask me how it could be that if there is a command-ment in the face, one can do the opposite of what the face demands. The face is not a force. It is an authority. Authority is often without force.[140]

In his essays on humanism, as well as in *Otherwise than Being*, Levinas also stresses that the relationship between the self and the Good does not consti-tute a 'natural tendency' or 'an altruistic or generous nature', nor does it pre-clude the possibility of human evil. The answer to Wyschogrod's question would therefore seem to be that ritual practice is needed not to enable us to hear the commandment, but to prepare us to respond to it in a positive fash-ion, acting in accordance with our responsibility. However, it must be said that Levinas' formulations are often somewhat ambiguous on this point. The argument that 'only someone who has been able to impose a severe rule on his own nature is able to recognize the face of the other' might seem to imply that adherence to the laws of Judaism (or perhaps a similar system of law) is a necessary condition for recognising the face of the other and the command-ment which proceeds from it. This interpretation is not only inconsistent with the texts quoted above, but was explicitly rejected by Levinas in the interview we have cited. When asked how, apart from Jewish observance, one can learn to 'recognize and welcome the face of the other', Levinas insist-ed that his ethical philosophy is entirely universal:

> I do not preach for the Jewish religion. I always speak of the Bible, not the Jewish religion. The Bible, including the Old Testament, is for me a human fact, of the human order, and entirely universal. What I have said about ethics, about the uni-versality of the commandment in the face, of the commandment which is valid even if it doesn't bring salvation, even if there is no reward, is valid independently of any religion.[141]

Elsewhere in the interview, Levinas states:

> [...It] is not difficult to recognize the face. There is the commandment, the form in which its excellence appears. It is a commanded excellence because it is not an excellence given simply, in an intuition. It is the being that we are, being itself, which prevents us from recognizing our ethical duties.[142]

Here again, the formulation is ambiguous. If it is not difficult to 'recognize the face', how can 'the being which we are' prevent us from 'recognizing our ethical duties'? The difficulty stems from using the verb 'to recognise' in two different senses. In the first instance, recognition of the face seems to amount simply to a realisation that the face issues a commandment, while the second usage of 'to recognise' implies a positive response to the commandment. In the passage we have quoted from *Difficile liberté,* Levinas seems to have been using the word in the second sense.

However, even once we have resolved this ambiguity regarding the verb 'to recognise', Levinas' claim that 'only someone who has been able to impose a severe rule on his own nature is able to recognize the face of the other' remains somewhat problematic. What, we might wonder, apart from the discipline of *halakha*, would constitute a sufficiently 'severe' rule? Levinas does not address this question in the essay in *Difficile liberté* and, as we saw above, when a similar question was put to him in 1986, his response was 'I do not preach for the Jewish religion.'[143] His refusal to 'preach' Judaism can be understood simply as a reflection of the fact that he is a philosopher rather than a pulpit rabbi. However, this reticence is also a reflection of the philosophical view that the other's responsibilities are 'his affair'. As we will see throughout the remainder of this study, Levinas' ethical reading of Judaism does not issue in a call to other Jews to take upon themselves the yoke of the law, whether this is understood as the acceptance of the *mitzvot* or as a symbol for ethical obligation. Instead, Levinas' interpretation of Judaism as ethical saying shows the meaningfulness of the texts and practices of the Jewish religion.

Let us return once again to the claim in *Difficile liberté* that it is necessary to impose a severe discipline on one's nature in order to prepare oneself to welcome the Other. Levinas frequently points out that his writings on Judaism are exegeses, and although the essay 'Une religion d'adultes' is not a commentary on any one text, it can be understood as an exposition of the 'text' of the tradition itself. If we understand the essay in this way, the claim about the necessity of discipline no longer seems to be a universal statement about the conditions for the possibility of ethical behaviour. Rather, it is Levinas' interpretation of the importance attributed to ritual law in Judaism.

Levinas' position, then, is that the commandment which issues from the face can always be recognised, but is not always obeyed, and the discipline of Jewish law can help prepare us to obey the Other. Whether or not there are other ways of preparing to welcome the Other remains an open question. This question will be considered below, in our discussion of Levinas' understanding of the relationship between the universal and particular aspects of Judaism.

In addition to characterising Jewish law as a 'severe discipline' which 'tends towards justice', Levinas has discussed the significance of the *mitzvot* in his essay '*Vieux comme le monde?*',[144] a commentary on pages 36b–37a of the talmudic tractate *Sanhedrin*. The talmudic texts opens with a *mishna* which describes the seating arrangements of the *Sanhedrin*, the high court. The *gemara* seeks scriptural authority for this *mishna* and finds it in a verse from Song of Songs (7: 8): 'Thy navel is like a round goblet, that never lacks blended wine: thy belly is like a heap of wheat, set about with roses.'[145] It is the phrase 'set about with roses' that is of importance for a discussion of the significance of the mitzvot. Rabbi Akha bar Hanina, who cites this verse as the source of the *mishna*, interprets it as referring to the *Sanhedrin*, and sees in the reference to a rose border the implication that the judges of the *Sanhedrin* will refrain from sin, even if they are separated from it only by a rose border.

Levinas understands Rabbi Akha bar Hanina's interpretation as meaning that the judges must be in complete control of their instincts. He concedes that this may be a utopian demand, but insists that without a virtuous tribunal, there would be only a mockery of justice. Furthermore, he insists that it is not sufficient for the judges to be virtuous in their public lives. The image of a rose border connotes private life.

> The rose border is tempting by itself; the hand is carried spontaneously towards the flower. In that which separates us from evil there resides an equivocal seduction. This enclosure is less than an absence of closure. When there is nothing between you and evil, one could refrain from crossing the distance, but when there are roses —all the literature of evil, *les fleurs du mal*—how can one resist?[146]

Levinas is not alone in seeing the image of the rose border as evoking private life. After presenting Rabbi Akha bar Hanina's interpretation of the verse cited above, according to which the subject of the description is the *Sanhedrin*, the Talmud cites Rabbi Kahana, who understands the verse as describing the Jewish people. It reports that a Sadducee once asked Rabbi Kahana how the *Halakha* can permit a married couple to be alone together at times when sexual relations between them are forbidden. Rabbi Kahana replied 'The Torah testifies this of us: "Set about with roses" —even through a hedge of roses they will make no breach.' Levinas emphasises that with this objection and the response to it, the discussion has moved from the virtue of the judges to that of the ordinary people. He insists that this exchange is of universal significance: 'Judaism conceives the humanity of man as open to a culture which preserves it from evil by separating it from evil by a simple rose border.'[147]

Levinas draws upon the teaching of the medieval commentator Maharsha[148] to explain how the rose border can provide protection from sin: 'Those things in the world which are charming, tempting, seductive, invite us to vigilance.'[149] The very temptation to sin is a call to refrain from sin. The aim of Judaism is, Levinas explains, to train us to reflect before acting. '[All] of Judaism has tried precisely to place a time of reflection between natural spontaneity and nature.' Judaism accomplishes this by means of the *mitzvot*, the system of commandments which govern even the most mundane actions.

This understanding of the purpose of the *mitzvot* is closely related to the idea of a 'severe discipline' presented above. In 'Une religion d'adultes', as we have seen, Levinas argues that the *mitzvot* can train one to submit his will to that of the other. The time of reflection between desire and act is, of course, the means by which this discipline is achieved. However, it is important to note that reflection separates man from nature regardless of whether he refrains from fulfilling his desire, and Levinas accords a positive value to this separation. It is not simply a question of yielding to the will of the other when there is a conflict of interest, but of demonstrating that man is not entirely governed by natural forces. For Levinas, following the *mitzvot* elevates human existence. Interpreting the image of a rose border in a somewhat different light, Levinas remarks:

> That which stops us is not at all the unbearable yoke of the Law which frightened Saint Paul, but a rose border. The obligation to follow the commandments—the *mitzvot*—is not a curse for us, but brings the first perfumes of paradise.[150]

In addition to seeing the system of *mitzvot* as a discipline leading to ethical behaviour and affirming man's difference from the rest of nature, Levinas also asserts that Jewish law and the texts which describe it enshrine universal truths and protect them from corruption. Levinas' argument to this effect, which appears in *Difficile liberté,* was presented earlier, in the context of our discussion of his comparison of Judaism and western humanism.[151] Unfortunately, Levinas' statement of the argument is extremely brief, and he does not give specific examples of the 'truths' of Judaism and the laws or texts in which they can be found. However, the supposition that biblical and talmudic texts embody significant truths of interest to contemporary thinkers is the basis of Levinas' talmudic readings. His method of uncovering these truths will be examined in the next chapter, when we consider the relationship between Levinas' philosophy and his understanding of Judaism.

For our present purposes, it is sufficient to note that Levinas' understanding of Judaism is not reductive. Whilst arguing that *halakha* embodies universal truths, Levinas insists on the importance of the concrete, particular nature of the *mitzvot* and the texts in which they are discussed. This insistence on the concrete, however, raises the question of the relationship between the universal and the particular aspects of Judaism.

## Universal versus Particular Aspects of Judaism

Levinas has made a few suggestive remarks concerning this question in his essay 'Assimilation and New Culture',[152] in which he points out that universality is one of the supreme values of western culture and philosophy. He sees western culture as being doubly universal: it is the 'common inheritance of humanity' in which every individual and every people can find a place, and it celebrates universality in its science, letters, arts and, especially, philosophy.[153] For Levinas, philosophy is, above all, language which has been able to 'sublimate metaphors into concepts and to express all lived experience, whatever the original language assumed by the experience and even if it were unsayable'.[154] The particularity of western nations is, Levinas continues, only the logical particularity of the individual member of a genus. Western nations are able to translate the essence of their experience into the universal language of philosophy; anything that cannot be so expressed is mere 'local colour'.[155]

Levinas, however, insists that Judaism comprises an irreducible moment of particularity. This moment of 'isolation and distancing',[156] which is present in both Scripture and rabbinic literature is not, he maintains, merely the result of the historical experience of exile. Rather, it is 'an essential return to oneself in the consciousness of a surfeit of responsibility towards humanity'.[157] Jewish particularity, the awareness of being chosen, does not entail extra privileges, but extra responsibility. The concept of 'election' is that of an awareness that one is obligated to the other, without demanding that the other take on the same obligations. This assymetry, however, is often misunderstood as a narrow, particularistic nationalism; a misunderstanding which, Levinas recognises, is widespread among Jews and non-Jews alike.[158]

Levinas argues that careful reflection on Judaism forces us to re-think the notion of singularity, because Jewish particularity is a singularity which in fact goes beyond universality. He claims that this singularity has been made manifest in Jewish history, long before the 'distinction between particular and universal appeared in the speculations of logicians'.[159] Since the Emancipation, Jewish thinkers have limited themselves to apologetics, to attempts at making the truths of the Torah conform to western models of truth.[160] The Torah, Levinas insists, demands more than this. We must try to explicate the meaning of a Jewish singularity which goes beyond universality.

Levinas cites three themes of the Torah which he believes require a more subtle explication than they have been receiving. These are, first, the idea of the Israelites as a people 'that shall dwell alone, and shall not be received among the nations' (Numbers 23: 9); second, the theme of Abraham being called 'Hebrew' (*ivri*) because he was 'able to remain alone to one side (*me'ever ehad*) when others remain on the other side' (*Bereshit Rabbah* 42: 8)[161] and third the idea that there are 613 commandments which Jews are required to observe, while the 'children of Noah' (i.e. the rest of humanity) are only required to keep seven. Levinas is concerned that these three themes have too often been subject to a 'summary reflection' which confuses separation with superiority.[162] He suggests that the limitation of universalism which appears to be present in the Torah actually serves to protect universalism from the danger of totalitarianism, by 'opening our eyes on the faces which illuminate and allow us to control the anonymity of the social'.[163] As such, Jewish particularity is not the symptom of an outdated stage of existence; rather, it reveals 'a "beyond" of universalism, which is what completes or perfects human fraternity'.[164]

Levinas regrets that this singularity has been left to feeling and faith and has not yet been expressed in philosophical language. He insists that this a very important lacuna. 'We are faced', he writes, 'with the great task of articulating in Greek those principles of which Greece had no knowledge. Jewish singularity awaits its philosophy.'[165] We will see in the next chapter that Levinas' philosophy in many ways accomplishes this task of translating Jewish principles into 'Greek', that is, into philosophical language. Before doing so, however, it will be useful to consider Levinas' remarks on Jewish singularity in more detail, particularly as these are related to his understanding of the significance of the *mitzvot*.

The seven Noahide laws, which Levinas mentions in 'Assimilation and New Culture', may at first glance seem to contradict the claim in *Difficile liberté* that 'Judaism does not take up its responsibilities […] and right away propose that others share them.'[166] However, the contradiction is only apparent. The claim that Levinas makes in this essay is not that Judaism does not assign any responsibility at all to non-Jews, but that it does not demand that others share the same degree of responsibility as Jews. This difference is similar to the asymmetry of the ethical relation described in Levinas' philosophical works: just as the self has no right to make the same demands on the other that he makes on himself, so the Jew may not expect the non-Jew to accept the excessive degree of responsibility represented by the 613 *mitzvot*. At the same time, however, this does not mean that Judaism completely exempts non-Jews from responsibility. Instead, the rest of humanity is expected to adhere to the seven Noahide laws which are understood to form the basis of a just society.[167] Again, a parallel can be drawn with Levinas' philosophical distinction between ethics and justice. The asymmetry which is essential to the ethical relationship is not characteristic of human relations considered on the level of justice. When thinking in terms of justice, I am permitted to think of myself in the same category as other individuals, and to consider not only my obligations towards them, but also their obligations towards me. 'Justice' is something that can be taught and preached, whereas I am not permitted to expect others to behave 'ethically'.[168]

However, in spite of these parallels, it should be noted that the division of obligations into the 613 mitzvot of Judaism and the seven Noahide Laws does not correspond to Levinas' distinction between 'ethics' and 'justice'. The responsibility revealed in the ethical relation is, ultimately, unrealisable, first because it is infinite, and second because, in reality, I am 'never alone in the world with the other.'[169] Judaism therefore cannot be considered a system of 'ethics'. In fact, a Jewish society governed by *halakha* would provide an excellent example of 'justice' in Levinas' terminology. He insists that justice is not static and that the truly just society is one which continually strives to become more just. The concern to improve justice by tempering its verdicts with mercy is apparent in the development and application of Jewish law. For example, the Rabbis were loathe to impose sentences of capital punishment, even though the Bible lists fifteen different capital offences.[170] The Rabbis of the *Mishna* and *Gemara* enumerated a number of provisions and restrictions which made it almost impossible to enforce the death penalty. For example, they ruled that two eye-witnesses were required to convict someone of a capital offence. This rule alone would severely limit the number of capital cases which could be tried, since serious crimes are rarely committed in the presence of two trustworthy witnesses. Another rule which the Rabbis enacted which is of particular interest was that no one who was thought to be lacking in compassion could be appointed to the court.

> The Talmud states that 'We do not appoint to a Sanhedrin an old man, a eunuch or a childless man' and Rabbi Judah adds 'one who is hard-hearted' (Sanhedrin 36b).[171]

This rule, with its emphasis on the importance of compassion, epitomises the Rabbis' concern to temper justice with mercy in their application of Jewish law. The history of the development of *halakha* reveals numerous similar instances of rabbinic attempts to soften the verdicts of the law in various domains.[172]

According to Jewish teaching, however, responsibility for improving justice does not rest solely with the judges and leaders of the community. Individuals are encouraged to forfeit their legal rights or accept responsibilities in excess of their legal obligations when ethical considerations suggest that it would be appropriate to do so. Moreover, according to many authorities, acting *lifnim mishurat hadin* ('beyond the requirements of the law')[173] is sometimes obligatory.[174]

Aharon Lichtenstein has suggested that halakhic Judaism includes two distinct realms of moral reasoning and obligation. The first is *din*, which 'consists of a body of statutes, ultimately rooted in fundamental values but which at the moment of decision confront the individual as a set of rules'. *Din* in this sense is formally similar to the Greek reasoning which, according to Levinas, has as its task 'comparing the incomparable'. The basic mode of *din*, Lichtenstein writes, is that of

> formulating and defining directives to be followed in a class of cases [...] and apply-ing them to situations marked by the proper cluster of features. [Its] judgments are essentially grounded in deductive, primarily syllogistic reasoning.[175]

The second domain is that of *lifnim mishurat hadin*, which Lichtenstein char-acterises as the sphere of 'contextual morality'. Paradoxically, the basis for making decisions in this domain is both more general and more specific than the formalistic procedures of *din*. The contextualist is not guided by class rules but by 'a minimal number, perhaps as few as one or two, of ultimate val-ues, on the one hand, and by the unique contours of the situation at hand, on the other'.[176] One of the most important details of a situation in this context is the needs and abilities of the individuals involved. For example, in a dis-pute between two parties, one of whom is wealthy, and the other poor, the former might be expected to forfeit his rights in favour of the latter, despite the fact that his case is upheld by the *din*.[177]

The notion of *lifnim mishurat hadin* is not only indicative of the ethical concern underlying the law, but is also of interest for our consideration of universality and particularity in Judaism. It shows that Judaism is not simply a two-tiered system, prescribing one set of obligations for Jews (represented by the 613 *mitzvot*) and another for non-Jews (the seven Noahide laws). Rather, each individual is expected to accept a level of obligation commensur-able with his capacity to fulfil it. A person is not simply viewed as a member of a group, with the obligations incumbent upon all the members of that group, but is also considered in his individuality.

In his philosophical works Levinas is equally insistent on the importance of viewing people not only as members of the genus man, but as individuals. As we saw in Chapter One, he argues that both the self and the other are refractory to the totalising force of the concept. In *Totality and Infinity*, he argues that 'when taken to be like a genus that unites like individuals the essence of society is lost sight of.'[178] Although the concept of a human race is useful and necessary in biology, it is not sufficient to explain the 'fraternity' of men.

> [...] the human community instituted by language, where the interlocutors remain absolutely separated, does not constitute the unity of a genus. It is stated as a kin-ship of men. That all men are brothers is not explained by their resemblance, nor by a common cause of which they would be the effect, like medals which refer to the same die that struck them.[179]

Instead, to understand 'fraternity' and society, we must focus on the responsibility that is revealed in the face-to-face relation.

> It is my responsibility before a face looking at me as absolutely foreign [...] that constitutes the original fact of fraternity. [...] In this welcoming of the face (which is already responsibility in his regard, and where accordingly he approaches me from a dimension of height and dominates me), equality is founded.[180]

The argument that responsibility is the basis of fraternity and society helps to illuminate Levinas' claim that Jewish particularity is a singularity beyond universality, revealing that which 'completes or perfects human fraternity'.[181] As we saw in the first chapter, Levinas argues that responsibility institutes a bond with the Good which is beyond being. The realm of the universal, however, is the realm of being. The meaning of Jewish singularity is not simply that the Jewish people are a particular example of the genus people, or that a Jew is a particular example of the genus human. Instead, their singularity is the fact that they are *singled out* for responsibility by that which is beyond being, and, therefore, beyond universality.

We noted above that, according to Levinas, this singling out occurs through the Revelation, understood as ethical saying. This understanding of the Torah as ethical saying helps to explain Levinas' suggestion that the Torah's apparent limitation of universalism actually serves to protect universalism from the danger of totalitarianism, by 'opening our eyes on the faces which illuminate and allow us to control the anonymity of the social'.[182] If the Torah were not ethical saying but merely a body of laws or universal principles, it would encourage us to view others (and ourselves) as members of the genus human. Such a body of laws and principles would be 'ontological' in Levinas' terminology and therefore 'violent'; although it might, strictly speaking, be 'just', it would not leave room for the 'mercy' which Jewish tradition sees as the necessary counterpart of the divine attribute of justice.[183] The Torah as ethical teaching, however, singles out the individual and calls upon him to be responsible, to turn towards the face of the other.

### The Significance of Prayer

Levinas suggests that this call to responsibility is present even in the silent prayer that the individual addresses to God. Although there is a common perception that prayer consists in asking God for something, he has devoted an entire essay[184] to expounding Rabbi Hayyim of Volozhin's view that 'prayer never asks for anything for itself'.[185] In 'Prayer Without Demand', Levinas describes the cosmology that underlies this view before discussing the approach to prayer itself. Significantly for us, even the cosmology, which is derived from Jewish mysticism, issues in a call to responsibility.

Levinas understands Rabbi Hayyim Volozhiner's book *Nefesh haHayyim* ('The Soul of Life') as 'an attempt to lay out the philosophical ideas implicit in Rabbinical study'.[186] He therefore has no hesitation in translating the language of this work, which is derived from Kabbalistic as well as Biblical and Rabbinic texts, into philosophical language. For example, Rabbi Hayyim argues that the existence of the 'worlds' depends on their 'association' with God and Levinas equates the existence of the 'worlds' with the contemporary notion of 'the being of countless beings':

> The existence of reality—the being of countless beings, as we say today—or in the terminology of *Nefesh haHayyim*, the being of creatures designated by the plural term 'worlds', is a sign of God's association with these worlds, which would return to nothingness or fall into decline if God withdrew from them.

We will see further examples of this work of translation below. For the moment, however, let us follow Levinas' exposition of Rabbi Hayyim Volozhiner's cosmology. The fact that the 'worlds' derive their being from divine energy entails that their being is 'equivalent to their holiness, their light and their spirituality'.[187] The worlds are arranged in a hierarchy. 'Each superior world gives life to the world beneath, governing, sanctifying and throwing light on it, and in turn receives movement, being and holiness from the world above it.'[188] God, of course, is situated at the top of this structure, as the 'soul' of the worlds. Man, however, introduces a complication into the system.

> Although he was created in the shadow of the worlds, out of substance taken from those worlds, man—thereby related to the worlds—is the element on which the whole structure depends (!); his body is situated at the lowest point, at the level of *doing*, the level of *work*, but his soul occupies the highest point, beside the 'throne of the Lord' from whose breath it comes.[189]

Because man's soul is higher than any of the other created worlds, man has the potential either to block or to facilitate the association of God and the lower worlds. Human actions (as well as thoughts and words) that are in accordance with the Torah sanctify and illuminate the worlds, but when they are contrary to the Torah, the very existence of the worlds is threatened. Human actions 'determine, in this way, the being or nothingness of all creatures'.[190] Levinas follows Volozhiner in deriving from this cosmology the claim that each individual is responsible 'for the life and death of all the other worlds and men'.[191] He quotes Volozhiner's plea:

> Let nobody in Israel—God forbid—ask himself: 'what am I, and what can my humble acts achieve in the world?' Let him rather understand this, that he may know it

and fix it in his thoughts: not one detail of his acts, of his words and of his thoughts is ever lost. Each one leads back to its origin, where it takes effect in the height of heights, in the worlds. [...] The man of intelligence who understands this in its truth will be fearful at heart and will tremble as he thinks how far his bad acts reach and what corruption and destruction even a small misdeed can cause.[192]

Significantly, Volozhiner does not entreat people to pay attention to their deeds out of fear of personal punishment or desire for personal reward, but out of concern for the cosmological repercussions of their actions. Levinas explains that when an individual understands his actions in this way, concern for others constitutes 'the meaning of his own self-identity'.[193] This responsibility makes man 'the *soul* of the world, as if God's creative word had been entrusted to him to dispose of as he liked, to let it ring out, or to interrupt it'.[194] Levinas claims that this is the ultimate meaning of the verse in Genesis 1:27 where man is said to be created 'in the image of God'. It is also the literal meaning of Genesis 2:7, where man is described as a 'living soul'; and of Isaiah 51:16,

'And I have put my words in your mouth, and hid you in the shadow of my hand, stretching out the heavens and laying the foundations of the earth.' Another verse which should be taken literally! It tells us that God's creative word was placed in the mouth of man: the being or non-being of the universe depends upon his adherence to the Torah.[195]

For Levinas, the responsibility that God has given man does not only demonstrate God's humility; it also points out the need for ethics in addition to ontology, by articulating 'the inability of being (*être*) *qua* pure being to provide beings (*étants*) with an adequate *raison d'être*'.[196] Levinas momentarily abandons Volozhiner's terminology in order to explicate the philosophical implications of his cosmology in the language of *Otherwise than Being*.

Onto-logy—that is, the intelligibility of being—only becomes possible when ethics, the origin of all meaning, is taken as the starting point. Humanity must irrupt into Being: behind the perseverance, in being, of the beings or worlds [...] behind their *conatus essendi* or their identity, affirming its own ego or egoism, there must figure [...] the responsibility of the *one for the others*. The *for itself* must be inverted, and become the *for the other*, the immediate fear of the one *for* the other.[197]

Having moved from the Rabbinic and Kabbalistic language of Rabbi Hayyim to the more philosophical language of *Otherwise than Being*, Levinas appropriately raises the question whether the ideas expressed in *Nefesh Hayyim* admit of a more universal interpretation.

Can we see, in this possibility given to humanity—that of being responsible for the other—the foremost meaning of Israel's historical existence? [...] Or should we understand this reversal of the self (*moi*) into the for-the-other as the Judaic endowment of all men?[198]

Conceding that an adequate answer to these questions lies beyond the scope of his discussion of Rabbi Hayyim's work, Levinas nevertheless asserts his belief that the work lends itself to the most universal interpretation. Acknowledging that Rabbi Hayyim's concern is with man's faithfulness to the Torah's commandments, he suggests that underlying the 'local and particularistic purposes' of the Rabbi's work, 'there is the affirmation of the idea that being-for-itself—and no doubt being-in-itself too—has as its condition the unconditioned responsibility of *being-for-the-other*'.[199]

The importance, for Levinas, of the universal interpretation of the cosmology of the *Nefesh HaHayyim*, becomes apparent in the next section of the essay, in which Levinas discusses the relationship between Rabbi Hayyim's cosmology and his understanding of prayer. As we saw above, Rabbi Hayyim argues that in true prayer, the individual never asks for anything for himself. Instead, Levinas explains, he sees the essence of prayer as man's act of blessing God.

> In his eyes, the essence of prayer lies in the moment of benediction, the generous act of offering that is necessary for God's association with the worlds. This offering 'feeds' the association—the existence or life of the worlds—in the same way as the food which guarantees the continued animation of living bodies even though the spiritual principle of animation has no need to consume this food.[200]

God, in other words, has no intrinsic need for blessings, but, at the same time, prayer is necessary for the continued existence of the world. Levinas cites the Bible to illustrate that God *desires* prayer.

> God desires prayer in the manner of Proverbs 15:8, where the verse is read for the most obvious meaning: 'the prayer of the upright is his delight (*désir*)'. He needs prayer, just as he needs man's fidelity to the Torah, to make his association with the worlds, their existence and elevation, possible.[201]

The type of prayer that Rabbi Hayyim has in mind is not the spontaneous expression of the individual, but the *Amidah*, the set prayer a Jew is expected to say every morning, afternoon and evening. He emphasises that the form of this prayer, composed by the Great Assembly (*keneset ha-gedolah*), is conducive to spiritual elevation.

> Its words are endowed with an unparalleled spiritual force, 'bringing thought to an extreme purity of intention and elevation', 'a privilege of that marvellous refinement which annuls all those vain ideas weighing down and impeding purity of thought and intention'.[202]

For Rabbi Hayyim of Volozhin, Levinas explains, prayer is 'far from being a demand addressed to God'; instead, it consists in the 'elevation, surrender and adherence of the soul to the heights'. The soul rises up, just as the smoke from a sacrifice does. One dis-inter-ests oneself (*se des-inter-esser*), loosens the ties of that unconditional attachment to being.[203]

Volozhiner also argues that prayer which arises out of an individual's own suffering is valid, if the individual is concerned with the suffering that this causes God, rather than simply with his own suffering.

> [...] Insofar as the suffering of any 'I' (*moi*) immediately becomes God's suffering—who suffers in this suffering of 'mine'—there is a way in which the suffering self can pray: by praying for the suffering of God who suffers through my human suffering. [...] The suffering self prays on behalf of God's suffering, for the God who suffers both through man's transgression and through the suffering by which this transgression can be expiated.[204]

Levinas summarises this view of prayer as follows: 'The meaning of any prayer can be found only in its relationship to God's need of the prayers of the just to bring the worlds into existence, to sanctify and elevate them'.[205] For Levinas who, as we saw above, chooses to understand Volozhiner's cosmology in the most universal terms possible, the necessity of prayer is of philosophical significance. Prayer represents the irruption of the ethical dimension into being. Combining his own terminology with that of the rabbi, Levinas reiterates what he sees as a central theme of *Nefesh Ha'Hayyim*:

> [...] it is not enough—and it is not possible—for the worlds to continue to be, by virtue of their power to subsist. They must be justified. The ethical must intervene! Man, and man's prayer are essential. In this way, prayer [...] refers, in the true sense of the term, to the task of edifying the worlds, or 'repairing the ruins of creation'. For the self (*moi*), prayer means that, instead of seeking one's own salvation, one secures that of others.[206]

Both Rabbi Hayyim's mystical view of prayer, and Levinas' philosophical interpretation of it, take us a long way from the ordinary conception of prayer as speech addressed to God, analogous to speech addressed to human beings. The necessity of such an abstract understanding of prayer becomes apparent, however, when we consider the question of prayer in relation to Levinas' insistence that God is beyond being. Although Levinas does not indicate, in this essay, his intended audience, one might surmise that it is similar to the audience of 'Revelation in the Jewish Tradition'. In the latter essay, Levinas points out that the Revelation does not constitute a philosophical problem for those Orthodox Jews who have remained untouched by modern intellectual developments in the secular world. He explains that he is not writing for such people, but for 'modern Jews [...] whose concern with the intellectual destiny of the West and its triumphs and crises is not simply borrowed'.[207] The question that he addresses for the sake of this audience is:

How can we make sense of the 'exteriority' of the truths and signs of the Revelation which strike the human faculty known as reason? [...] how can these truths and signs strike our reason if they are not even of this world?[208]

In other words, the problem of Revelation is: how can a human being receive communication from God, who is beyond being? The problem of prayer is the same problem in reverse: how can a human being speak to a God who is beyond being? The answer to both these questions is that through the irruption of the ethical, in the form either of the 'ethical saying' of the Revelation, or of the 'for-the-others' that is the meaning of true prayer, a person can enter into relation with what is beyond being. In other words, the relationship with God (understood not as the Supreme Being, but as beyond being) can only be enacted through the ethical.

## CONCLUSION

Levinas' philosophy provides the orientation for an understanding of Judaism as ethical teaching. Revelation, the system of *mitzvot*, and even the very private act of individual prayer, are understood via their ethical significance. Revelation is not a discourse about God, but commandment, or 'ethical saying'. Observance of the *mitvzot*, even the purely ritual ones, prepares the self to act ethically, to 'welcome the other.' Even the individual's daily prayers are understood as affirmation that he does not live for himself, but for the others.

By interpreting the texts and teachings of Judaism as 'ethical saying', Levinas has shown that Judaism remains meaningful in the face of both biblical criticism's challenge to belief in revelation and the calling into question of traditional faith brought about by the *Shoah*. Despite Levinas' appreciation of the '614th commandment' and the important affinities between his work and that of Fackenheim, Levinas differs from the latter thinker in that his understanding of Judaism as essentially 'ethical teaching', rather than Revelation understood as 'God's presence in history', is not threatened by the *Shoah*. On the contrary, as Levinas' essay on 'Yossel ben Yossel of Rakover' highlights, adherence to the precepts of the Torah is all the more necessary in a world from which God is painfully absent.

1   Richard Rubenstein, *After Auschwitz: Radical Theology and Contemporary Judaism*, London, Collier Macmillan, 1966, p. 49.
2   'Useless Suffering', p. 162.
3   Emil L. Fackenheim, *God's Presence in History*, New York, Harper and Row, 1970, p. 84.
4   *Difficile liberté*, pp. 201–6. This essay has been translated by Seán Hand under the title of 'Loving the Torah more than God' (*Difficult Freedom*, pp. 142–45). However, as there are a few inaccuracies in this translation, we have instead used an earlier one by Helen A. Stephenson and Richard I. Sugarman ('To Love the Torah More than God', *Judaism* 28, 2, 1979, pp. 216–223).

5   The monologue was translated into French by Arnold Mandel and published anonymously in *La terre retrouvée* a French Zionist periodical. However, the version that Fackenheim refers to is attributed to Zvi Kolitz, and was published in *Out of the Whirlwind*, ed. Albert H. Friedlander, New York, Doubleday, 1968, pp. 390–99. Both the monologue and Levinas' essay are reprinted in Zvi Kolitz's book *Yossel Rakover Speaks to God: Holocaust Challenges to Religious Faith* (Ktav: Hoboken, New Jersey, 1995), which also includes a number of essays responding to the monologue.

6   'To Love the Torah More than God', p. 217.

7   Ibid., p. 218.

8   Idem.

9   In the Jerusalem Talmud, God is portrayed as saying 'So should it be that you would forsake Me, but would keep my Torah' (Jer. Hag 1:7). It should be noted that Hand's translation mistakenly has Yossel echoing 'the whole of the Torah' rather than the Talmud (*Difficult Freedom*, p. 144).

10   'To Love the Torah More than God', p. 219.

11   Ibid., pp. 217–18.

12   Ibid., p. 218.

13   Levinas' argument against theodicy is developed in his essay 'Useless Suffering'.

14   'To Love the Torah more than God', p. 219.

15   Idem.

16   Ibid., p. 219.

17   Ibid., p. 218.

18   Ibid., p. 219.

19   This is one of Fackenheim's main criticisms of Rosenzweig, for whom nothing of significance for Jewish theology could happen between Sinai and the messianic days. In his later work, as we will see, Fackenheim came to insist that neither theology nor philosophy can be immune to history.

20   'The People Israel Lives', in *The Jewish Return into History: Reflections in the Age of Auschwitz and a New Jerusalem* (hereafter cited as *Jewish Return*), New York, Schocken, 1978, p. 52. As we will see below, it is not difficult to discern the 'ethical' concern that motivates Fackenheim.

21   Idem.

22   Emil L. Fackenheim, *God's Presence in History*, New York, Harper and Row, 1970.

23   'The Trace of the Other', pp. 358–59. As was pointed out in the previous chapter in the context of our discussion of this essay, Levinas speaks of God as always already having passed in the sense of Exodus 33.

24   We shall use the term '614th commandment' as a shorthand notation for Fackenheim's claim that 'Jews are forbidden to hand Hitler posthumous victories.' However, it should be noted that as early as *God's Presence in History*, Fackenheim preferred to avoid the theological language of that expression and wrote instead of an unidentified 'commanding Voice which speaks from Auschwitz' (see note 28, below).

25   *La Presence de Dieu dans l'histoire*, translated by M. Delmotte and B. Dupuy, Lagrasse, Verdier, 1980. 'La Souffrance Inutile' was first published two years later in *Giornale di Metafisica* 4 (1982), pp. 13–26. In addition, in 1981 Levinas published a short article entitled '*Le 614e commandement*' (*L'Arche*, n. 291, Juin, pp. 55–57).

26   *God's Presence in History*, p. 70. Quoted by Levinas in 'Useless Suffering', p. 162.

27   'Useless Suffering', pp. 163–64.

28   Fackenheim claims to have substituted a 'theologically neutral "Commanding Voice"' for his original, theological '614th commandment'. See *To Mend the World: Foundations of post-Holocaust Jewish Thought*, Bloomington, Indiana University Press, 1994, p. 26. Hereafter cited as *To Mend the World*.

29   However, the theological language in which the commandment is articulated clearly invites such an interpretation, as for example when Fackenheim identifies the 'unthinkable Jewish *sin*' (italics added) of today as responding to Hitler 'by doing his work'.

30   It is, he writes, 'as old as a certain reading of the Bible' ('Useless Suffering', p. 161).

31   'Useless Suffering', pp. 161–62.

32   Ibid., p. 161.

33 'A Reply to My Critics: A Testament of Thought', in *Fackenheim: German Philosophy and Jewish Thought*, edited by Louis Greenspan and Graeme Nicholson, University of Toronto Press, 1992, p. 296. Hereafter cited as 'A Reply to my Critics'.

34 Ibid., p. 163.

35 'Useless Suffering', p. 163.

36 Or, as Fackenheim suggests elsewhere, a Kantian-style imperative. See *To Mend the World*, p. 26, on *God's Presence in History*, p. 92.

37 Ibid., p. 164.

38 Idem. Italics added.

39 Fackenheim describes the book in this way in his 'Preface to the Midland Edition' of *To Mend the World*, p. xxviii. However, our discussion of the relationship between Levinas and Fackenheim will focus primarily on Fackenheim's earlier work.

40 It should be noted that in the later work Fackenheim is concerned not so much with articulating the commandment to survive, but in assessing the philosophical significance of the fact that the commandment is being obeyed. He dismisses his earlier claim that 'The Commanding Voice which *bids* endurance also *gives* the power of it' as far too glib. (*To Mend the World*, p. 24).

41 'A Reply to My Critics', p. 281.

42 'Fackenheim and Christianity', in *Fackenheim: German Philosophy and Jewish Thought*, pp. 176–202.

43 Ibid., p. 196. Baum seems to have Kierkegaard in mind; it is not clear why has substituted the word 'theological' for the word 'teleological' in this expression.

44 Idem.

45 In 'A Reply to My Critics' Fackenheim describes the Kierkegaardian 'teleological suspension of the ethical' as a doctrine 'rejected by me even in its own context, and horrifying in this one' (p. 282).

46 In 'Jewish Faith and the Holocaust: A Fragment', Fackenheim wrote the following: 'To be a Jew after Auschwitz is to have wrested hope—for the Jew and for the world—from the abyss of total despair. In the words of a speaker at a recent gathering of Bergen-Belsen survivors, the Jew after Auschwitz has a second *Shema Yisrael*: no second Auschwitz, no second Bergen-Belsen, no second Buchenwald—anywhere in the world, for anyone in the world!' (*Jewish Return*, p. 31).

47 *God's Presence in History*, p. 84. Fackenheim is here quoting from his earlier essay 'Jewish Faith and the Holocaust', published in *Commentary*, vol. 46, no. 2, August 1968, pp. 30–36.

48 'Fackenheim and Christianity', p. 196.

49 *God's Presence in History*, p. 85.

50 *Jewish Return*, p. 13.

51 Idem.

52 It should be noted that for Fackenheim the threat of annihilation remains actual. (See, for example, the references to the Gulf War in 'A Reply to my Critics'.) However, a discussion of this perception of the present situation is of course beyond the scope of the present study.

53 *God's Presence in History*, p. 87.

54 See Chapter Two, above.

55 *L'Audelà du verset,* p. 21.

56 *Shabbat* 31a.

57 Levinas' understanding of the *mitzvot* will be discussed in greater detail below.

58 Levinasian ethics is radically particular in that it singles me out for responsibility. It is, however, universal in scope insofar as to encounter the face of the other is to become aware of my responsibility for all the others. On this point, see Peperzak, *To the Other*, p. 168 ff.

59 Indeed, even if this is not precisely Baum's position it is worth considering since it is the position of many alienated Jews who sees the Jewish establishment's preoccupation with Jewish issues as parochial.

60 However, according to Levinas' analysis, guilt will be the consequence of any course of action I choose, given that my responsibilities are infinite and my resources finite. Whomsoever I choose to help, I will be guilty of neglecting all the others.

61 Levinas makes this point in the context of a discussion of Zionism in *L'Audelà du verset*. He writes that we must not forget that '*my* family and *my* people are, despite the possessive pronouns, my "others" [...] and that they demand justice and protection' (p. 14).

62 See our discussion of Levinas' essay 'Assimilation and New Culture', below.

63 Fackenheim insists that although it is obviously true that 'the death of a Jewish child at Auschwitz is no more lamentable than the death of a German child at Dresden', we must nevertheless 'refuse to dissolve Auschwitz into suffering-in-general.' 'Jewish Faith and the Holocaust', p. 27.

64 Michael Wyschogrod, 'Faith and the Holocaust', *Judaism*, Vol. 20, No. 3, 1971, pp. 288–89.

65 'A Reply to My Critics', p. 287.

66 'Useless Suffering', p. 162. Levinas' emphasis.

67 *To Mend the World*, p. 6.

68 Levinas criticizes Buber for his neglect of the rabbinic commentaries on the Torah, which led him to 'read the Bible as if he possessed the entire Holy Spirit all by himself'. ('Martin Buber's Thought and Contemporary Judaism' in E. Levinas, *Outside the Subject*, translated by Michael B. Smith, London, Athlone, 1994, p. 13.)

69 See Chapter One of *The Jewish Bible after the Holocaust; A re-reading*, (hereafter cited as *Jewish Bible*) Manchester, Manchester University Press, 1990 (pp. 1–26) and *To Mend the World*, pp. 16–18 and passim.

70 *Nine Talmudic Readings*, p. 6.

71 Idem.

72 *Jewish Bible*, pp. 67–8.

73 Levinas italicises these words. *Nine Talmudic Readings*, p. 93.

74 Translated by Sarah Richmond in *The Levinas Reader,* pp. 191–210.

75 Ibid., p. 191.

76 Ibid., p. 192.

77 See our discussion of humanism and anti-humanism in Chapter Two.

78 'Revelation in the Jewish Tradition', pp. 192–93.

79 Ibid., p. 193.

80 Idem.

81 Idem.

82 Ibid., p. 194.

83 Idem.

84 Ibid., p. 195.

85 Idem.

86 Idem.

87 Ibid., p. 196.

88 Idem.

89 Ibid., p. 197.

90 Ibid., p. 197 our emphasis.

91 Idem.

92 Idem.

93 Idem.

94 Idem.

95 Ibid., pp. 197–98 our emphasis.

96 Ibid., p. 201.

97 Ibid., p. 198.

98 Ibid., p. 199.

99 Ibid., p. 200.

100 Ibid., p. 201.

101 Idem.

102 Idem.

103 Idem.

104 Ibid., p. 202.

105 Idem.

106 Idem.

107 Idem.

108 Idem.

109 Ibid., p. 203.

110 Idem.

111 Ibid., p. 204.

112 Idem. Cf Maimonides *Mishneh Torah, Hilkhot yesodey hattorah*, 7.1 and 8.1.

113 Idem.

114 See Glossary.

115 The translation used here and below is that of Rev. M. Rosenbaum and Dr. A.M. Silbermann, *Pentateuch with Targum Onkelos, Haphtaroth and Rashi's Commentary*, New York, Hebrew Publishing Company, 1976. Emphasis added.

116 'Revelation in the Jewish Tradition', p. 205 .

117 Idem.

118 Idem.

119 Idem.

120 Ibid., p. 207.

121 Idem.

122 For an analysis of the relationship between Levinasian ethics and Kantian morality, see Peter Carey Atterton's PhD thesis, cited in the previous chapter.

123 'Revelation in the Jewish Tradition', p. 207.

124 It should be noted that in the translation in *The Levinas Reader*, the verse is misleadingly rendered 'All that the Lord has spoken we will do and we will be obedient (listen to it)'. (Levinas' version reads 'Tout ce que l'Eternel a dit, nous le ferons et nous l'écouterons'.) This translation misses the point, which is that the expression for obedience (*naaseh*, we will do, *nous ferons*), precedes that for understanding (*nishma*, we will hear/understand, *nous écouterons*).

125 Levinas elaborates on the significance of this verse in '*La tentation de la tentation*', which we will discuss in Chapter Five.

126 'Revelation in the Jewish Tradition', p. 206.

127 Ibid., pp. 206–7.

128 Ibid., p. 207.

129 Idem.

130 Ibid., p. 208.

131 Idem.

132 Idem.

133 Ibid., p. 209.

134 Edith Wyschogrod, *Emmanuel Levinas: The Problem of Ethical Metaphysics*, The Hague, Martinus Nijhoff, 1974, p. 165. Hereafter cited as *The Problem of Ethical Metaphysics*.

135 'Revelation in the Jewish Tradition', p. 200.

136 Ibid., p. 203.

137 *Difficile liberté*, p. 34.

138 *The Problem of Ethical Metaphysics*, p. 165.

139 *Totality and Infinity*, pp. 198–99.

140 'The Paradox of Morality', p. 169.

141 Ibid., p. 177.

142 Idem.

143 Idem.

144 *Quatre lectures talmudiques*, Paris, Editions de Minuit, 1968, pp. 149–87.

145 The translation of this verse has been altered to agree with Levinas' version.

146 Ibid., p. 171.

147 Ibid., p. 173.

148 Rabbi Shmuel Eliezer Edels (1555–1631).

149 Ibid., p. 176.

150 Idem.

151 See Chapter Two.

152 Translated by Roland Lack in *The Levinas Reader*, pp. 283–288.

153 'Assimilation and New Culture', p. 285.

154 Ibid., translation slightly altered.

155 Idem.

156 Ibid, p. 286.

157 Idem., translation slightly altered.

158 Examples of such attitudes are not difficult to find, even amongst scholars in the field of Jewish studies. For instance, Ze'ev Levy argues that the Jewish doctrine of chosenness is implicitly arrogant. He insists that 'The rationalist notion of a universal God cannot be reconciled with the personalist conception of a "choosing" God. It does not befit him to be a "choosing" God in the first place.' Contra Levinas, he insists that 'chosenness does not go hand in hand with otherness, that is, with unconditional respect of otherness.' ('Judaism and Chosenness', in *A People Apart: Chosenness and Ritual in Jewish Philosophical Thought*, edited by Daniel H. Frank, SUNY series in Jewish Philosophy, SUNY Press, Albany NY, 1993, pp. 103–4.)

159 'Assimilation and New Culture', p. 286, translation slightly altered.

160 Fackenheim makes a similar point in the introduction to *Encounters Between Judaism and Western Philosophy: A Preface to Future Jewish Thought*, New York, Schocken Books, 1973.

161 'Assimilation and New Culture', p. 286.

162 Ibid., p. 287.

163 Idem.

164 Idem. These claims will be analysed below.

165 Ibid., p. 287. Translation slightly altered.

166 *Difficile liberté*, p. 398.

167 For a detailed discussion of these laws and their significance, see Aharon Lichtenstein, *The Seven Laws of Noah*, New York, Rabbi Jacob Joseph School Press, 1981. It should be noted that, according to Lichtenstein, the seven 'laws' are actually categories which include most of the civil and criminal law of the Torah.

168 See 'The Paradox of Morality', p. 176.

169 Ibid., p. 174. As we saw in Chapter One, the unrealisable responsibility of the ethical relation calls for the institutions of justice.

170 See 'Judaism and the Death Penalty', by Israel J. Kazis in *Contemporary Jewish Ethics: Theory and Practice,* edited by Menachem Marc Kellner, New York, HPC, 1978, pp. 326–30.

171 Ibid., p. 328.

172 Whether or not today's rabbinic establishment is similarly concerned to seek a 'better justice' is of course an important topic of debate, but one that Levinas himself does not take up.

173 Although 'beyond the requirements of the law' is an accepted translation of the phrase *lifnim mishurat hadin*, it should be noted that the Hebrew preposition *lifnim* literally means 'within', not 'beyond'.

174 For an analysis of the significance of *lifnim mishurat hadin* see Aharon Lichtenstein's article 'Does Jewish Tradition Recognize an Ethics Independent of Halakha?' in *Modern Jewish Ethics: Theory and Practice*, Edited by Marvin Fox, Ohio, Ohio State University Press, 1975, pp. 62–88.

175 Ibid., p. 78.

176 Idem.

177 See, for example, the story of Rabba the son of Rav Huna, who was obliged to pay his porters' wages despite the fact that they had been negligent in performing their assigned task (Baba Metzia 83a).

178 *Totality and Infinity*, p. 213.

179 Ibid., pp. 213–14. Cf Mishnah Sanhedrin 4.5.

180 Ibid., p. 214.

181 'Assimilation and New Culture', p. 287.

182 Idem.

183 See, for example, Rashi's comment on the use of the divine name in Genesis 1:1.

184 'Prayer without Demand', translated by Sarah Richmond in *The Levinas Reader*, pp. 227–34.

185   Ibid., p. 232.
186   Ibid., p. 229.
187   Ibid., p. 230.
188   Idem.
189   Idem.
190   Idem.
191   Idem.
192   Idem.
193   Idem.
194   Ibid., pp. 230–31.
195   Ibid., p. 231.
196   Idem.
197   Idem.
198   Idem.
199   Ibid., pp. 231–32.
200   Ibid., p. 232.
201   Ibid., p. 233.
202   Idem.
203   Ibid., pp. 232–33.
204   Ibid., p. 234.
205   Idem.
206   Ibid., p. 233.
207   'Revelation in the Jewish Tradition', p. 192.
208   Idem.

# Chapter 5

## 'TRANSLATING THE BIBLE INTO GREEK' —LEVINAS' ETHICAL HERMENEUTICS

### INTRODUCTION

The previous two chapters have argued that neither Levinas' philosophy nor his understanding of Judaism are theological in nature; instead, each is better described as a 'humanism of the other man'. This chapter analyses the relationship between these two sides of Levinas' work, beginning with an examination of three of Levinas' talmudic commentaries.

### LEVINAS' TALMUDIC COMMENTARIES

The congruity of Levinas' ethical philosophy and his understanding of Judaism is nowhere more evident than in his talmudic commentaries, in which notions central to his philosophy are frequently employed to elucidate the text. In his introductions to the commentaries, Levinas emphasises that he is not interested in the Talmud as an historical document, but as a text in which universally significant themes are addressed in the particularistic language of the Rabbis.[1] Levinas terms the task of expressing these themes in modern language that of 'translating the wisdom of the Talmud "into Greek"'.[2]

### 'La Tentation de la Tentation'

One of the themes that is often present in Levinas' talmudic commentaries is the question of the relationship between Jewish and western thought. In 'La Tentation de la tentation',[3] for example, the suggestion is made that the Bible and Talmud describe a rationality profoundly different from western, or 'Greek', thought.

'La Tentation de la tentation' is a commentary on pages 88a and 88b of the tractate *Shabbat*. The talmudic text opens with a bold interpretation of Exodus 19:17, which is usually translated as 'And Moses brought the people out of the camp to meet with God; and they stood at the foot of the mountain.' Rab Abdimi bar Hama, one of the sages, claims that this verse means that the mountain was actually suspended over the people, and God threatened that if they did not accept the Torah, Sinai would become their tomb. This strange claim rests on his interpretation of the preposition in the phrase translated as 'at the foot of the mountain'; Rab Abdimi bar Hama understands the word *betachtit* in its literal sense of 'underneath'. This intentional 'misreading' produces the image of the mountain hovering over and threatening the Israelites, suggesting that there was some sort of compulsion for them to accept the Torah.[4]

On Levinas' understanding, Rab Abdimi is asking 'Are we not already responsible in choosing responsibility?' He suggests that Rab Abdimi is denying that freedom can begin in freedom.

> The Israelites coming out of Egypt are going to receive the Torah: the negative freedom of freed slaves will be transformed into the freedom of the Law engraved on stone,[5] into the freedom of responsibilities. Is one already responsible when choosing responsibility?—this is the problem that Rab Abdimi is suggesting. Does freedom begin in freedom? This would be a vicious circle, according to Rab Abdimi.[6]

If the Israelites did not freely choose the Torah, what did occur? Levinas offers two possibilities: either the choice was, in some sense, 'Torah or death', and they were compelled to choose the former, or the disjunction between freedom and non-freedom does not apply to this case. He argues the latter, suggesting that the decision to accept the Torah was of a different nature than decisions that one makes after careful consideration of a situation, and that the distinction between freedom and non-freedom does not apply. It was, he argues, a decision made in a time somehow prior to the dichotomy of freedom and non-freedom.[7]

Levinas continues this line of interpretation with his consideration of the text's reference to the Israelites' undertaking to act before understanding. As we saw in Chapter Four, in Exodus 24:7 the people say 'All that the Eternal has spoken we will do and hearken.' The second verb in the Hebrew phrase 'we will do and hearken', *lishmo'a*, can mean both 'to hear' and 'to understand'.[8] The talmudic text cites Rab Simai's teaching that when the Israelites agreed to do before understanding, 600,000 angels descended to attach to each Israelite two crowns: one for doing and one for understanding. It goes on to cite Rabbi Eliezer, who said that when the Israelites committed themselves to doing before understanding, they were acting like angels, who also do before understanding. Levinas stresses this comparison to the angels, for this reversal of the normal, logical way of proceeding may at first seem naive and child-like. Although it would be possible to read the verse as 'we will do in order to understand',[9] he rejects this interpretation. Instead, he argues that, rather than simply being a reversal of normal procedure, the inverted order of doing and understanding lends new meaning to these notions, and represents a profound structure of subjectivity. The 'doing' in question, he maintains, is not simply *praxis* as opposed to theory, but a way of 'actualizing without beginning with the possible', a way of 'knowing without examining'.[10]

Levinas sets out this 'knowing without examining' in opposition to a characterisation of the 'western' mode of knowledge which he presents as an introduction to the talmudic commentary. As Wyschogrod explains, for Levinas

> [...] the difficulty of Western man is rooted in his need to experience everything which can be experienced. He is eager to taste all the possibilities which life affords. [...] The paradigms of Western man are Ulysses [...] and Don Juan [...][11]

Levinas, of course, is not suggesting that all westerners try to emulate Ulysses and Don Juan. He points out, however, that both Christianity and western secular culture presuppose the life of temptation. A dominant theme of Christianity is the need to battle with temptation; even the saints experience temptation, although they always overcome it.[12] Levinas explains that, in experiencing and overcoming temptation, the self is able to enjoy the excitement of whatever tempts it without suffering the consequences of giving in to that temptation. The self, he writes, 'can come within a hair's breadth of evil, know evil without succumbing to it, experience it without experiencing it'.[13] It is this experience which is not experience that Levinas terms 'the temptation of temptation'.

Moving away from the religious or moral notion of temptation, Levinas identifies a similarly ambiguous relationship to experience at the heart of the western idea of knowledge. The essence of the 'temptation of temptation' is that the self remains simultaneously engaged in, and disengaged from, that which tempts it; the self is, 'at the same time, outside of everything and participating in everything'.[14] The temptation of temptation is, therefore, the temptation to know.[15]

> The temptation of temptations is philosophy, opposed to wisdom, which knows everything without experiencing it. It begins with a self which, in engagement, is assured a permanent disengagement. The self is perhaps nothing other than that. A self purely and simply engaged is naive.[16]

Levinas argues that, apart from naiveté, there is another alternative to this subordination of action to knowledge. This alternative is represented by the priority of doing over understanding. The 'yes' of the Israelites' undertaking 'to do and hearken' cannot, he argues, be a simple engagement to do as such, an undertaking of 'some sort of miraculous praxis, prior to thought, whose blindness [...] would lead to catastrophe'.[17] The Torah and Talmud would not be condoning a naive and precipitous commitment to do something which is not understood, for that would only lead to disaster. Levinas claims, rather, that the Talmud attributes to the Israelites 'a lucidity aware [averti] like doubt, but engaged like doing'. This is a lucidity 'without trial and error, not preceded by a knowledge-hypothesis, by an idea [...]'.[18] Levinas insists that the western ideal of understanding being completely disengaged from action does not apply. The Israelites spoke first of 'doing' and only secondly of 'understanding' because they possessed an absolute knowledge which was in itself a commitment to do as they were commanded. As Gibbs explains,

> [...To] accept the Torah is not irrational, but is rather a kind of reasoning 'prior' to Greek reason. There is a truth here that is not based on hypotheses [...] a truth prior to the separation of knowing/doing.[19]

Levinas concludes his description of this absolute knowledge with the statement that 'such knowledge is that of which the messenger is, at the same time, the message itself.'[20] This concluding comment is important because it emphasises that the absolute knowledge of which Levinas writes is of a very specific nature; he is not talking about concepts of which one might have an intuitive or absolute knowledge. Instead, his interest is in a 'message' delivered by a 'messenger'. The case in question in the talmudic text is of course that in which God is the messenger, but Levinas generalises the structure of revelation by asserting that 'to hear a voice which speaks to you is *ipso facto* to accept an obligation towards the one who speaks.'[21]

It is at this point that Levinas' commentary most obviously departs from the plain meaning of the text, for there is no reference to relations between people in this excerpt. What, then, are we to make of Levinas' claim to be 'translating talmudic wisdom into Greek'? It would appear, from this commentary, that such a translation is not an attempt to express theological beliefs in philosophical terms. Indeed, we saw in the previous chapter that Levinas sees the Bible as primarily an ethical text, and that he insists that statements about God are meaningless unless they are somehow concerned with ethical relations between people. Levinas' work of 'translation' seems rather to consist in uncovering philosophical, which almost invariably means ethical, meaning in the Bible and Talmud.

The philosophical claim that 'to hear a voice which speaks to you is *ipso facto* to accept an obligation towards the one who speaks' can thus be seen as Levinas' translation of one aspect of revelation, that which is expressed by the formula 'we will do and we will hear'. Moreover, if we look at Levinas' philosophical texts, we see that various aspects of the structure of revelation which he discerns in the talmudic text, appear in diverse forms throughout his work on the 'ethical relation'.

Rab Abdimi's difficulty in accepting that responsibility can be freely chosen is echoed in many places in Levinas' philosophical works. In *Totality and Infinity*, as we saw in Chapter One, Levinas claims that the self's freedom is called into question by the appearance of the other person. 'The welcoming of the Other', he writes, 'is *ipso facto* the consciousness of my own injustice—the shame that freedom feels for itself.'[22] It is evident from this formula that responsibility is not freely chosen; rather, recognition of responsibility leads to awareness of the arbitrariness of freedom. Yet, this is not a negation of freedom, but its 'investiture'.

> We think that existence *for itself* is not the ultimate meaning of knowing, but rather the putting back into question of the self, the turning back to what is prior to oneself, in the presence of the Other. The presence of the Other, a privileged heteronomy, does not clash with freedom but invests it.[23]

Levinas argues that the calling into question of freedom by responsibility, in the guise of the encounter with the Other, does not negate that freedom, but elevates it.

> The shame for oneself, the presence of and desire for the other are not the negation of knowing; knowing is their very articulation. The essence of reason consists not in securing for man a foundation and powers, but in calling him in question and in inviting him to justice.[24]

This structure is reminiscent of the idea that true freedom emerges from responsibility, which was put forth in the interpretation of the talmudic text. Only by recognising its responsibility, Levinas argues, is the self able to realise its full (i.e. moral) potential.

> The marvel of creation does not only consist in being a creation *ex nihilo*, but in that it results in a being capable of receiving a revelation, learning that it is created, and putting itself in question. The miracle of creation lies in creating a moral being.[25]

In *Otherwise than Being*, there are also striking similarities between Levinas' philosophical arguments and his interpretation of the talmudic text. The idea of a responsibility that not only has not been freely chosen, but that is itself prior to freedom, is a dominant theme of the work. Often, as in the following passage, the idea is expressed in terms, such as 'commandment', which are borrowed from religious language.

> In proximity is heard a command which has come as though from an immemorial past, which was never present, began in no freedom. This way of the neighbour is a face.
>     The face of a neighbour signifies for me an unexceptionable responsibility, preceding every free consent, every pact, every contract.[26]

Although Levinas does not refer to it in 'La Tentation de la tentation', the idea of being faithful to a commandment which one has received in a past that has never been present, also features in Jewish tradition. The *Midrash* relates that the soul of every Jew who would ever live, including those who would convert to Judaism, witnessed the Revelation at Sinai, and joined in the Israelites' declaration 'We will do and we will hear'.[27] This is the *Midrash*'s way of resolving the difficulty inherent in claiming that all generations of Jews are bound to observe the laws of the Torah: how can the individual be bound by an agreement to which he was not party? Despite the *Midrash*'s insistence that all Jewish souls were present at Sinai, for the individual in subsequent generations, the event of Revelation clearly belongs to 'a past which has never been present', if not to an 'immemorial past.'

We have seen that several major ideas which Levinas expounds in 'La Tentation de la tentation' not only appear in his exegetical writings, but are also crucial elements of his philosophical work. In the talmudic commentary, the ideas are presented in the context of a discussion of the Revelation. In the philosophical texts, the context is an analysis of the self's relationship to the human other. Yet the ideas are remarkably similar in both contexts. The notions in question include the claim that responsibility precedes, and is necessary to freedom, and thus that responsibilities are not freely chosen; the claim that responsibility has been recognised, or a commandment received, in an 'immemorial past'; and the related conception of 'doing before understanding', that is, of accepting that one is commanded to do something without having examined the content of the commandment—accepting it because 'to hear a voice which speak to you is *ipso facto* to accept an obligation towards the one who speaks'.[28]

*'Judaïsme et Révolution'*

A second talmudic commentary that is of particular interest for us is *'Judaïsme et révolution'*,[29] in which Levinas discusses the 'humanist' and 'revolutionary' content of pages 83a and 83b of the tractate *Bava Metsia*. These pages of the Talmud, which contain both halakhic and aggadic material, are largely concerned with the obligations of the employer towards his employees. In his introduction to the commentary, Levinas points out that this text is representative of the 'Jewish humanism' of the Bible and the Talmud.

> Our ancient text affirms the rights of the person [...]. The Mishna intends to impose a limit on the arbitrariness of the economy and on the [resultant] alienation. Let us again emphasize a detail of the situation in which the Mishna places itself here [...] the man whose rights it is proper to defend, is, in the first instance, the other man, it is not initially me. It is not the concept 'man' which is the foundation of this humanism, it is the other.[30]

Let us now consider some of the points at which Levinas discerns a 'humanism of the other man'. The talmudic text opens by citing a *mishna*, in which the following story is related:

One day, Rabbi Yohanan ben Mathia said to his son, 'Go hire some workers.' The latter included food among the terms of employment. When he returned, the father said, 'My son, even if you made them a meal equal to that which King Solomon served, you would not have discharged your obligation to them, because they are the descendants of Abraham, Isaac and Jacob. While they have not yet started work, go and specify: 'you will only be entitled to bread and dried vegetables'.[31]

Levinas interprets this story as indicating that the rights of the other person are practically infinite—even by providing a splendid feast, such as those King Solomon used to present, Rabbi Yohanan could not fully meet his obligation to supply his workers with food. Levinas acknowledges that the *Mishna* places a condition on the infinite rights of the other: the other in question is described as the 'descendant of Abraham, of Isaac and of Jacob'. Yet he resists a narrow interpretation of this expression, insisting that those who would understand talmudic references to 'Israel' as applying only to a particular ethnic group lose the universal meaning of the idea expressed. 'Israel', Levinas explains, signifies 'a people having received the law and, consequently, a humanity which has reached the plenitude of its responsibilities and of its consciousness of itself.'[32] Towards such people, he claims, our obligations are without limit.

Yet even this formulation appears insufficient. Do our obligations to the other depend on the degree to which the other is conscious of himself and aware of his responsibilities? A passage which occurs later in the talmudic text indicates that it is not so. The context is a discussion of the Mishna's teaching that some conditions of work, such as hours and the standard of meal the employer is required to provide, are decided according to local custom. However, the Talmud records the teaching of Resh Laqish that the worker must return home on his own time, but that he goes to work on his employer's time. Resh Laqish offers a verse from Psalms in support of this teaching. But, the text asks, what need is there for this teaching and its scriptural 'proof', given that the *Mishna* has already established that the hours of work depend on local custom? The answer given is that the case in question is that of a new city, whose inhabitants are of diverse origins; or, that of an employer who wishes to say to his workers, 'I am engaging you according to the laws of the Torah.'[33]

Levinas is intrigued by the hypothesis of new cities, whose inhabitants come from many different places:

Resh Laqish has enough imagination to foresee a society without customs, the so-called 'inhuman' society which is constituted, for example, in the mushroom-cities [*villes-champignons*] of our industrial world. These men living at the beginning of the Middle Ages already conceived of American cities! Everything has been thought.[34]

Resh Laqish's prescience impresses Levinas not only because of its imaginative anticipation of 'American cities',[35] but because of the underlying assumption that, in Levinas' words, 'there exist beings without history'.[36] Moreover, the fact of being without history, of not being able to claim Abraham, Isaac and Jacob as ancestors—or, in less symbolic terms, of not belonging to a humanity conscious of its history, a humanity which is organised and structured—does not deprive a person of human rights. Resh Laqish's intention, as Levinas understands it, was that Torah law be independent of the particularities of time and space: 'an eternal law attached to the person as such, even in his individualistic isolation'.[37] Resh Laqish did not intend merely to provide a special law for those without history, but to teach that one may engage workers following the laws of the Torah alone. Levinas concludes his commentary on this section of the text with the following short summary: 'It is not the long historical tradition that counts, it is the personal character of persons that counts.'[38]

In addition to discovering in the talmudic text indications that one's obligations to the other—regardless of the other's ancestry and history—are practically infinite, Levinas also finds teachings regarding the relationships between ethics and politics and between ethics and law. He claims that the text's allusion to the meals served at King Solomon's palace is not an arbitrarily chosen symbol of splendid fare.[39] Rather, he sees this reference to the king as representing the State:

> All the splendour of King Solomon would not suffice to insure the dignity of the descendants of Abraham. There is more in the family of Abraham that in the promises of the State [...]. It is not through the State and through political progress that the humanity of the person will be satisfied—which certainly does not exclude the State from the necessary conditions for this satisfaction. But the family of Abraham establishes the norms.[40]

It is not simply by progressing in the political realm that humanity can realize its highest potential, but by living in accordance with the high ethical standards transmitted from Abraham to his descendants. In this commentary, as in his philosophical work, Levinas emphasises the distinction between the ethical and political realms and stresses the primacy of the ethical. On his view politics can, at best, only be the handmaid of ethics.[41]

Levinas also finds in this story about Rabbi Yohanan's son hiring workers a clue to the origin and nature of contracts. Apparently, Rabbi Yohanan does not see the contract as a means of defending his own rights and interest, but as a method of limiting his obligations. In truth, he believes, his obligation to provide food for his workers is almost infinite in scope but, with the agreement of the workers, the contract serves to limit his obligation.

Commenting on Rabbi Yohanan's behaviour, Levinas puts forward the general claim that the true function of a contract is to impose limits on otherwise infinite obligations. He argues that the contract cannot be produced in a world of violence, a world in which 'man is a wolf for man'.[42] A system of laws cannot evolve from violence. 'In the forest of wolves, no law can be introduced.'[43] Only the 'descendants of Abraham', that is, people who are aware of their obligations towards one another, are morally mature enough to establish contracts.

The talmudic text imposes an interesting condition on the use of a contract to limit an employer's obligation to provide food for his workers. In the course of its discussion of the *Mishna*'s story about Rabbi Yohanan and his workers, the text raises the question of whether the meal being offered consisted of bread and dried vegetables or bread made of dried vegetables. The decision reached is that it was bread and vegetables, and that the 'and' is absolutely necessary. The text states that 'This conjunction is here as important as the rudder is necessary for navigating a dangerous river.'[44] Levinas understands from this emphasis on the conjunction 'and' that the limitation of obligations through contracts also has its limits. In the case of Rabbi Yohanan, the limit is that a meal offered to the other—even when the other is a hired worker—must always be a meal and not just unappealing nourishment such as one might feed an animal. 'It is necessary, when feeding the other, to humour his fancies, to some extent.'[45] The general point being made is that although the other may accept a contract which severely limits his otherwise infinite rights, no contract can legitimate treating the other as less than human.

Levinas' interpretation of this talmudic text has established that Judaism recognizes inalienable human rights. He has shown that the other's rights are independent of his ancestry and history, and that they do not emerge in the realm of politics but in that of ethics. Moreover, even the other himself cannot forfeit, via a contract, his right to be treated as human; for the very concept of 'human' initially arises not from me, but from the other.

'LA TRADUCTION DE L'ECRITURE'

The two commentaries that we have examined thus far are similar in that each talmudic excerpt contains a large proportion of aggadic material. Levinas has a stated preference for commenting on aggadic, rather than purely halakhic, texts. The commentary entitled 'La traduction de l'Ecriture'[46] is exceptional in that the talmudic text (pages 8b and 9a–9b of the tractate *Megilla*) contains a long and very complex discussion of a question in Jewish law. Although the talmudic excerpt is therefore not typical of Levinas' usual choice of text, it is representative of the halakhic reasoning with which students of the Talmud must grapple. Since it is our task to analyse Levinas' way of reading the Talmud, and not just the aggadic material it contains, it will be helpful to look at this excerpt, which, being focused on a practical issue in Jewish law, is representative of a large proportion of talmudic material. Moreover, the excerpt Levinas has chosen is an excellent illustration of the diversity of opinions expressed by the sages. We will see also that the halakhic question under discussion has implications for the relationship between Judaism and other cultures, and, on Levinas' reading, especially for the relationship between Jewish and Greek thought. Both the form and the content of this commentary are, therefore, relevant to our discussion of the relationship between Judaism and philosophy in Levinas' work.

The talmudic text under discussion opens by citing the following teaching from the *Mishna*.

> There is no difference between books [of Scripture] and *tefillin* and *mezuzot* save that the books may be written in any language whereas *tefillin* and *mezuzot* may be written only in Assyrian.[47] R. Simeon b. Gamliel says that [the sages] only extended permission for books [of the Scripture] to be written in Greek.[48]

Although this *mishna* appears to be about the permissibility or otherwise of translating scriptural texts into languages other than Hebrew, the *Gemara* understands the question to be not whether the act of translation is permissible, but whether translated texts retain their spiritual authenticity. However, the *Gemara* does not approach the question by discussing 'spiritual authenticity' in abstract terms but asks the halakhic question of whether or not a translated text 'makes one's hands impure'. Levinas offers his own interpretation of this notion of 'making one's hands impure' in another context.[49] For our present purposes, however, it is sufficient to understand the question of whether or not a text makes one's hands impure as asking whether it enjoys the status of a sacred text. The *Mishna* states two opinions on this question. According to the first, *tefillin* and *mezuzot* may not be translated, whereas books can be translated into any language, without losing their status as sacred texts. According to the second opinion, books can only be translated into Greek.

Levinas interprets the first opinion as representing an understanding of Judaism that calls for both universality and particularism. The possibility of translating the Bible into any language without compromising its status as a sacred text represents the 'unlimited universality of the Bible and of Judaism'.[50] On the other hand, the insistence that the texts contained in *mezuzot* and *tefillin* must be written in Hebrew represents the particularism of Jewish ritual. It is, Levinas comments, as if

> [...] it were necessary to add the authenticity of the Hebrew original to the meaning of the verse, in order to confer on these objects their full liturgical force. In addition to the universal Jewish spirit, there is here a need for the Hebrew 'materiality'. The Hebrew 'body' would be indispensable![51]

The second opinion, however, expresses a limitation of universality. Yet Levinas suggests that in allowing only translations into Greek, this teaching may be foreseeing a universality of a different nature,

> [...] a supplementary universality in Greek, the language of Europe. Does it not have the excellence of an intelligibility which is privileged in its own way? Does it complete or equal the excellence of Hebrew?[52]

We will see that Levinas addresses these questions in the course of his commentary.

The *Gemara* presents an objection to the first opinion in the *Mishna*. It cites a *baraita*[53] which holds that books must be written in Hebrew, and in the classical script which is called 'Assyrian' rather than in ancient Hebrew script.

> BOOKS MAY BE WRITTEN IN ANY LANGUAGE. The following seems to conflict with this. '[A Scriptural scroll containing] a Hebrew text written in Aramaic or an Aramaic text written in Hebrew, or [either] in [ancient] Hebrew script, does not defile the hands. it does not do so until it is written in Assyrian [i.e. classical Hebrew] script upon a scroll and in ink!'[54]

Levinas points out that this *Baraita* represents an extreme particularism, an 'untranslatable Judaism', which 'holds to the "letter" of the text in the most literal sense'. Such a Judaism might be open to converts, but only on the condition that the conversion be one of 'the entire soul', that is, of one's 'entire culture'.[55]

The position of the *Baraita* would therefore seem to conflict with both opinions expressed in the *Mishna*. The *Gemara* presents a series of attempts to resolve the contradiction. For Levinas, the diverse ways in which various sages attempt to solve this problem represent 'as many ways of understanding the relationship between Judaism and other cultures and nations, and notably between Judaism and European discourse'.[56] Although Levinas analyses the reasoning of the sages in some detail, we will not attempt to reproduce the complicated legal argument, but will outline the various positions and present Levinas' understanding of each sage's approach to the question of the relationship between Jewish and other cultures.

The first attempt to resolve the contradiction is made by Raba, who argues that the *Mishna* is speaking about texts written in classical Hebrew characters, whereas the *baraita* is speaking about texts written in foreign script. According to Raba's position, translation does not compromise the spiritual authenticity of a text as long as Hebrew characters are used. Levinas sees this position as insisting on the importance of custom (represented by the traditional script) whilst accepting that the meaning of the Bible is translatable. It is as if 'the fluctuations of meaning in the language of translation matters less to the spirit if, in its corporeity, the text remains in a traditional form.'[57] Levinas suggests that some contemporary Jews have adopted a similar position, and points to Yiddish in modern Europe, and Arabic at the time of Maimonides, as examples of non-Hebrew languages written in Hebrew script.

The next speaker, Abaye, rejects this position, and argues that the *mishna* expresses the opinion of the Rabbis, whereas the *baraita* expresses that of Rabbi Simeon ben Gamliel. For Levinas, this way of resolving the contradiction testifies to the 'importance of the very possibility of different opinions [...] at the heart of a monotheistic Revelation'.[58] However, Levinas points out that in this case the argument is flawed; the *baraita's* extreme particularism is contradicted by Rabbi Simeon ben Gamliel's statement, in the second part of the *mishna*, that Scripture can be translated into Greek.

The next position, presented anonymously in the *Gemara*, is that the *mishna* refers to books, whereas the *baraita* refers to *tefillin* and *mezuzot*. Levinas' interpretation of this position is the same as his understanding of the first opinion in the *Mishna*: there would be two aspects in Judaism, a universal spiritual culture 'open to all languages', alongside the particularistic, ritual life of the synagogue.[59]

Although this may be a tenable position on the general issue of the relationship between Judaism and other cultures, Levinas emphasises that it does not actually resolve the contradiction. The next interpretation refers to the *baraita's* ruling that Aramaic words must not be written in Hebrew, and Hebrew words must not be written in Aramaic. Since there are no Aramaic words in the biblical verses contained in *tefillin* and *mezuzot*, the *baraita* cannot be referring to these objects. Instead, the *baraita* would, on this interpretation, be referring to the Scroll of Esther, in which two Aramaic words occur. The *baraita*, according to this opinion, is only refusing to allow translation of the Book of Esther. The argument that the Book of Esther loses its sacred status in translation is based on the phrase in Esther 8:9 'to the Jews, according to their writing and according to their language'. Levinas concedes that this argument may be somewhat forced, but he discerns, in the content of the book, reasons for denying translations the status of sacred books. He points out that the Book of Esther is unique amongst biblical books in that it takes place in the Diaspora, and relates an episode of persecution of the Jews.

The Scroll of Esther, a book about persecution, a book about anti-semitism, is only intelligible to Jews according to their language and according to their writing. The pain of the anti-semitic persecution is only related in the language of the victim: it is transmitted by signs which do not claim to be interchangeable. Regardless of what sociologists have to say about it, this is not a particular case of a general phenomenon, even if all the other problems approached in Scripture are interhuman and can be translated into all languages.[60]

This insistence on telling the story of persecution in the language of the victims provides an important counterpoint to Levinas' claim, in *Difficile liberté*, that western thought '[...] has never been able to understand failures, nor to comprehend [*penser*] a history to which the vanquished and persecuted could lend any valid meaning'.[61] However, Levinas points out that the Talmud neither affirms nor refutes this understanding of the refusal to allow translations of the Book of Esther.

The next interpretation cited by the *Gemara* is that of Rab Ashi, whose position refers back to the second opinion in the *Mishna*, i.e. Rabbi Simeon ben Gamliel's view that Scripture can only be translated into Greek. According to Rab Ashi, permission to translate the Bible into Greek is an exception to the general rule that translation negates the sacred status of books. Moreover, he insists that the exception was made only for the translation into Greek of the Pentateuch, which was commissioned by King Ptolemy of Egypt, an exception which, Levinas remarks, was 'itself exceptional'.[62] Rab Ashi cites the following teaching of Rabbi Judah regarding the miraculous events involved in the production of the Septaguint.

It is related of King Ptolemy that he brought together seventy-two elders and placed them in seventy-two [separate] rooms, without telling them why he had brought them together, and he went in to each one of them and said to him, 'Translate for the me the Torah of Moses your master'. God then prompted each one of them and they all conceived and wrote for him 'God created in the beginning' [...][63]

The first verse of Genesis (*Bereishit bara elohim et hashamayim v'et haaretz*) can be construed in many different ways, some of which would, according to the talmudic tradition, constitute heresy. Although it would be possible to understand the Hebrew verse as saying, for example, that something created *elohim*, or that several gods rather than one God created, the seventy-two translators chose to render the verse as 'God created in the beginning'. The *Gemara* goes on to list fourteen more 'corrections' to the Hebrew text, which all the translators made without consulting one another.

Levinas does not examine each of the corrections individually, but points out the exigency to which they answer. As we saw in the last chapter, the Hebrew text of the Bible calls out for interpretation, and hence for the Oral

Law. As such, the Jewish reading of the Torah is biased [*prévenu*]. One never approaches the text on one's own, without preconceived notions; rather one always already belongs to the community of readers and interpreters. However, the task of translating the Bible into Greek is that of presenting a text which does not call for the traditional interpretations, but can be understood by a reader who has had no special preparation for approaching this text. The translators, therefore, could not reproduce the ambiguity of *Bereishit bara elohim* in the Greek text, because they could not appeal to the commentaries for protection against heretical readings. Instead, they had to choose the best of the possible interpretations and translate it in the clearest possible way.

For Levinas, both the Jewish, 'biased', mode of reading, and the Greek, 'unbiased' one, represent 'essential possibilities of the Spirit'.[64] As such, the translation into Greek of the Bible is 'an essential test for the Torah'.[65] Levinas argues that the miracle that is reputed to have occurred in the process of translating the Torah represents divine approbation for this work and, therefore, that the translation is 'spiritually necessary'.[66]

After relating the story of the translation, the *Gemara* returns to the second opinion in the *Mishna*, (i.e. that of R. Simeon b. Gamliel), and offers scriptural support for allowing translations into Greek, but no other language.

> And Rab Yohanan said 'What reason did R. Simeon b. Gamliel give [for his opinion]? The verse says [Gen. 9:27] 'May God enlarge Japheth, and may he dwell in the tents of Shem'—may the speech of Japheth dwell in the tents of Shem![67]

Levinas points out, however, that Japheth had many sons; how, then, do we know that this verse refers to the Greek language? The answer, given by Rab Hiyya bar Abba, plays on the Hebrew word *yaft*, which was translated as 'enlarge' in the phrase 'May God enlarge Japheth' (itself a play on the name, which in Hebrew is *yefet*). Since the word *yafe* means 'beautiful', Rab Hiyya bar Abba understands the phrase as referring to what is most beautiful amongst Japheth's descendants, the Greek language.

Levinas acknowledges that the Talmud is not always so complimentary about the Greeks. However, he cites the teaching in the *Gemara* (*Baba Kamma* 83a) that it is necessary to distinguish between the Greek language and Greek wisdom (*sagesse*), the first of which the Rabbis admired greatly, while deploring the second. This distinction is not, as it might appear, one between form and content, but, as Levinas suggests in his commentary 'Modèle de l'Occident', between usages to which the Greek language lends itself.[68] On Levinas' understanding, the Rabbis admired the science and philosophy of the Greeks, but, like Plato, objected to and feared the degeneration of these disciplines into rhetoric. Greek philosophy is open to sophistry, and Greek science can be pressed into the service of politics.

In the introduction to this book, we discussed the exchange between Ben Dima and Rabbi Yishmael on the subject of Greek wisdom. Rabbi Yishmael, it will be recalled, said to his nephew 'Find an hour which is neither day nor night and study Greek wisdom then.' Although in that context we focused on Levinas' suggestion that it is not necessary to understand this reply as a blanket prohibition, but rather as an allusion to 'hours of uncertainty when the recourse to Greek wisdom would be possible, perhaps even necessary', it should be noted that in the same commentary Levinas offers another interpretation of Rabbi Yishmael's reply, this time according to the obvious meaning. He explains Rabbi Yishmael's complete prohibition of the study of Greek wisdom as arising from this fear of rhetoric.

> There would exist in purely human wisdom the power of inverting into lies and ideology. This is why, in the reply to Ben Dima, the exclusion of Greek wisdom would be radical. Not because it is knowledge, but because, in a purely human knowledge without Torah, in pure humanism, this deviation already slides towards rhetoric and all the betrayals against which Plato himself fought. Perhaps the style of the Talmud, which makes it so difficult to translate, is also precisely this battle against rhetoric.[69]

The difficulty of translating the Talmud, on the other hand, points to a reason for allowing the study of Greek. In the 'twilight' eras of uncertainty, when Israel is neither 'master of its difficult wisdom' nor 'blindly submitted to its tradition' (nor, we might add, completely ignorant of its tradition) a Greek translation of the Torah would be better than no Torah at all.

In his discussion of the translation of the Septuagint, Levinas similarly argues that it was the Jewish population's ignorance of its own texts that made necessary the translation of the Bible into Greek. He points out that, at the time of King Ptolemy, the majority of Jews in Alexandria were highly assimilated, and no longer capable of understanding the Hebrew of the Bible.[70] The royal authority therefore conceived the plan of providing the Jewish community with a translation of the Bible which would constitute their national law. In the debate that followed Levinas' delivery of this lecture, he emphasised that his commentary did not concern the dissemination of the Greek version of the Bible to a general audience, but only its use within the Jewish community.[71] Thus, when Levinas describes the task of translating the Bible into Greek as that of presenting it to an 'unbiased', 'Greek' reader, the reader in question is, in fact, the assimilated 'Greek' Jew of Alexandria. The parallel with Levinas' work as an interpreter of talmudic texts is obvious, for his commentaries are addressed, in the first instance, to the 'Greek' Jews who attend the annual *Colloques des intellectuels juifs de la langue française*.

However, in the concluding paragraph of '*La Traduction de l'écriture*', Levinas acknowledges that his view of the Greek language may differ significantly from that of the Rabbis.

> But of course, I have advanced all alone in attributing Greek speech to order, to clarity, to method, to the concern for a progression from the simple to the complex, to intelligibility, and above all to the lack of prejudice in the European language; or, at least, to the language of the university, such as it should be [...].[72]

The fact that Levinas' understanding of so central a notion as the significance of the Greek language may differ profoundly from that of the Rabbis raises the question whether, and in what sense, Levinas' commentaries can accurately be called 'translations'. We will address this question below. However, before doing so, let us consider the understanding of Jewish and Greek thought, as presented in 'La Traduction de l'Ecriture' and 'La Tentation de la tentation', in relationship to Levinas' more general remarks on 'Athens and Jerusalem'.

## ATHENS AND JERUSALEM

### Levinas' Characterisations of 'Greek' and 'Hebrew' Thought

In his talmudic commentaries and other writings on Judaism, Levinas has set up an opposition between Hebrew and Greek thought. The description of the former focuses on the approach to sacred texts, and on the notion of Revelation in general. Both are characterised by personal involvement. Revelation, according to Levinas, is ethical saying and as such is an appeal to the subjectivity of the subject. It does not appeal to man *qua* member of the genus human, but *qua* individual. The response to Revelation, expressed in the formula 'we will do and hear', is not based on detached, objective reasoning, but on a reasoning that is always already engaged, an understanding that is already a commitment to do. For Levinas, this commitment is not the expression of piety, but of the ethical awareness that 'to hear a voice which speaks to you is *ipso facto* to accept an obligation towards the one who speaks.'[73] Similarly, interpretation of sacred texts is not an exercise of objective reason, but a personal engagement with a text that cannot be read without prior knowledge and involvement. Levinas argues that the enigmatic style of the Hebrew Bible calls for interpretation; in order to guard the text from purely subjective readings, it must be approached via the Rabbinic commentaries. Moreover, although the writings of the Rabbis deal with universal themes, Levinas has shown, in his talmudic commentaries, that these are expressed in a particularistic language, characterised by its concern with the practicalities of Jewish law.

Greek, on the other hand, represents the antithesis of this model of reasoning. Greek thought is described as objective, unbiased, concerned with expressing universal, abstract truths in clear language. As we have seen, Levinas often equates 'Greek' thought with 'justice'. He describes the other as 'unique', and points out the difficulty inherent in this characterisation: the fact that there is more than one 'other' in the world entails that one must compare the incomparable.

> Now, when there are two unique beings, the genre reappears. From this moment on, I think of the other in the genre. [...] The thought of comparison, of judgment, the attributes of the subject, in short, the entire terminology of Greek logic and Greek politics appear.[74]

Levinas' opposition between Hebrew and Greek thought, however, should not be taken too literally. In characterising Jewish thought as 'ethical' and Greek as the language of 'justice', Levinas is by no means claiming that rabbinic thought is intrinsically incapable of the conceptualisation necessary for the work of 'comparing the incomparable'. This would be an absurd claim since, as we saw in Chapter One, there can be no 'system' of ethics, and no society can exist without the necessary violence of 'justice'. Levinas does not deny that Rabbinic thought deals with concepts; he emphasises, however, that the sages of the Talmud like to derive as much as possible from concrete examples. In the debate following his lecture on the translation of Scripture, Levinas was asked whether the necessity for turning to Greek thought arose from the Hebrew language's lack of access to concepts. In response, Levinas stated that talmudic thought

> does not consist in jumping straight into the concept; it remains a certain time with sensible representations, which are much richer. Always returning to the example, it is a paradigmatic thought, with a special fruitfulness. But at the end of the day, one speaks of all this in conceptual language.[75]

Just as Hebrew is not incapable of dealing with concepts, it would seem that Greek is not entirely incapable of expressing the ethical. If the Bible is ethical saying, and the Greek translation of the Bible retains its spiritual authenticity, it would stand to reason that the translation is also ethical saying, although it might lack some of the power of the original. Moreover, we have seen in Chapter One that for Levinas reason itself begins in the ethical relation, and, in Chapter Two, that the texts of western humanism, which are written in 'Greek', i.e. the language of the universities, nevertheless bear witness to the ethical relation. There would thus seem to be a 'Hebrew' moment inscribed in Greek thought, and vice versa.

According to Levinas, the Bible and Greece are the two complementary sources of western culture.[76] The strength of Jewish thought is that it articulates the concern with the ethical which, he claims, is the underlying motivation for justice itself. Greek thought, however, lends itself more easily to the tasks of conceptual reasoning which are necessary in any society. In addition, the objectivity of Greek thought means that it is universally accessible. Unlike the language of the Bible and Talmud, which calls for personal engagement and endless interpretation, Greek is a language which 'everyone can enter', one that 'can say everything to everyone because it never presupposes anything in particular'.[77]

### Are Levinas' Talmudic Commentaries 'Translations'?

Having looked at Levinas' understanding of Jewish and Greek thought, let us now consider the interplay between Judaism and philosophy in his own work. As we have seen, Levinas states that contemporary Jewish thinkers face the task of translating the Bible, and the Talmud, into Greek. As Wyschogrod explains, this means that 'it is the task of the thinker to bring into the clarity of philosophical reflection the ethical insights found in the teachings of the [Bible and the] Talmud and the paradigmatic activities of the rabbis.'[78] Our discussions of Levinas' talmudic commentaries and other essays on Judaism have, however, illustrated that this task of translation is not as straightforward as it may seem. Levinas' emphasis on the need for the individual reader to actively interpret both the Bible and the Talmud entails that, *qua* translator, he is also a writer or 'scribe'. His personal outlook, moreover, influences not just the meaning that he finds in the texts, but also his choice of texts on which to comment. In the introduction to *Quatre lectures talmudiques* he writes, 'In the sea of the Talmud we have preferred to navigate close to the coasts, by choosing to comment on passages which support a fairly easy exegesis.'[79] Elsewhere, he emphasises that this 'sea' consists of over three thousand folio pages; as a 'talmudiste du dimanche' he cannot pretend to have mastered this vast text, with its generations of commentaries upon commentaries.[80]

It should also be noted that, in his commentaries, Levinas occasionally seems to depart fairly radically from the immediate concerns of the talmudic text, as for example when, in 'La Tentation de la tentation', he generalises the structure of Revelation and states that 'to hear a voice which speaks to you is *ipso facto* to accept an obligation towards the one who speaks.'[81] Levinas' awareness that his reading of the text may be extremely personal is indicated in the concluding section, where he writes 'may we be permitted to add to this commentary some philosophical considerations which it inspires or which inspired it'.[82] As we saw above, in the concluding section of 'La Traduction de l'écriture', Levinas similarly acknowledges that his understanding of the significance of Greek may not reflect that of the Rabbis, and as such, might constitute a significant departure from the talmudic text under consideration.

Levinas' general understanding of Judaism also seems to differ markedly from that of other Jewish philosophers, both medieval and modern, if not from that of the Rabbis. For example, the contemporary Israeli philosopher Yeshayahu Leibowitz (writing in the 'Greek' Hebrew of the Hebrew University), takes an opposite view of the *mitzvot* from that of Levinas. He argues that Judaism does not recognize a separate category of 'ethics', and that all *mitzvot* are to be understood on the basis that they are ways of fulfilling God's will.[83] We saw in the last chapter that Levinas also sees an important difference between his philosophical understanding of Judaism, and that of Maimonides. The latter does not see God as 'beyond', or 'otherwise than', being, but as the Supreme Being.[84]

In addition to having a novel way of understanding the texts to be interpreted, Levinas also has a very specific understanding of the language of the translation. Levinas himself points out that his characterisation of 'Greek' as a language 'which does not imprint itself in what it says', and which always leaves open the possibility of 'unsaying that to which you were obligated to have recourse in order to show something' is contested by Derrida.[85] A complete discussion of this disagreement is, of course, beyond the scope of the present study; we have pointed it out only to highlight the fact that Levinas is by no means a neutral site of the intersection of Greek and Hebrew thought. On the contrary, his own understanding of each language and tradition inevitably shapes his 'translations'.

It is, however, useful to describe Levinas' talmudic lectures as 'translations' rather than, for example, 'commentaries', because the latter term does not convey the sense that the second order text is operating in a different language from the original. Provided that we keep in mind that different 'languages' indicate different cultural assumptions and even different modes of reasoning, and that the interpretation of a text is also a form of writing, Levinas' talmudic commentaries can be usefully described as translations of excerpts from the Talmud.

*Are Levinas' Philosophical Works 'Translations'?*
To similarly describe Levinas' philosophical work as a 'translation' of the Bible (or 'Jewish thought') into Greek, would, however, be misleading. 'Translation', even broadly defined, carries the implication that there is an

original text which is authoritative, insofar as a translation is evaluated on the basis of its success in conveying the meaning of the original.[86] Yet, as Levinas repeatedly emphasises, his philosophical works do not appeal to the Bible or Talmud to prove his theses. Instead, these texts provide illustrations and examples. *Totality and Infinity*, for example, is not to be evaluated on the strength of its presentation of Jewish ideas, but on its philosophical merits. Whether or not the theses of *Totality and Infinity* reflect those of Judaism is a separate issue.

Some commentators, however, tend to give this question undue emphasis. For example, Wyschogrod remarks that, 'while Levinas refrains from the use of religious language in his philosophical work, it is not difficult to discern the religious perspective in which these themes arise.' She sets herself the task of bringing to light 'the religious sources from which his phenomenological analyses emerge' and argues that:

> It is from talmudic sources that Levinas derives his emphasis upon the unique rela-tion with the other not only as the most immediately given datum of experience, but as a datum which is ethical in its very upsurge.[87]

While this characterisation of the relationship between Levinas' readings of the Talmud and his phenomenological analyses may be accurate on a bio-graphical level, it is more of a hindrance than a help to our understanding of Levinas' work. To say that Levinas developed his notion of the face-to-face while reading the Talmud is like saying that Newton developed the notion of gravity when an apple fell on his head: it is to substitute anecdote for explana-tion. What needs to be explained is the concept itself, and not the circum-stances of its discovery.

In her chapters on Levinas' phenomenological works, Wyschogrod does evaluate the phenomenology on its own merits. However, remarks like the ones we cited above are extremely misleading, suggesting that we can turn to the pages of the Talmud to acquire a better understanding of Levinas' phe-nomenological analyses. Such a suggestion is unfortunate, not only because talmudic exegesis is a 'difficult science', but because, as we have seen, Levi-nas' readings of the Talmud are highly idiosyncratic. It is only when we are already in a position to execute a 'Levinasian' reading of the Talmud that the talmudic text can illuminate Levinas' philosophical work. If this were not the case, other philosophically minded readers of the Talmud would have come up with notions similar to the 'face-to-face' and the 'otherwise than being'.

In other words, although it may be true that Levinas developed his notion of the face-to-face through his readings of the Talmud, we must ask what he brought to the text that allowed for these 'ethical' readings in the first place.

It could be argued that a partial answer to this question lies in the pre-philosophical experiences which Levinas identifies at the basis of phenomenological descriptions. Without his readings of the Talmud, he might never have become self-reflectively aware of these pre-philosophical experiences;[88] but without these experiences, he could not have discerned the ethical meaning of the Talmud.

The congruity of Levinas' understanding of Judaism and his ethical philosophy, which we have illustrated throughout this study, does not entail that there must be a one-way, causal relation, in either direction, between them. Instead, Levinas' reflections on Jewish texts and on the ethical relation should be seen as mutually illuminating paths of enquiry. The danger of characterising the relationship between them as Wyschogrod does, or of describing Levinas as a 'Jewish Philosopher',[89] is that one is tempted to think that in understanding Judaism one has understood Levinas, or vice versa. In so doing, one is led to overlook the originality of Levinas' work, his contributions to both western philosophy and Jewish thought.

Having said this, however, there are contexts in which Levinas can be usefully described as a 'Jewish philosopher', and in which an examination of the relationship between the 'Judaic' and 'Greek' content of his thought is of great importance. These are, firstly, when examining Levinas writings on Judaism and, secondly, when considering the general question of the nature of western culture. In both instances, however, it is important to realise that the term 'Jewish philosopher' does not help to explain Levinas' work, but to indicate the value that it may have for modern readers. We have seen that, in the role of philosophical interpreter of the Bible and Talmud, Levinas offers modern Jews[90] a way of reading these texts that shows their relevance to the contemporary world. Levinas, qua 'Jewish philosopher', also makes a broader contribution to western thought by pointing out that western culture is not only Greek, but also biblical. However, this would hardly be a notable contribution if it were not for the fact that Levinas understands the Bible not as a work of theology or mythology, and not as a historical document, but as 'ethical saying'.

It must be asked, however, why Levinas uses the term 'biblical' at all. As noted earlier, he defends the use of biblical quotations in his philosophical work by arguing that, as a source of examples and illustrations, the Bible has as much right to be quoted as any other work of literature. However, more needs to be said. Given that Levinas has always tried to keep his philosophical and religious writings separate, one might wonder why he has not attempted to keep the former free of religious language generally, and of biblical allusions and quotations in particular.

In order to answer this question, it is useful to consider Levinas' use of examples on two different levels. Firstly, each example must obviously be considered within its immediate context. As readers approaching the text on this level, we should take the biblical examples in the way that Levinas has indicated, i.e. as 'literary' illustrations of the phenomena (or non-phenomena) under discussion. Thus, for example, when Levinas describes the asymmetry of the face-to-face relationship, it does not matter whether the illustrations he chooses come from the Bible, the Talmud, or Dostoyevsky. Our first concern, as readers, should be to understand what the example is intended to illustrate, even if our own interpretation of the literary text differs from that of Levinas. Moreover, on this level of interpretation, the source of the illustration should not affect our evaluation of Levinas' argument, or analysis of a phenomenon. If, for instance, the reader believes that Dostoyevsky's portrayal of human existence is more accurate than that of the Bible, he should not, on this basis, accept Levinas' analyses that are illustrated with examples from Dostoyevsky whilst rejecting those that are illustrated with biblical verses.

In addition to this local approach to the examples, a more global approach is called for by Levinas' discussions of the need for literature itself. In Chapter Two we presented his argument that literature (and philosophy) are needed in order to bring the 'beyond being' into the said, even though it will inevitably be betrayed. This argument, however, should not be seen as an imperative addressed to Levinas' reader ('Write ethical literature'), so much as an invitation to uncover the ethical saying in the literature that we already possess, that is, a call for an ethical hermeneutics. Levinas' use of literary examples is an illustration of such a hermeneutics. On this level, rather than simply illustrating his ideas, the examples illuminate the literary texts and indicate an approach the reader can take to other works of literature (secular or religious).

The notion of a Levinasian ethical hermeneutics is helpful to answer the question raised above as to why Levinas does not avoid religious language and biblical allusion, in order to safeguard his work from theological interpretations. Levinas' relationship to the texts of western culture is ambivalent. He criticises the violence inherent in the ontological thought of western philosophy, but insists that we cannot do without this thought, and, more importantly for our present purposes, he uncovers ethical moments within the philosophical canon.[91] Similarly, he criticises humanist thought and literature for its tendency to degenerate into empty rhetoric, but rather than joining the chorus of anti-humanists, tries to resurrect the word by disclosing the underlying ethical concern of humanist texts. Levinas' approach to sacred texts should be viewed in the same way. Although he does not devote much time to criticising them (or, more precisely, their received interpretations), his writings on Judaism, addressed to 'modern' Jews, presuppose the centuries of 'enlightenment' and 'demythologisation' which preceded them. Levinas therefore more or less skips over the negative work of attacking theological interpretations, and proceeds to the positive task of revealing the ethical meaning of Scripture.

Admittedly, for Levinas, the ethical meaning lies closer to the surface in biblical and rabbinic texts than in most of the texts of western culture. However, we should not allow this fact to obscure the implied negative aspect of Levinas' approach to sacred texts. Levinas substitutes his ethical reading of Scripture for the more traditional theological ones, just as he strives to produce ethical readings of the texts of western culture. The presence of biblical quotations in his writings is due to the fact that he finds the Bible so readily amenable to ethical interpretation, and thus the best text on which to demonstrate an ethical hermeneutics.

Although Levinas does not use specific literary examples as proofs of his arguments, the cumulative effect of his readings of literature is to lend some credence to his phenomenological analyses. However, this effect can only obtain if the reader is somehow able to recognise the experiences in question; indeed, the role of literature would be to highlight and articulate these experiences. Levinas' thought can be characterised as an uneasy combination of transcendental and empirical philosophy. His use of literary examples would seem to bolster the empirical side, by calling attention to certain key experiences that are represented in literature.[92]

In addition to providing illustrations of the ethical relation, Levinas' practise of ethical hermeneutics expresses a certain humility concerning his thought. Unlike Descartes, who attempted to develop his philosophy completely independently of other thinkers, Levinas is acutely aware of the value of his intellectual heritage. He even goes so far as to suggest that 'everything has always already been thought […] at least in the Mediterranean basin during the few centuries which preceded and followed the start of the common era.'[93] Levinas' humility regarding his work does not only concern the originality or otherwise of his ideas, but also the fate and effect of his books. In *Otherwise than Being*, for example, Levinas acknowledges that in spite of its attempts to enact and describe the 'saying', it, like all books, becomes a 'pure said', thus betraying the saying. 'Books', he writes, having stated that his own book is no exception,

have their fate; they belong to a world they do not include, but recognize by being written and printed, and by being prefaced and getting themselves preceded with

forewords. They are interrupted, and call for other books and in the end are interpreted in a saying distinct from the said.[94]

Thus Levinas acknowledges that his own work is neither radically original,
since everything has always already been thought, nor is it the last word, the
end of philosophy. Instead, *Otherwise than Being* and the rest of his writings,
which are responses to other books, call, in their turn, for interpretation and
more books, which will call for yet more interpretation and more books, and
so on *ad infinitum*.

Levinas' ethical hermeneutics, however, may make some change in this
chain of interpretation, if readers try to emulate him by uncovering the ethical
meaning of texts, the 'saying' behind the 'said'. Moreover, we saw in Chapter
Two that Levinas is dubious about the capability of abstract thought to transmit universal truths and protect them from distortion; he argues that talmudic
reasoning, with its emphasis on concrete situations, and the embodiment of
the truths in a text that requires interpretation, is better suited to protecting
the truth from corruption. Levinas' hermeneutics may similarly be seen to
represent an approach which he feels is more useful than the simple statement
of theses in abstract language. For example, rather than simply stating
propositions about the nature of the relationship between the self and the
other, he invites us to discover this relationship by contemplating literary
examples.

To summarise: the importance of Levinas' ethical hermeneutics should
not be underestimated. The 'intertextuality' of his writing, the appeal to both
literary examples and the 'marginalised' ethical concern of philosophical
texts, are essential to his work. Firstly, the appeal to other texts is necessary
because without some 'evidence' of the ethical relationship in the texts of
European culture, Levinas would find it difficult to believe that his phenomenological analyses transcended his subjective experience, and he would find
it even more difficult to persuade anyone else. Secondly, his interpretations
of other texts are needed to indicate the approach to be taken to his own
writings, that is, the continuous struggle to uncover the saying in the said.
We have argued that Levinas uses biblical quotations because the Bible lends
itself so easily to an ethical interpretation, and not because Levinas attributes
any special authority to Scripture.

## LEVINAS' TALMUDIC HERMENEUTIC

In the previous section, we discussed Levinas' ethical hermeneutics as a
general approach to interpreting the texts of both Judaism and western
culture, a way of seeking the 'saying' that lies beneath the 'said'. Levinas'

interpretations of talmudic texts are grounded in this general approach, but are also governed by specific principles of talmudic exegesis. Our initial readings of the talmudic commentaries in this chapter, focused as they were on the philosophical content, did not explicitly address Levinas' approach to interpreting the Talmud. Moreover, our concern with pointing out the similarities between the confessional and philosophical writings may have created the impression that Levinas' hermeneutics, when applied to the Talmud, simply consists in seeking proof-texts for the theses of *Totality and Infinity* and *Otherwise than Being* in the *Mishna* and *Gemara*. In an attempt to correct this impression, by 'unsaying' what we have said, we shall now return to the talmudic commentaries, this time focusing on Levinas' method.

For our present purposes, the most important question about Levinas' method of interpretation is one which he himself raises within the commentaries: what prevents his readings from being merely subjective? How can we distinguish between philosophical reflections which arise from the commentaries and those which inspire them?[95]

The first question can be answered by looking at the specific techniques that govern Levinas' readings of the Talmud and an analysis of these principles will prepare us to address the second question. Levinas, as discussed in the previous chapter, insists that the Bible cannot be read without the mediation of the rabbinic commentaries. Similarly, he argues that the Talmud too must be approached not with 'naked hands' but via the generations of commentary upon commentary.[96] As Aronowicz explains, 'this passage through the tradition [...] curbs, trains, molds one's own subjectivity.'[97] Although there are relatively few explicit references to commentaries on the Talmud in Levinas' writings,[98] he makes it clear that his own approach to the Talmud was learnt from his teacher, Mordechai Shushani.[99]

Levinas points to two further rabbinic principles of interpretation. Firstly, the Rabbis insist that the interpreter has to pay careful attention to both the local details of a passage, and to the context from which it is taken, i.e. the whole of the Talmud. Secondly, the interpreter must be open to life: to 'the city, the street, other human beings'.[100] One does not seek to uncover the 'truths' of the Talmud by withdrawing from the world, in the manner of Descartes, but by bringing the concerns of the others, one's concern *for* the others, to one's reading.

The first part of the first principle means that one must treat the talmudic text as though nothing in it were arbitrary, neither its choice of words and images, nor the ordering of its parts. For example, we saw above that Levinas reads great significance into the allusion to the feasts of King Solomon in 'Judaïsme et révolution'. The same commentary also points out the importance of even the shortest possible word—the one-letter conjunction [*vav*] 'and' of the phrase 'bread and dried vegetables'. The Gemara itself tells us that 'This conjunction is here as important as the rudder is necessary for navigating a dangerous river' and Levinas interprets this statement as meaning that it is imperative to provide a person with food that retains the character of a meal, however modest.

The second principle is related to Levinas' claim, which we examined in the previous chapter, that despite its origin in antiquity, the Talmud belongs to the modern intellectual history of Judaism, and thus can be fruitfully consulted about contemporary problems. This consultation does not have to take the form of a quest for purely halakhic solutions, not only because Levinas is reluctant to enter the deep waters of Jewish law, but because he insists that the Talmud is meaningful even for people who do not feel bound by its precepts. As noted in the previous chapter, Levinas argues that the Talmud extracts from the written Torah 'ethical meaning as the ultimate intelligibility of the human and even of the cosmic'.[101] This ethical meaning is one that can be appreciated by any reader, secular or religious, Jewish or non-Jewish, in any place and at any time. As such, the teachings of the Talmud are eternal, not because they have their source in an eternal supreme Being, but because they allow us to step outside history and judge it.

Clearly, there is a certain amount of tension between the first principle, which demands close attention to the articulations of the text, and the second, which insists on openness to the life and concerns of the *polis*. Although we have said that the Talmud provides a perspective from which contemporary society can be judged, the relationship between the world of the text and that of the interpreter is a complex one. In order to judge society on the basis of the Talmud one must first engage in the difficult task of interpreting its teachings; but the interpreter inevitably brings to this task the concerns and assumptions of contemporary society. The continual movement back and forth between text and world that takes place in Levinas' commentaries is not simply an illustration of the 'hermeneutic circle', but an indication of the manner in which the talmudic text can continue to signify in different cultural contexts. Levinas insists that each individual's interpretation of the Revelation is itself part of revelation; these interpretations will of course be influenced, if not determined, by the historical situation of the individuals concerned. Thus the passage of time and changes in society do not make the Talmud progressively less intelligible; instead, they allow for a continual renewal of its meaning.

This approach to interpreting the Talmud clearly depends upon the assumption that the text retains a certain authority *vis-à-vis* its readers. On one level this is an important difference between Levinas' confessional and philosophical writings; as we have seen, in the latter Levinas draws on sacred texts only for illustrations, never for proofs. However, it should be noted that the authority granted to the Talmud in the commentaries is that of teaching, not that of legislating. As Handelman points out, Levinas arrives at the assumption of authority in a non-dogmatic manner.

> [Levinas] is dissatisfied with the options contemporary thought has offered for a free, nondogmatic exegesis [of the Talmud]—options such as historicism, sociology, philology, or formalistic analyses. He aims, instead, to read these texts as 'teachings,' and not merely remnants of ancient mythologies. One could say that in this sense, he returns to the fundamental assumptions of the rabbis themselves about the power of the text to instruct us, but he comes to this position independently of any dogmatic authority. The 'other as teacher' is the fundamental presupposition of all his work.[102]

At this point it will be useful to return to the second question raised above, which we might rephrase as: to what extent does Levinas extract ethical meaning from the talmudic texts, and to what extent does he read it into them? Aronowicz, noting that this is Levinas' own question, suggests that it is un-answerable.[103] She makes an important comparison between the ethical self and the self engaged in the task of talmudic interpretation. Both the ethical self and what we might call the hermeneutic self are characterised by an extreme attention to what is 'outside' the self: respectively, the human other and the text. Yet the attention paid to the 'outside' is so extreme that it blurs the distinctions between inside and outside. Aronowicz writes that for Levinas,

> the primary sense of subjectivity is not a private universe, a sealed interiority, but an unparalleled attention, a response to what is outside, the most outside of which is the other human being. Thus, when Levinas talks of the necessity of the specific person of the interpreter in the act of interpretation, the lines we are accustomed to draw between subjectivity and objectivity blur. His is a redrawing of the lines in which a total subjectivity is at the same time a total attention to the object.[104]

Aronowicz's analogy can be taken further. I can never have an adequate idea of the human other, nor can I have an adequate idea of the text, i.e. an interpretation that exhausts its meaning. The encounter with both the human other and the talmudic text issues in a teaching, a call to responsibility. This responsibility, whilst calling into question the egoism of the self, does not negate selfhood. Levinas, as we saw in Chapter One, insists that the two poles of the self-other relation must be maintained. The encounter with the human other does not lead to the negation of economic existence; instead, the ethical self must draw on its labour and possessions to serve the other.

Similarly, to interpret the Talmud one must immerse oneself in the world of the text at the same time as drawing on all one's resources to understand it.

Foremost amongst the resources available to Levinas qua talmudic exegete are his own philosophical insights into the nature of the ethical relation. Does the ethical philosophy determine in advance the interpretation of the talmudic passages? Aronowicz argues that the question is unanswerable because 'the hermeneutic, the way of entering the text, is already an incarnation of precisely that for which it is seeking.'[105] The best example is Levinas' manner of interpreting the word 'God' in his talmudic commentaries. In the philosophical writings, as we have seen in Chapter Three, the references to 'God' can always be understood as part of the quasi-phenomenological analysis of the ethical. Similarly, Aronowicz points out that Levinas always contextualises the word 'God' in his talmudic commentaries. She notes that he neither leaves the term untranslated, assuming that it is readily understandable to everyone, nor does he allegorise it. 'God' does not become equivalent to, say, 'Reason', or 'Society'.[106] Aronowicz insists that 'the key to the meaning of the term cannot come from the outside but must rely on the context, the place in the text, in which the term appears.'[107] Although in this sense the word 'God' has many meanings in Levinas' readings of the Talmud,[108] its meaning always 'comes to light through an ethical stance, a defense of the specificity of the human being, the other man'.[109]

Aronowicz points out that the talmudic context of the term 'God' in Levinas' commentaries is always an interhuman one: God enters the text in its discussions of the human interactions. But that is also, according to both Levinas the philosopher and Levinas the exegete, how God enters the world.

> An act such as the protection of strangers, for instance, conceals within it a dimension of reality for the indication of which the use of the word 'God' comes to mind. What the text teaches, according to Levinas, is that it is through *action*, not through the fixing of the idea of God in our mind, that the wholly other, transcendent dimension is made accessible. Thus, the content of the text, its teaching, is parallel to the hermeneutic by which this teaching is uncovered.[110]

According to Aronowicz, Levinas' talmudic hermeneutic is itself an embodiment of his understanding of the content of Jewish tradition. Thus the lines between 'inside' and 'outside' are blurred and the question as to whether Levinas is extracting meaning from the text or reading meaning into it becomes unanswerable. In a certain sense it is also unimportant. One of the central themes of Levinas' philosophy is the priority of the search for the Good over the search for the True. Worrying about the accuracy of Levinas' 'translations' of talmudic thought, their success or otherwise in rendering the content of the original in a different language, is akin to focusing on the philosophical quest for truth. Perhaps we should focus instead on the manner in which the commentaries serve the Good, that is, the way in which they can be of service to the others.

CONCLUSION

In spite of the congruity between Levinas' ethical philosophy and his writings on Judaism, it is somewhat misleading to categorise the work of the former as 'translating the Bible into Greek', or to describe it as a work of Jewish philosophy. Translation implies an authoritative original text, against which the accuracy of the translation can be assessed; however, we have argued that Levinas' philosophical texts do not refer to the Bible as a source of proof, but a source of literary examples, equivalent in philosophical status to those drawn from other works of literature. Although Levinas finds indications of the 'ethical relation' and the 'beyond being' both in the Bible and and in the margins of the western philosophical canon, the originality of his thought consists in his development and analysis of these notions, and in his ethical hermeneutics, through which the 'ethical saying' can be uncovered in the 'said' of the text.

When this ethical hermeneutics is applied to the Talmud, a blurring of the distinction between text and interpreter occurs, such that it is difficult, if not impossible, to distinguish between meanings that are discovered in the text and meanings that are read into it. However, the most important consideration is not the accuracy of Levinas' translations' of the Talmud, but their capacity for serving the Good. Reflections on this capacity, not only of Levinas' talmudic commentaries but of his entire *œuvre*, form the conclusion to this book.

---

1 See the introduction to *Quatre lectures talmudiques*, pp. 9–25, as well as the introductions to the individual talmudic readings in this and the other collections.

2 *Quatre lectures talmudiques*, p. 24. We will examine this notion, and the related idea of 'translating the Bible into Greek', below.

3 Ibid., pp. 67–109.

4 Ibid., p. 81.

5 Levinas is alluding here to Avot 6:2 where the word *harut*, 'engraved' in Exodus 32:16 is read as *herut*, 'freedom', so that the phrase is translated 'freedom on the tablets of stone' with the explanation 'no man can be free unless he engages in the study of Torah'.

6 Ibid., p. 81. Unless otherwise indicated, all translations of passages from Levinas' talmudic commentaries are my own.

7 Ibid., p. 82.

8 The importance of doing before understanding is also discussed in Chapter Four, in our consideration of Levinas' essay 'Revelation in the Jewish Tradition'.

9 Levinas points out that Buber translated the verse in this way, p. 93. R. Ovadiah Sforno's understanding is syntactically similar: 'We will do [what God commands] for the purpose of obeying His

command, like slaves who serve their master without the expectation of reward [...]' (cf Mishnah Avot, 1:3). (*Be'ur haSforno al haTorah*, edited by A. Darom and Z. Gottlieb, Jerusalem, Mossad haRav Kook, 1980.)

10  Ibid., p. 95.

11  *The Problem of Ethical Metaphysics*, pp. 189–90.

12  *Quatre lectures talmudiques*, p. 73.

13  Ibid., p. 74

14  Idem.

15  Idem.

16  Idem. Wyschogrod's translation, from p. 190 of the work cited. Punctuation slightly altered.

17  *Quatre lectures talmudiques*, p. 104.

18  Idem.

19  *Correlations*, p. 162.

20  *Quatre lectures talmudiques*, p. 104.

21  Ibid., pp. 104–5.

22  *Totality and Infinity*, p. 86.

23  Ibid., p. 88.

24  Idem.

25  Ibid., p. 89.

26  *Otherwise than Being*, p. 88.

27  Shemot Rabbah 28:4.

28  *Quatre lectures talmudiques*, pp. 104–5.

29  *Du Sacré au saint, cinq nouvelles leçons talmudiques*, Paris, Editions de Minuit, 1977, pp. 11–53. Hereafter cited as *Du Sacré au saint*.

30  Ibid., p. 17.

31  Ibid., p. 17. My translation of Levinas' translation.

32  Ibid., p. 18.

33  Ibid., pp. 30–31.

34  Ibid., p. 30.

35  As Annette Aronowicz points out, Levinas' anachronistic allusions introduce humour into the commentaries and 'draw attention to his own subjectivity and to the process of interpretation itself'. 'Translator's Introduction' to *Nine Talmudic Readings*, p. xvi.

36  *Du Sacré au saint*, p. 30.

37  Ibid., p. 31.

38  Idem.

39  Indeed, it is one of the central tenets of Levinas' hermeneutics that the Talmud's symbols are never arbitrary. In the 'Preface' to *Du Sacré au saint*, he writes that one must always 'take into account the nonrhetorical character of this Talmudic speaking and read it without neglecting its articulations, which may seem to be contingent but in which the essential is often hidden and in which one can almost hear its spirit breathing.' *Nine Talmudic Readings*, p. 92.

40  *Du Sacré au saint*, p. 20.

41  For an analysis of the differences between Levinas' view of politics as expressed in *Totality and Infinity* and *Otherwise than Being*, see Gibbs, *Correlations*, pp. 240–41 and passim.

42  *Du Sacré au saint*, p. 21.

43  Idem.

44  Idem.

45  Ibid., p. 22. Cf. Levinas' analysis of enjoyment in *Totality and Infinity*.

46  *A L'Heure des nations*, Paris, Editions de Minuit, 1988, pp. 43–65.

47  The term appears to mean Hebrew written in 'Assyrian' characters rather than (for example) the ancient Hebrew script.

48  Soncino translation, p. 8b. Translation slightly altered. *Tefillin* (phylacteries) and *mezuzot* are ritual objects containing scrolls of parchment with scriptural verses. *Tefillin* are worn on the head and arm during prayer; *mezuzot* are affixed to gates and doorposts.

49  In *La Bible au présent, Données et débats*, edited by Jean Halpérin, Paris, Gallimard, 1982, pp. 327–329.

50  *A l'heure des nations*, p. 50.

51  Idem.

52  Idem.

53  A teaching of comparable age to those that make up the *Mishna*.

54  Soncino translation, p. 8b. Translation slightly altered to reflect Levinas' version. Block letters indicate a quotation from the *Mishna*.

55  *A L'heure des nations*, pp. 51–52.

56  Ibid., p. 52.

57  Idem.

58  Ibid., p. 53. We have considered the diversity of opinions in more detail in Chapter Four, in our discussion of 'Revelation in the Jewish Tradition'.

59  Ibid., p. 55.

60  Ibid., pp. 56–57.

61  *Difficile liberté*, p. 392

62  *A l'heure des nations*. p. 58.

63  Megilla 9a, Soncino translation.

64  *A l'heure des nations*, p. 62.

65  Idem.

66  Ibid., p. 58.

67  Megilla, 9b. My translation of Levinas' version.

68  'Modèle de l'Occident', in *L'au delà du verset*, pp. 29–50. Levinas discusses the attitude of the Rabbis towards the Greek language and Greek wisdom on pp. 42–45.

69  Ibid., p. 44.

70  *A l'heure des nations*, p. 59.

71  'Débats', in *Israel, le judaïsme et l'Europe: Acts du xxiiième Colloque des intellectuels juifs de la langue française*, Textes présentés par Jean Halpérin et Georges Levitte, Paris, Gallimard, 1984, p. 367. Hereafter cited as *Israel, le judaïsme et l'Europe*.

72  *A L'heure des nations*, pp. 64–65.

73  *Quatre lectures talmudiques*, pp. 104–5.

74  'The Paradox of Morality', pp. 174–75.

75  *Israel, le judaïsme et l'Europe*, p. 368.

76  See, for example, 'The Paradox of Morality', p. 174, where Levinas states 'I think that Europe is the Bible and Greece.'

77  Ibid., p. 178.

78  *The Problem of Ethical Metaphysics*, p. 160.

79  *Quatre lectures talmudiques*, p. 22.

80  *L'Au-delà du verset*, p. 143.

81  *Quatre lectures talmudiques*, pp. 104–5. See our discussion, above.

82  Ibid., p. 106.

83  Yeshayahu Leibowitz, *Judaism, Human Values and the Jewish State*, Edited by Eliezer Goldman, translated by Eliezer Goldman et. al., Boston, Harvard University Press, 1992, pp. 18–19.

84  'Revelation in the Jewish Tradition', in *The Levinas Reader*, p. 205.

85  'The Paradox of Morality', p. 179. See also Derrida's essay 'Violence and Metaphysics'.

86  However, Robert Gibbs, Annette Aronowicz and Susan Handelman, amongst others, point out the Rosenzweigian sense of 'translation' that Levinas may have in mind when he speaks of translating the Bible into Greek. (See, for example, Handelman, *Fragments of Redemption: Jewish Thought and Literary Theory in Scholem, Benjamin and Levinas*, Bloomington, Indiana University Press, 1991, pp. 309–15.) If translation is understood in this way as reflecting 'the very essence of language as relation, as bridge among persons' (Handelman, p. 310) then clearly the image of translating the Bible into Greek applies to all of Levinas' writings.

87  *The Problem of Ethical Metaphysics*, p. 159.

88  But who can say? Perhaps his readings of Dostoyevsky would have sufficed.

89  See the debate in *Autrement que savoir,* in which Levinas refuses the epithet 'Jewish philosopher' and insists that he is a 'philosopher' *tout court* (p. 83).

90  We refer here to 'Jews' specifically, and not just to modern readers, because Levinas' texts on Judaism, particularly his talmudic lectures, were initially intended for an audience of university educated Jews.

91  See *Otherwise than Being,* p. 178.

92  It is important to note, however, that for Levinas, secular literature is amenable to ethical exegesis regardless of whether the self's obligations are an obvious theme of the work in question. According to Levinas, all literature is prophetic in that it 'awaits or commemorates' Scripture, whether to profane or celebrate it (*L'Audelà du verset,* p. 8). For a discussion of Levinas' view of the prophetic quality of secular literature, see Handelman, *Fragments of Redemption,* pp. 282–90.

93  *Quatre lectures talmudiques,* pp. 15–16.

94  *Otherwise than Being,* p. 171.

95  *Quatre lectures talmudiques,* p. 106.

96  See, for example, Levinas comments to this effect in 'Revelation in the Jewish Tradition', p. 196.

97  'Translator's Introduction' to *Nine Talmudic Readings,* p. xxi.

98  Levinas occasionally cites Rashi, Maharsha, Rabbi Israel Salanter and Rabbi Chaim of Volozhin.

99  Shushani was an enigmatic, itinerant teacher of Talmud with whom Levinas studied after the war. He is the 'excellent master' to whom Levinas occasionally refers in the course of his commentaries. See for example *Du Sacré au saint,* pp. 26–27.

100  'Translator's Introduction', p. xvii. Aronowicz is here quoting from *L'Au-delà du verset,* p. 136.

101  Levinas italicises these words. *Nine Talmudic Readings,* p. 93.

102  *Fragments of Redemption,* p. 308.

103  'Translator's Introduction', p. xxii.

104  Ibid., p. xxi.

105  'Translator's Introduction', p. xxii.

106  Idem.

107  Idem.

108  For example, Aronowicz explains that in 'Toward the Other', 'God' is 'the refusal to acquiesce to the judgment of the State, of history, at the expense of the person whom this history or this State crushes in order to arrive at its goal'. Ibid., p. xxiii.

109  'Translator's Introduction', p. xxii.

110  Idem.

# Conclusion

We began our enquiry by noting that, for Levinas, Jewish philosophy belongs necessarily to the twilight—not Nietzsche's twilight of the idols, but a shadowy period of uncertainty when Jews are neither masters of their traditional wisdom, nor blindly submitted to it. Jewish philosophy, understood as the translation of 'Hebrew' teachings into 'Greek', would find its justification in this uncertainty.

The late twentieth century is clearly such a twilight period. The majority of Jews today lack the linguistic competence to read the Bible and the Talmud in the original, let alone the ability to 'master' this ancient wisdom. Moreover, the erosion of traditional religious belief has entailed that many do not even see such mastery as desirable. In this context, Levinas' work as a 'translator' of the Talmud obviously serves an important function. His talmudic commentaries demonstrate that ancient Jewish texts can be fruitfully consulted about contemporary problems, without necessarily accepting the legislative authority of *halakha*. Works such as *Nine Talmudic Readings* show that the Talmud is not the sole preserve of rabbis, yeshivah students and academic philologists; instead, it is a repository of wisdom of relevance to all of Jewry and indeed to all of humanity.

Although Levinas' confessional writings can be justified on the basis of this need for a 'translation' of Jewish teaching, his contribution to Jewish thought is not simply to have demonstrated that a seemingly out-moded 'Hebrew' text can be revived by translating it into 'Greek', the language of philosophy. The contemporary era is characterised not only by Jewish uncertainty, but by philosophical uncertainty as well—a lack of certainty that extends to the nature and value of philosophy itself. Levinas' quasi-phenomenological account of the ethical relation provides the basis for a far-reaching critique of the western philosophical tradition. However, equally importantly, his philosophical works also present a justification for 'Greek' thought: the entry of the third person necessitates comparing the 'incomparable' others, and hence calls for politics, justice, institutions, and so forth.

In showing that philosophical reason is justified and Judaism meaningful, even in a post-Holocaust world, Levinas does not claim to have overcome the uncertainty that is endemic in contemporary thought. On the contrary, the central teaching of both his confessional and philosophical writings, the inescapable obligation of the self to the other, is not a thesis capable of demonstration or proof. Nor is it a notion that can be adequately and unambiguously expressed in language. As *Otherwise than Being* shows, philosophical language can only state it obliquely, through complex linguistic stratagems. Religious language too, according to Levinas' analysis of Judaism, does not offer unambiguous, abstract statements of this obligation. Rather, the ethical teaching of Judaism is embedded in ritual actions and texts that require interpretation.

Levinas' contribution to both Jewish and philosophical thought is not to have replaced out-moded religious beliefs or philosophical systems with yet another new system. Instead, his writings both bear witness to the anarchic call to responsibility which can never itself become part of a philosophical system, and demonstrate the ethical hermeneutics through which the saying beneath the said in the texts of both Judaism and western thought can be revealed.

However, the ethical meaning that is uncovered through interpretation provides us neither with a new certainty, nor with an exhaustive expression of the ultimate signification of the text in question. As Levinas himself warns us in a different context, revelation 'does not leave worry behind'.[1] The ethical meaning that is uncovered signifies only enigmatically; the alterity that disturbs the same enters so subtly that 'unless we retain it, it has already withdrawn'.[2] Moreover, the saying is inevitably betrayed when expressed in the said. Thus, the ethical interpretations arrived at through a Levinasian hermeneutics can never claim to be final; they in turn call for a new interpretation, another attempt at bringing the otherwise than being into the said.

Let us return, in closing, to the verse in Joshua which we cited in the introduction: 'This book of the Torah shall not depart out of thy mouth; but thou shalt meditate therein day and night.' The perpetual obligation to bring the saying into the said can perhaps be understood as an instance of 'translation into Greek', a philosophcial articulation of the perpetual obligation of *Talmud torah*. However, we might ask, as did the sages, whether the verse in Joshua really is an expression of obligation. Should we not instead follow Rabbi Jonathan and Rabbi Samuel b. Nahmani, and read it as a blessing rather than a commandment?[3] To meditate day and night on the otherwise than being and continually seek to bring the saying into the said is to respond to an obligation that can never be fully discharged. But it is also to discover an inalienable meaning in one's own life, and a way of reading that can uncover the ethical saying beneath the sometimes violent 'said' of our culture's texts. In this twilight era of philosophical and religious uncertainty, is that not indeed a blessing?

1 'Revelation in the Jewish tradition', p. 203.
2 'Phenomenon and Enigma', *Collected Philosophical Papers*, p. 66.
3 Menachot 99b.

# Bibliography

WORKS BY EMMANUEL LEVINAS

## French versions

*A L'Heure des nations*. Paris: Editions de Minuit, 1988.

*Autrement qu'être ou au-delà de l'essence*. La Haye: Martinus Nijhoff, 1974.

*De Dieu qui vient à l'idée*. Paris: Vrin, 1986.

*Difficile liberté: Essais sur le judaïsme*. Paris: Albin Michel, 1976.

*Du Sacré au saint: cinq nouvelles leçons talmudiques*. Paris: Editions de Minuit, 1977.

'Ecrit et sacré', in *Introduction à la philosophie de la religion*, pp. 353–62. Edited by Francis Kaplan and Jean-Louis Viellard-Baron. Paris: Editions du Cerf, 1989.

*Entre Nous: Essais sur le penser-à-l'autre*. Paris: Editions Grasset, 1991.

'Entretien avec Emmanuel Lévinas', *Revue de Métaphysique et de Morale*, vol. 90, no. 3 (1985) pp. 296–310.

*Hors sujet*. Paris: Fata Morgana, 1987.

*Humanisme de l'autre homme*. Paris: Fata Morgana, 1972.

*L'Au-delà du verset: Lecteurs et discours talmudiques*. Paris: Editions de Minuit, 1982.

*Le Temps et l'autre*. Paris: Fata Morgana, 1979.

*Noms propres*. Paris: Fata Morgana, 1976.

*Quatre lectures talmudiques*. Paris: Editions de Minuit, 1968.

*Totalité et infini. Essai sur l'extériorité*. La Haye: Martinus Nijhoff, 1961.

## English Translations

'Assimilation and New Culture'. Translated by Roland Lack, in *The Levinas Reader*, pp. 283–88. Edited by Seán Hand. Oxford: Basil Blackwell, 1989.

*Beyond the Verse*. Translated by Gary D. Mole. London: The Athlone Press, 1994.

*Collected Philosophical Papers*. Translated by Alphonso Lingis. The Hague: Martinus Nijhoff, 1987.

*Difficult Freedom: Essays on Judaism*. Translated by Seán Hand. London: The Athlone Press, 1990.

*Ethics and Infinity, Conversations with Philippe Nemo*. Translated by Richard A. Cohen. Pittsburgh, Pa.: Duquesne University Press, 1985.

'Franz Rosenzweig'. Translated by Richard A. Cohen. *Midstream*, vol. 29, no. 9 (1983) pp. 33–40.

'God and Philosophy'. Translated by Richard A. Cohen and Alphonso Lingis, in *The Levinas Reader*, pp. 166–89. Edited by Seán Hand. Oxford: Basil Blackwell, 1989.

'Ideology and Idealism', translated by Arthur Lesley and Sanford Ames, in *Modern Jewish Ethics: Theory and Practice*, pp. 121–38. Edited by Marvin Fox. Ohio: Ohio State University Press, 1975.

*In the Time of the Nations*. Translated by Michael B. Smith. London: The Athlone Press, 1994.

*Nine Talmudic Readings*. Translated by Annette Aronowicz. Bloomington: Indiana University Press, 1990.

*Otherwise than Being or Beyond Essence*. Translated by Alphonso Lingis. The Hague: Martinus Nijhoff, 1981.

*Outside the Subject*. Translated by Michael B. Smith. London: The Athlone Press, 1993.

'Revelation in the Jewish Tradition'. Translated by Sarah Richmond in *The Levinas Reader*, pp. 191–210.

'The Contemporary Criticism of the Idea of Value and the Prospects for Humanism', in *Value and Values in Evolution*, pp. 179–87. Edited by Edward A. Maziarz. New York: Gordon and Breach, 1979.

'The Paradox of Morality: an Interview with Emmanuel Levinas'. Translated by Andrew Benjamin and Tamra Wright, in *The Provocation of Levinas: Rethinking the Other*, pp. 168–80. London: Routledge, 1988.

'The Trace of the Other'. Translated by A. Lingis in *Deconstruction in Context*, pp. 345–59. Edited by Mark Taylor. Chicago: University of Chicago Press, 1986.

'To Love the Torah more than God'. Translated by Helen A. Stephenson and Richard I. Sugarman. *Judaism,* vol. 28, no. 2 (1979) pp. 216–223.

*Totality and Infinity: An Essay on Exteriority.* Translated by Alphonso Lingis. Pittsburg: Duquesne University Press, 1969.

*The Levinas Reader.* Edited by Seán Hand. Oxford: Basil Blackwell, 1989.


## OTHER WORKS

Aronowicz, Annette. 'Translator's Introduction' to *Nine Talmudic Readings.* Bloomington: Indiana University Press, 1990, pp. ix–xxxix.

Atterton, Peter Carey. *Ethics and Justice; The Problem of Kantian Rationality in the Philosophy of Emmanuel Levinas.* PhD thesis, submitted to the Dept. of Philosophy, University of Essex, May 1990.

Berkovits, Eliezer. *Faith After the Holocaust.* New York: Ktav, 1973.

Bernasconi, Robert and David Wood, editors. *The Provocation of Levinas: Re-thinking the Other.* London: Routledge, 1988.

Bernasconi, Robert and Simon Critchley, editors. *Re-Reading Levinas.* London: The Athlone Press, 1991.

Bernasconi, Robert. 'Levinas: Philosophy and Beyond', in *Philosophy and non-Philosophy Since Merleau-Ponty,* pp. 232–58. Edited by Hugh J. Silverman. London: Routledge, 1988.

Bernasconi, Robert. 'Rereading *Totality and Infinity*' in *The Question of the Other: Essays in Contemporary Continental Philosophy,* pp. 23–34. Edited by Arleen B. Dallery and Charles E. Scott. Albany: State University of New York Press, 1989.

Bernasconi, Robert. 'The Silent Anarchic World of the Evil Genius' in *The Collegium Phenomenologicum: the First Ten Years,* pp. 257–72. Edited by G. Moneta, J. Sallis and J. Taminiaux. London: Kluwer Academic Publishers, 1988.

Bouckaert, Luk. 'Ontology and Ethics: Reflections of Levinas' Critique of Heidegger', *International Philosophical Quarterly,* vol. 10 (1970), pp. 402–19.

Brown, David. *Continental Philosophy and Modern Theology: An Engagement.* Oxford: Basil Blackwell, 1987.

Burrgraeve, Roger. 'The Ethical Basis for a Humane Society according to Emmanuel Levinas', translated by C. Vanhove-Romanik, in *Emmanuel Levinas,* pp. 5–57. Leuven: The Centre for Metaphysics and Philosophy of God, 1981.

Burrgraeve, Roger. *Emmanuel Levinas. Une bibliographie primaire et secondaire (1929–1985).* Leuven: The Centre for Metaphysics and Philosophy of God, 1986.

Chalier, Catherine and Miguel Abensour, editors. *Emmanuel Levinas,* Cahiers L'Herne. Paris: Editions de l'Herne, 1991.

Chalier, Catherine. *Figures du Féminin. Lecture d'Emmanuel Lévinas.* Paris: La Nuit Surveillée, 1982.

Ciaramelli, Fabio. 'Le role du juadaïsme dans l'œuvre de Levinas', *Revue philosophique de Louvain,* vol. 81 (1983) pp. 580–600.

Cohen, Richard, editor. *Face-to-face with Levinas.* Albany: State University of New York Press, 1986.

Critchley, Simon. 'The Chiasmus: Levinas, Derrida and the Ethical Demand for Deconstruction', *Textual Practice,* vol. III, No. 1 (1988) pp. 91–106.

Critchley, Simon. *The Ethics of Deconstruction: Derrida and Levinas.* Oxford: Blackwell, 1992.

De Fontenay, Elisabeth. 'Levinas lecteur du Talmud', *Les Nouveaux Cahiers,* Vol. 13–14 (1968) pp. 139–32.

De Greef, Jan. 'Ethique et religion chez Levinas', *Revue de théologie et de philosophie,* vol. 103, part 1 (1970) pp. 36–51.

Decloux, S. 'Existence de Dieu et rencontre d'autrui', *Nouvelle Revue Theologique,* vol. 86, No. 7 (1964) pp. 706–24.

Derrida, Jacques. 'Violence and Metaphysics: An essay on the Thought of Emmanuel Levinas', in *Writing and Difference,* pp. 79–195. Translated by Alan Bass. London: Routledge and Kegan Paul, 1978.

Descombes, Vincent. *Modern French Philosophy.* Translated by L. Scott-Fox and J.M. Harding. Cambridge: Cambridge University Press, 1989.

Fackenheim, Emil L. *Encounters Between Judaism and Modern Philosophy: A Preface to Future Jewish Thought*. New York: Schocken Books, 1973.

Fackenheim, Emil L. *God's Presence in History*. New York: Harper and Row, 1970.

Fackenheim, Emil L. *To Mend the World: Foundations of Post-Holocaust Jewish Thought*. Midland Book Edition. Bloomington: Indiana University Press, 1994.

Fackenheim, Emil. L. *The Jewish Bible after the Holocaust: A Re-reading*. Manchester: Manchester University Press, 1990.

Fackenheim, Emil. L. *The Jewish Return into History: Reflections in the Age of Auschwitz and a New Jerusalem*. New York: Schocken, 1978.

Ferry, Luc and Alain Renaut. *La pensée 68*. Paris: Gallimard, 1988.

Forthomme, Bernard. *Une philosophie de la transcendance: la métaphysique d'Emmanuel Levinas*. Paris: Vrin, 1984.

Gans, Steven, 'Ethics or Ontology', *Philosophy Today*, vol. 16, no. 2 (1972) pp. 117–21.

Gaviria Alvarez, Olmedo 'L'idée de création chez Levinas: une archéologie du sens', *Revue philosophique de Louvain*, vol. 72 (1974) pp. 509–38.

Gibbs, Robert. *Correlations in Rosenzweig and Levinas*. Princeton: Princeton University Press, 1993.

Greenberg, Irving. 'Cloud of Smoke, Pillar of Fire: Judaism, Christianity and Modernity After the Holocaust', in *Auschwitz: Beginning of a New Era? Reflections on the Holocaust*, Edited by Eva Fleischner. New York: KTAV Publishing House, 1977.

Greenspan, Louis and Graeme Nicholson, Editors. *Fackenheim: German Philosophy and Jewish Thought*. Toronto: University of Toronto Press, 1992.

Guttmannn, Julius. *Philosophies of Judaism: A History of Jewish Philosophy from Biblical Times to Franz Rosenzweig*. New York: Schocken Books, 1964.

Halpérin, Jean and Georges Levitte, editors. *Israel, le judaisme et l'Europe: Acts du xxiiième Colloque des intellectuels juifs de la langue française*, Paris: Gallimard, 1984.

Halpérin, Jean, editor. *La Bible au présent, Données et débats*. Paris: Gallimard, 1982.

Handelman, Susan. *Fragments of Redemption: Jewish Thought and Literary Theory in Scholem, Benjamin and Levinas*. Bloomington: Indiana University Press, 1991.

Heidegger, Martin. 'Letter on Humanism', in *Martin Heidegger: Basic Writings, From Being and Time to the Task of Thinking*, pp.193–242. Translated by David Farrel Krell. New York: Harper & Row, 1976.

Heidegger, Martin. *Being and Time*. Translated by John Macquarrie and Edward Robinson. Oxford: Basil Blackwell, 1962.

Holub, Robert C. *Reception Theory: A Critical Introduction*. London: Methuen, 1984.

Jospe, Raphael. 'Jewish Particularity from Ha-Levi to Kaplan: Implications for Defining Jewish Philosophy', in *Go and Study: Essays in Honor of Alfred Jospe*, pp. 319–31. Edited by Raphael Jospe and Samuel Z. Fishman. Washington: Hillel Foundation, 1980.

Kasher, Menachem M, editor. *Encyclopedia of Biblical Interpretation: a Millenial Anthology*, Genesis: Volume I. Translated under the editorship of Rabbi Dr. Harry Freedman. New York: American Biblical Encyclopedia Society of New York, 1953.

Katz, Steven T. *Post-Holocaust Dialogues: Critical Studies in Modern Jewish Thought*. London: New York University Press, 1985.

Kazis, Israel J. 'Judaism and the Death Penalty' in *Contemporary Jewish Ethics: Theory and Practice*, pp. 326–30. Edited by Menachem Marc Kellner. New York: HPC, 1978.

Laruelle, François, editor. *Textes pour Emmanuel Levinas*. Paris: Jean-Michel Place, 1980.

Leibowitz, Yeshayahu. *Judaism, Human Values and the Jewish State*. Edited by Eliezer Goldman. Translated by Eliezer Goldman et. al. London: Harvard University Press, 1992.

Libertson, Joseph. *Proximity, Levinas, Blanchot, Bataille and Communication*, Phaenomenologica, 87. The Hague: Martinus Nijhoff, 1982.

Lichtenstein, Aharon. 'Does Jewish Tradition Recognize an Ethics Independent of *Halacha*?' in *Modern Jewish Ethics: Theory and Practice*, pp. 62–88. Edited by Marvin Fox. Ohio: Ohio State University Press, 1975.

Lichtenstein, Aharon. *The Seven Laws of Noah*. New York: Rabbi Jacob Joseph School Press, 1981.

Maia Neto, José R. 'The String that Leads the Kite: Steven S. Schwarzschild's (1924–1989) View of Jewish Philosophy', *Judaism*, vol. 40, no. 2 (1991) pp. 224–34.

Malka, Salomon. *Lire Levinas*. Paris: Le Cerf, 1984.

Manning, Robert John Sheffler. *Interpreting Otherwise than Heidegger: Emmanuel Levinas' Ethics as First Philosophy*. Pittsburgh, Pennsylvania: Duquesne University Press, 1993.

Maybaum, Ignaz. *The Face of God After Auschwitz*. Amsterdam: Polak and Van Gennep Ltd., 1965.

Meskin, Jacob. 'The Other in Levinas and Derrida: Society, Philosophy, Judaism', in *The Other in Jewish Thought and History*. Edited by Laurence J. Silberstein and Robert L. Cohn. London: New York University Press, 1994, pp. 402–23.

Nietzsche, Friedrich. *The Gay Science*. Translated by Walter Kaufmann. New York: Vintage, 1974.

Peperzak, Adriaan. *To the Other: An Introduction to the Philosophy of Emmanuel Levinas*. West Lafayette, Indiana: Purdue University Press, 1993.

Peperzak, Adriaan. 'Beyond Being', *Research in Phenomenology*, No. 8 (1978) pp. 239–61.

Peperzak, Adriaan. 'Emmanuel Levinas: Jewish Experience and Philosophy', *Philosophy Today*, vol. 27 no. 4 (1983) pp. 297–306.

Peperzak, Adriaan. 'From Intentionality to Responsibility: On Levinas's Philosophy of Language', in *The Question of the Other: Essays in Contemporary Continental Philosophy*, pp. 3–22. Edited by Arleen B. Dallery and Charles E. Scott. Albany: State University of New York Press, 1989.

Petitdemange, Guy et. al. *Emmanuel Levinas—Autrement Que Savoir*, Paris: Osiris, 1988.

Petrosino, Silvano and Jacques Rolland. *La vérité nomade. Introduction à Emmanuel Levinas*. Paris: Editions La Découverte, 1984.

Poiré, François. *Emmanuel Levinas, Qui êtes-vous?* Lyon: La Manufacture, 1987.

Ricoeur, Paul. *Hermeneutics and the Human Sciences*. Edited and Translated by John B. Thompson. London: Cambridge University Press, 1984.

Robbins, Jill. *Prodigal Son/Elder Brother: Interpretation and Alterity in Augustine, Petrarch, Kafka*, Levinas. London: The University of Chicago Press, 1991.

Rolland, J., editor. *Les Cahiers de la nuit surveillée*, no. 3. Lagrasse: Verdier, 1984.

Rose, Gillian. *Judaism and Modernity: Philosophical Essays*. Oxford: Blackwell, 1993.

Roth, Cecil, editor. *Encyclopaedia Judaica*. Jerusalem: Keter, 1971–2, 16 vols.

Rubenstein, Richard. *After Auschwitz: Radical Theology and Contemporary Judaism*. London: Collier Macmillan, 1966.

Schwarzschild, Steven S. 'Modern Jewish Philosophy' in *Contemporary Jewish Religious Thought*, pp. 629–34. Edited by Arthur A. Cohen and Paul Mendes-Flohr. New York: Scribner, 1987.

Smith, Steven G. *The Argument to the Other: Reason Beyond Reason in the Thought of Karl Barth and Emmanuel Levinas,* American Academy of Religion: Academy Studies, no. 42. Chico, California: Scholars Press, 1983.

Soper, Kate. *Humanism and Anti-Humanism*. London: Hutchinson, 1986.

Sosevsky, Moshe Ch. 'Introduction', *Jewish Thought: A Journal of Torah Scholarship,* vol. 1, no. 1 (Elul 5750/1990) pp. 9–11.

Valevicius, Andrius. *From the Other to the Totally other: The Religious Philosophy of Emmanuel Levinas*. New York: Peter Lang, 1988.

Wyschogrod, Edith. *Emmanuel Levinas: The Problem of Ethical Metaphysics*. The Hague: Martinus Nijhoff, 1974.

Wyschogrod, Michael. 'Faith and the Holocaust', *Judaism*, vol. 20, no. 3 (1971) pp. 288–89.

# Index